Jc

Breast Cancer

With Love and Compliments
from the
Author!

Jayashree Thatte Bhat, Ph.D.

DIAMOND BOOKS

Disclaimer!

All the characters in the present book are fictitious. Their resemblance to any living or dead persons is purely coincidental.

ISBN : 81-8419-387-4

Published by

DIAMOND POCKET BOOKS (P) LTD.

X-30, Okhla Industrial Area, Phase - II
New Delhi - 110 020
Phone : 011-41611861
Fax : 011-41611866
E-mail : sales@dpb.in
Website : www.dpb.in

Edition : 2008

Printed at
Star Prion-o-Bind, New Delhi-110020

Journey through Breast Cancer
by: *Jayashree Thatte Bhat, Ph.D.*

I dedicate this book to

All the women who, while giving a
fight to breast cancer with support
from their families and friends,
took the world on the path of
Positive thinking through their
Silent eloquence!

About the Book

I migrated to Canada forty years ago from India. After I completed my Post-Graduate degrees in Biochemistry from York University of Toronto, Ontario; I started working as a Research Associate in the medical research field, first in Toronto, and then in Calgary.

During all this time, I was writing stories about my new adopted country, Canada, in Marathi. (My mother tongue and a language spoken by about one hundred million people in India). These stories covered varied topics, many among them on topics of medical research.

My very first collection of stories won a coveted award and writing honor for literature in India[1]. The stories based on medical science in this book received a huge welcome and appreciation by the readers. This encouraged me to focus my writing on medical science in a story format, each story covering some specific area of this science. I published three more books after that, two being collections of science stories and the third one, a science novel dealing with the problem of 'infertility'. All these books received rave reviews, and one of them received an award again given for writing in the field of scientific literature in India[2]. In this book, one story was based on breast cancer. The story caused quite a stir among women readers. It had struck the nerve of women readership of Marathi language. This response brought to my attention the fact that the topic of breast cancer carried a big social stigma among women, even the well-educated ones, in India. Women who had developed this disease were quite reluctant, sometimes totally opposed, to talk about it openly with anyone, including their own family members.

---

1. 'Datar' award, given for best literature in Marathi.
2. Award given by 'Akhil Bharateeya Vidnyan Sahitya Parishad' (All India Science Council) for scientific literature.

By the time this book went into its second edition a few local organizations invited me during my frequent visits to India, for giving a brief talk on breast cancer. These talks were usually followed by a Question-Answer ('Q/A') period for their fellow members. I accepted their invitations gladly. The opportunity to meet and address hundreds of women in one place at one time and the Q/A period, *especially the Q/A period*, offered me a direct contact with many women. Talking with them gave me an excellent insight into the severity of the problem, problem of total ignorance and lack of information about breast cancer.

In one of my extended visits to India, I went on many lecture tours and met with leaders of many social organizations. I returned to Canada with a thought of publishing a book totally dedicated to the subject of breast cancer, geared specially for this audience in India. After returning to Calgary, I contacted the Reach to Recovery organization, a special wing of the Canadian Cancer Society; dedicated completely to support the women and their families victimized by breast cancer. That is where I met all these wonderful women, who had faced this disease sometime in the past. I expressed my desire to all of them about writing a book on breast cancer targeted for readers in India. I wished to interview some of the women members, and if possible, to gather some personal data from them, for giving a human face to my writings. They gladly accepted my request. I had an excellent opportunity of interviewing as many as one hundred and seven women members of this organization. These women opened their hearts and held absolutely nothing back. They told me everything they could. In a few incidents, even the husbands participated in the interviews. I offer my heartfelt thanks to these women for allowing me to get a complete insight into their lives as breast cancer patients and survivors.

This experience was overwhelming. It made me realize one more thing; and that was, these women, *Canadian* women, were not too different from those I met in India. They were as frightened and sad as those I met in India. Many of them had faced hysteria and sometimes acute depression after the diagnosis of breast cancer. However, the big difference between the two sets of women was that most of the women in Canada had overcome the initial shock and grief with the help of their doctors, friends, therapists and other support groups; and they were miles ahead in beating the disease because of information and awareness. Having accurate medical information and awareness about the disease alone had made all the difference in their battle with the disease. As against that, women in India, due to the social inhibitions, coupled with total lack of knowledge and awareness, were lagging much too behind the women in Canada.

This observation transpired my decision of writing a book on this topic in Marathi. I did some serious library research and found out that almost all the books on this subject were written by either doctors, cancer specialists, psycho-social workers or breast cancer survivors. I belong to none of these categories. However, in addition to my many years of experience in medical research field, I had gained a tremendous experience while conversing and dealing with breast cancer patients and survivors in India, and had seen a totally different side of this disease. That finalized my decision.

A year and a half later, in 1997, the Majestic Publications of Mumbai, India, published my book, (in Marathi.), under the title *"Samna breast cancershi"* (meaning 'fight with breast cancer'). The main focus here was on what I had learnt while interviewing all the breast cancer patients and their families in Canada, on the kind of support that was available to these women through many sources, and primarily on what I had seen over and over again with most of these women, that being their tremendous will power and positive attitude in their fight with the disease. What I had felt, time and again, while talking with them was how they had summoned uncommon courage during the fight with cancer. There was a mutual give-and-take support system in place for them; meaning, they had help of an excellent support system in their distress, and they gave optimism to their families with their own courage. That impressed me a lot. Along with that, I tried to give all the necessary medical information about the disease and its treatment in this book.

The book became a great success. Not because it reached a vast readership, not because a play based on this book for Marathi Stage became successful; but because it had helped, albeit to a small extent, eradicate ignorance and disseminate some valuable information about breast cancer, create awareness and propagate knowledge about it among Marathi speaking people. It had, to some degree, helped inculcate the importance of open communication between patients and their family members, while taking the medical help during cancer treatment. I was very happy to see such results because of this book.

Invitations to give talks based on this book, followed by a Q/A period have increased considerably since this book (on breast cancer) was published. More and more social organizations in India, both women's as well as others, have started showing interest in conducting such activities for their members. The Q/A sessions after the talks have provided me with a good understanding of the gravity of the situation[3].

Creating awareness about this disease among people, especially women, is a dire necessity in India. A support system for establishing a healthy, two-way communication between the affected women and the doctors, social workers and their family members during the breast cancer treatment is vital. For the last ten years, since the publishing of this book, I have made it my 'calling' to visit India, go on lecture tours especially in smaller towns and rural areas and try to spread the knowledge and awareness about this disease among people, especially among women in an attempt to break their silence, as best as I possibly can. I pursue this work very diligently every year for four months; and this work, in turn, gives me a feeling of tremendous satisfaction and fulfillment.

With such a success of my book in Marathi, I just received a request to write a book based on the same topic, breast cancer; and in the same style, in English, from an equally established and reputed publishing house, Diamond Pocket Books (P) Ltd., based in New Delhi, India.

English, considered to be a universal language, is much more commonly used in India than all regional languages including Hindi, the national language of the country. In this book also, I have adopted the same style as my Marathi book, *i.e.* a story format where various characters with their varied situations, conflicts, clashes, passions, emotions, etc. play roles in erecting colorful sets; and through these sets, or a plot if you will, relevant factual medical information is deciphered by a doctor's or a scientist's character. The purpose for this style is to entertain the readers while giving them valuable medical information on the given topic. And hence this work in English, and in this style![4]

---

3. I have published an article, named 'Stories Based on Realities-Breast Cancer in India', in **Women's Studies Quarterly**, Volume XXXI- Numbers 1 & 2, Spring/Summer 2003. This is an Educational Project of the Feminist Press at the City University of New York in Cooperation with Rochester Institute of Technology. .
I have also been invited to give a speech on this subject for the staff at the ***'Lifetime'*** Television Network in New York, NY.
4. I have developed this style of giving factual scientific information (non-fiction) through the dialogues of fictionally created characters, in a story format. I follow this style for writing all my books on science. This style may be considered as **'Creative Non-fiction'** by some!

Some of my experiences with women on both sides of the Atlantic Ocean very clearly identified one more facet of the situation. When a woman is diagnosed with breast cancer, it is a very frightening time in her life. Cancer to any part of the body is bad, and if terminal, it could kill the person. But to a woman, cancer of her breast is especially devastating. Her whole emotional equilibrium is lost due to this disease. Be that a woman in Canada, a world of openness and freedom; or India, a world of old traditions and customs, be that a woman of young age or an old one, breast cancer stirs a woman emotionally. What is it about *breast* cancer that frightens a woman the most? The fact that she may have to undergo surgery, meaning lose her breast, completely devastates a woman. There is no exception to this. Why? This question turned into a puzzle for me. I was thinking constantly about this puzzle when one day the answer came to me, almost as a revelation.

The answer entails significance of two factors in her life. They are, a woman's attitude towards her breasts and secondly, their importance to her own identity as a woman. And the reason for the significance of these two factors, according to my judgment is; a woman goes through many roles in her life; that of a daughter, a sister, a friend, a neighbor, a wife or a lover and a mother. Of all these roles, she adores and enjoys two roles the most, that of a wife or a lover and that of a mother! Both these roles have a very close relationship with her breasts. Her two breasts, that give her a satiated feeling of utmost erotic pleasures in romantic love-making with her partner, also give her the maximum pleasure of total contentment and the utmost maternal pleasures when she nurses her infant. There is that special relationship she has with her breasts. And when this very part of her body is attacked by cancer, it seems as if a tornado has hit her and shaken her whole being from inside out.

In addition to the emotional loss, there is that fear of the disease itself. When a woman is newly diagnosed with breast cancer, she is confused with numerous questions flooding simultaneously in her head. 'Why me?' is the first question that arises in her mind. A close second is 'what will my children do?' especially if she has young children. The effects upon a woman discovering that she has breast cancer and subsequently will have to undergo surgery, meaning possibly losing a breast, followed by radiation and chemotherapy, meaning loss of hair, nails, etc.; are severe. They often lead to psychological crisis. Fears of loss of self esteem and femininity, incapability of fulfilling accustomed roles, poor health, and possible end of life in sight, can cause acute mental anguish.

For newly diagnosed breast cancer patients, the shock phase begins with a confirmation of their diagnosis. The shock phase makes a gradual transition into a reaction phase. This reaction phase is directly dependent upon many factors, such as, the age of their children, the younger they are, the more intense is the women's reaction; the family situation; the staging of their cancer; and type and length of treatment they would receive. It has been observed that women with breast cancer may seem serene outwardly, but more often than not, beneath the surface there is all chaos.

At such times, helping a woman cope with her fears, answering her questions, giving her accurate information about the disease so that she can make the right decisions about the treatments, and information about the treatment itself, is absolutely necessary. The process of supporting her, mentally and emotionally, begins with the diagnosis of her disease. This is where a support group or a support centre is needed. A team of doctors, nurses, medical professionals and dieticians help the newly diagnosed women with breast cancer in their treatment of the disease. Simultaneously, a team of spiritual helpers, social workers and psychotherapists can help them cope with their anger and fear of the disease, anxiety of the treatment, feeling of loss of control and guilt, grief and sadness. Other breast cancer survivors can have a wonderful role in this process too, as helpers and advisers, since they themselves have already gone through the process before. With such support, when the process of coping begins, many women feel more in control of their lives and their future. The disease becomes less of a 'bugbear' or a 'bugaboo', and its treatment seems within the grasp. A strong and robust support can achieve this result. The focus of this book is precisely the same.

Five women, Anita, Ritu, Maya, Virani, and Shaina, coming from five different regions of India, five different walks of life and five different familial backgrounds are diagnosed with breast cancer. They meet in the metropolis of Mumbai and decide to create a support group with the help of their doctor, Dr. Vimal, a cancer specialist, and Meeraben, a psychotherapist, in combating the disease.

Their journey starts when they are newly diagnosed with breast cancer. Each one's disease is slightly different from the others'. Although, all five of them have breast cancer, their own reactions and their family responses to the disease differ significantly. How each one copes with her fear and anxiety is also remarkably different from the other four. However, with the help of their doctor, they gain enough information and knowledge about their disease and treatment. And with the help and assistance of the psychotherapist, each one manages to develop a positive attitude. With accurate information, awareness and positive attitude, they gain enough courage to give a fight to the disease. I have called these the major milestones on their journey when all these attributes are inculcated in these women.

Throughout the book, I have tried to emphasize how each one of these five women, although devastated initially, exhibits strong faith in herself and after developing a positive attitude with the help of professionals, does not lose it until her fight is over. These women share a strong thread of optimism throughout their journey, and try to help other women like themselves.

I have described each woman's background in detail, to make a point that *cancer does not discriminate*! It can develop in anyone, from any economic stratum, from any social class, rich or poor, young or old! However, to give a fierce fight to this disease, the means and measures to fight this war are the same. As such, all these five women, although suffer acutely through the initial shock and hopelessness, and even depression; develop and exhibit empowerment throughout the journey. They are ordinary, every-day women, loving their husbands and children, putting their heart and soul for the betterment of their families, some of them working hard outside their homes to provide for their families, and enjoying simple things of life. The same ordinary women, when attacked by breast cancer, refuse to be defeated by this deadly disease. They overcome their initial shock with a keen desire to fight the disease. I have shown them to be the first rate soldiers combating breast cancer with hope and self-confidence. Each woman's journey comes to an end with a success, success defined in their own terms, of course!

The entire focus of this book is 'positive thinking'! I have tried to maintain the same note throughout the book, without ever changing even the pitch of this note.

I created these five women characters, Anita, Ritu, Maya, Virani, and Shaina and was writing about them for almost a whole year. Over the period of this year, I fell in love with all of them. Each one of them taught *me* something. That is because, although each and every one of them was born out of my own imagination, each one of them reminded me of someone I met somewhere in my own journey of life. Each one of them represented a set of attributes that strikingly resembled someone that attracted me. Therefore, putting them on paper and bringing them to you all, readers, is giving me immense pleasure, right now. I have enjoyed their company tremendously. I hope so will you!

–Jayashree Thatte Bhat
M. Sc. M. A. Ph.D.

Address in Canada:
8340 Edgevalley Drive NW,
Calgary, Alberta,
T3A 4X2
Canada

Address in India:
'AmitShree'
Housing Society,
Flat No.5,
852 Bhandarkar Institute Road,
Pune- 411 004 (India)

E-mail Address: jthattebhat@hotmail.com

About the Author

Born and brought up in Hyderabad, India, Jayashree completed her Bachelor of Science degree in Biology and Chemistry at Osmania University. On coming to Canada after marriage, she completed her Post-Graduate Studies in Biochemistry at York University in Toronto and pursued a professional career as a Medical Researcher in Research Centres and hospitals in Toronto and Calgary, for nearly 15 years*. During all these years, she was fortunate to have worked with some prominent scientists like Dr. Doris Nicholls, Dr. Dave Logan, Dr. Morley Hollenberg, Dr. Eva Turley, Dr. Susan Friedman, et al. who are renowned scientists and considered as authorities in their own special fields of medical research.

Throughout her career in the Medical Research field, her area of interest has been cancer research. As a Researcher, Jayashree is also inclined towards the 'whys and why-nots' of every topic dear to her heart. Breast cancer area is one such area in which she has done considerable amount of research and studies on the social impacts the victim's family has to endure during such trying times. She has visited many "Support Centres" in Canada to ascertain the benefits such centres provide, by facilitating forums for patients and their families and friends to exchange ideas and share experiences, gather some solace along the way from each other, dissemination of most up-to-date information on treatments etc. She has gained very valuable insight into these Support Centres and has realized the tremendous value they provide.

During her frequent visits to India, she noticed a considerable lack

* She switched her career from the field of Medical Research to that of Computer Technology and Technical Writing in the Oil and Gas Industry of Calgary, Canada, and worked for nearly fifteen years in this field.

of awareness and availability of proper and latest information to women, especially in relation to the concept of support centres. So, as a first step, Jayashree wrote and published a book in Marathi language (her mother tongue) on fighting breast cancer. She wrote this book in a story format in order to make it more easily readable to the masses, thereby generating awareness and spreading scientific knowledge.

This book has been received extremely well by the readership in India, and a Support Centre – first of its kind in India- has been established. She regularly visits India for lecture tours and conducts workshops primarily in smaller towns and non-urban and rural areas of the country.

This overwhelming positive response from people in India and the cross-cultural work she has done, has resulted in Jayashree receiving a many scholarships and coveted awards, including *'Chaturastra Chatura'* award in India, and the *'Alberta Centennial Gold Medal'* from the government of Alberta, in Canada.

After leaving the gainful employment of almost thirty years in the technical field, Jayashree pursued a Doctorate degree in Indian Classical Music and now spends her time in her two passions; writing and publishing stories based primarily on science, and teaching and performing classical music in Canada, the United States of America, Europe, and India.

She lives in Calgary, Canada, with her husband, Suresh, and is blessed with two daughters, Dr. Tejashree and Meghana, both married and settled in the U.S.A., and four grand children, Amruta, Arjun, Vikram and Jahnavi.

•••

Sincere Thanks

In the first and foremost place, I pray the Almighty God for the eternal blessings and Grace upon me, without which nothing would have been possible.

During my Graduate studies and my career as a medical researcher, I have had the good fortune of working with and learning from some of the finest members of the world of medical research. They are Dr. Doris Nicholls, Dr. Dave Logan, Dr. Morley Hollenberg, Dr. Eva Turley and Dr. Susan Friedman. I sincerely thank all these Gurus! During the preparation for this book, I had many opportunities of personally meeting Dr. Alexander Paterson of Tom Baker Cancer Centre of Calgary, Canada. I extend my sincere thanks to him for his continuous support and help.[5]

The basic idea of a Support centre that is presented in this book is derived from what I observed and studied carefully in Tom Baker Cancer Centre of Calgary, Canada. This centre is one of the finest cancer centres of the world, if I can say so myself. I am grateful to all the staff who gave me their valuable time and helped me with this book.

With the help of Barbara Cameron and Carol Dyte[6], who themselves are breast cancer survivors, Barbara still actively working as 'cancer representative' in the Tom Baker Cancer Centre of Calgary, Canada; and Dr. Anuradha. Sowani, who is a renowned chemotherapy specialist for breast cancer in Pune, India, and who has written a brilliant foreword to my previous book on breast cancer (in Marathi), I got a good insight into the disease and all its related problems. I offer my sincere thanks to all of them.

---

5. Dr. Paterson had guided and helped me for my earlier book in Marathi as well.
6. They were at the time, with Reach to Recovery, a wing of the Canadian Cancer Society.

During the collection of the data for this book, I met literally hundreds of women in Canada[7] and India[8], who exhibited enthusiasm and offered me full co-operation in responding to all my questions and inquiries, a few being a little personal, without any reservations. I have no words to express my gratitude for their input into this work. I fully recognize the fact that they have been instrumental in my taking this subject for the present book.

This note of thanks will not be complete unless I mention my dear husband, Suresh, for the love and strong support I have received from him all the time; and for going through this manuscript a few times and offering me 'a set of fresh and layperson's eyes'!

Lastly, and most importantly, I wish to state here that without the publishers, any idea presented in a written form can not reach the readers unless it is published in a book form. For this important task, I extend my sincere thanks to Mr. Narendra Kumar Verma and

Diamond Pocket Books (P) Limited, a very reputable publishing company based in New Delhi, India; for showing complete faith in my work and publishing this fine book for my readers.

●●●

7. Through various sub-divisions of the Canadian Cancer Society, including Reach to Recovery.
8. Through many women's organizations and various Rotary Clubs of India.

CONTENTS

As the Journey begins...

There is a large community centre in one corner of the city which is quite popular among all the citizens of the city. It has many unusual facilities, such as a swimming pool, games room, weights room and a small gymnasium, on its main floor. As you go upstairs to the second floor, there are four rooms of medium size that are ideal for holding group meetings or small parties. The rooms are available to anyone, any group or association on rent as long as the person who books them is a member of the community. The rent for these rooms is very reasonable; so most of the communities and associations, especially the non-profit organizations of the city, rent these rooms for holding their meetings. The centre has a small parking lot for a few cars and provides free parking. In addition, its location near a major train station also becomes its asset for its popularity.

Right now, there is a meeting going on in one of these rooms. It seems like an unusual meeting; for, the chairs are arranged in a circle instead of facing the small stage in the room and there is no public announcement system set up. There are only seven chairs and except for one, all are occupied by women. It looks odd at a glance to see that no one is talking and all are just quietly glancing at the empty chair. From time to time, each woman is dabbing her eyes with a tissue paper. They all look quite sad. Just then, one of them gets up from her chair, and after blowing her nose and clearing her throat, starts speaking.

"One day, our chairs will also remain unoccupied like that one..."

The speaker, Anita Dixit, a woman in her fifties or so, is addressing the remaining women. They start listening to her intently. "We all know we have a disease that will end our lives, perhaps sooner than we expect. As cancer patients, we all know that, but we are not going to just sit and shed tears, or feel sad like this just looking at that chair."

She says after surveying the situation.

"Instead we are going to hold the occupant of that empty chair as an example to follow. You all know who sat in that chair with us until last month." Everyone nods.

"Her chair may be empty today but remember, her life never was so. Not even after she discovered she was a victim of breast cancer in its final stage. It was remarkable that her joyful bearing remained so till the end. We are going to remember that spirit of hers at all times. She was such a tremendous source of strength to me when I myself underwent mastectomy." Anita waits for a few seconds. She takes a deep breath and continues.

"You all know that I had to have my left breast removed when cancerous lumps were detected in it, right?" All of them nod again.

"When I was lying on the hospital bed, all depressed and feeling helpless, she visited me regularly and brought magazines and interesting books for me to read. Sometimes she read some passages from them to me; sometimes she brought poetry books and recited a few of the poems to me. She knew that poetry was something of my great interest."

Then Anita glances at another woman who looks of about forty years of age and says, "Ritu, she was not an accomplished singer like you are but when she recited those poems, the whole inner meaning of the poems seemed to come to the surface. That was so beautiful." Anita sighs and becomes abruptly quiet for a moment. Everyone in the room sighs too and there is complete silence for a moment.

"I tried everything medically possible for her but just could not save her." Dr. Vimal Sant, a reputed breast cancer specialist of the city, also in her forties, breaks the silence. Her voice seems heavy with sorrow.

"When she came to me, her cancer had already gone to its terminal stage. In the x-ray, it showed that both her lungs were cancer invaded. It was just too late to do anything." She adds.

"But did she not have any tumors or lumps or anything in her breasts?" One woman inquires.

"Of course, she did. Her right breast was filled with lumps, one of them the size of a small lemon, I would say."

"Then how is it that she did not notice them earlier? Say, while changing clothes or in shower? Mine was only of a small pea size when I discovered it." Maya Patel, a woman who looked to be in her late fifties or early sixties, asks.

"That's true, but Maya, do you remember, your daughter forced you to go to your gynacologist for some other problem and that's when your gynacologist felt a lump in your breast. Thankfully, she referred you to me immediately. When I examined you and looked at your mammogram, that's when your lump was detected, although it was still quite small, like a pea as you said. When we found out that it was malignant, we immediately started your treatment. It was in the very early stage and needed only a lumpectomy. That's why your breast was saved. Right?" Maya whole heartedly nods with a big sigh of relief that is also mixed with sad memories of her lost friend.

"Poor thing!" Dr. Vimal Sant continues. "She never realized that she had breast cancer. It would have been possible to do something to save her had she come to me for examination early." Dr. Vimal Sant says. "Particularly, as you all know by now, in cancer cases, time is very important. Time is the essence. The earlier it is discovered, the better it is. Early discovery followed by immediate treatment is what is needed. If you delay any one of these two, there is no pardon. The demon is sure to get you."

All of them look at the empty chair. The demon did take their friend's life. No one says anything for a long while. There is a brief and uneasy silence spread in the room.

"We are not here to lament but to recall and appreciate how courageously she spent her year after her cancer was detected." Anita once again takes charge of the proceedings.

"If that is so, then get that damn empty chair out of sight. It is very depressing to even look at it." A much younger looking woman, perhaps in her late twenties or early thirties, very graceful with a shapely body, grabs the chair and starts pushing it to a far away wall. The whole place reverberates with a loud noise coupled with the tic-tock sound of her high heeled shoes. For a moment, everybody is speechless and just stares simultaneously at the young woman and the chair she is pushing. The young woman returns to her own chair, readjusts it and asks her neighbor to shift her chair a bit.

"What? Umm...what? What's it you want?" The neighbor, Virani, another relatively young woman, perhaps this one also in her late twenties or early thirties, doesn't quite realize what is going on.

"I said pull your chair a bit so that six of us will form a proper circle. Right now, it looks a bit crooked." Virani gets up and pulls her chair where she thinks would be the right place for her seat.

"Are you settled now, Shaina? And you, Virani?" Anita looks at both of them with a smile and adds, "Shaina, you are absolutely right. Good you removed that empty chair from our sight. It did emit some 'vibes' of depression, especially for all of us who are victims of breast cancer, isn't it?"

"Well, except me, I suppose." Says Dr. Vimal.

"That's right Dr. Vimal. You are the specialist here. As a matter of fact, you are the one who has called this meeting today. Shall we proceed with the agenda of this meeting now?"

"Yes, yes." All the women agree to proceed with the meeting.

"Ladies," Dr. Vimal starts talking, "this meeting is specially called for a novel idea, an idea for developing a support group and thereby a major support centre for all breast Cancer victims." And the meeting of that day progresses as per the agenda.

Dr. Vimal clears her throat and starts talking, "Ladies, first of all, thank you all for coming to this meeting today in spite of such a short notice. To give you all a brief background of why I have called this meeting today is, in one of my casual meetings with Anita, I just mentioned to her the idea of the Breast Cancer Support Centre. To my utter surprise, Anita just took to that idea like wild fire. In theory, it is not a new idea. What we term as 'group therapy' is being practiced in many other countries today. So, a Support Centre as such is nothing new. It is just that it is not there yet in India and perhaps in many other countries with older cultures, such as ours. Women discussing openly about problems such as breast cancer is still a big taboo here, isn't it?" Dr. Vimal briefly looks at everyone and sees them nodding.

"But when I visited Canada for a two-year research fellowship in Oncology, I came across many Cancer Centres in Canada that offer group therapy to women. This service is offered to women with breast cancer in addition to their medical treatment. I was so impressed with their work that right then and there, I took a decision that; after getting back to India, I should start a similar project based on the same concept, for women with breast cancer. As a doctor, especially as a breast cancer specialist, I felt that this was my calling. And when I mentioned this to Anita, she just loved the idea." Dr. Vimal briefly looks at Anita and smiles.

"As you all know, she is a very well recognized social worker, and also a breast cancer survivor, herself gone through mastectomy. I thought she might be the best candidate for discussing this idea with you all in detail. And that is the purpose of this meeting, my dear ladies. Her role here will be what we can call, a 'patient representative'. How do you like that?"

Everyone claps at Dr. Vimal's suggestion. They unanimously declare Anita as the 'patient representative'.

"Thank you ladies" Anita says with a smile and modesty.

"As a doctor and a breast cancer specialist, I shall help you. I'll also send all my other patients to this group for support, including those in the future..." Dr. Vimal says.

"And I feel confident that all the patients will gladly join this group on Dr. Vimal's recommendation. We are indeed fortunate that we are starting such a project as a 'group therapy' here for support." Anita says.

There is again a light applause from the rest of the women in the room.

Dr. Vimal looks quite pleased with their response. She starts talking again to the group. "It is better not to think of what a woman goes through when one or both of her breasts are required to be removed in a mastectomy procedure. By now, I know each one of you very well and you all as a group provide an excellent sample for me and many other researchers like myself to know what any woman goes through mentally and emotionally during such times." She looks at her audience. Each woman is listening to her intently.

"We have had many interactions between us and I know each one of your case-histories very well. I have seen and met your family members and I have seen their reactions and responses to your disease, especially your husbands and children. However, during all our interactions, I always felt that you were not opening up completely. I felt that you were a bit detached from me. Then I realized that that could be because I was your doctor and not a friend or a fellow patient. Judging from this experience, I came to a conclusion that there must be a different way of communication, some other channel to establish some kind of bond between two women patients suffering from the same disease; so that there could be a distinct openness between them. The more I thought about it, the more I was determined to bring this idea of 'group therapy' for support into practice. The first name to come to my mind was Anita's." Dr. Vimal looks in the direction of Anita and smiles again.

"Anita was my very first patient on my return from Canada. It was a couple of years ago. When was it Anita?"

"Exactly two years ago. I remember even the day, date and time." These words from Anita amuse everyone there.

"I had a two year research fellowship at a renowned Cancer Centre in Canada." Dr. Vimal starts talking again.

"I spent those years in cancer research with some top caliber scientists there. I thought that the Centre was an extraordinary place. Every possible advanced research tool was available there. For me, it was like entering a wonderland. What impressed me the most, however, was its method of giving moral support to the patients. A portion of this Centre is dedicated completely to this activity. Support centre is an important part of this Centre, as important as the Centre's research and treatment wings. It is dedicated primarily for giving moral support to the cancer patients and their family members. It offers awareness, education and counseling on all aspects of the disease. It's a big help to the patients."

It is only Dr. Vimal's voice that is heard. All others are listening to her with utmost attention.

"There are qualified psychologists and psychiatrists among the counselors. There are many survivors of breast cancer as well, like our Anita, who are working there as patient advocates and patient representatives, most of the times, on volunteer basis."

Dr. Vimal looks at Anita with gratitude to signal her genuine appreciation. "These women volunteers, or patient representatives, share their experiences. They talk to women who are newly diagnosed with the disease and give them courage. For the awareness and educational activities, there are various workshops conducted on various topics relating to breast cancer and all other forms of cancer. In a separate hall, termed as the conference hall, researchers and doctors meet these social workers to discuss each other's work. I have seen doctors and scientists from all over the world coming to this centre. Adjacent to this hall are two rooms of moderate size, one with Indian décor and the other with décor from the Far East. Demonstrations of Yoga are regularly arranged in the room with Indian décor. People there firmly believe that the practice of Yoga offers peace of mind to the patients. In the other room, emphasis is laid on relaxation techniques practiced in the Far Eastern countries. I would say that this part of the centre is specifically designed for only moral support and is an essential and integral part of the main Cancer Centre." Dr. Vimal looks around to see how her idea is received by her listeners.

The listeners look fully engrossed in her speech. At the same time, they also look absolutely still, like statues, as though only their bodies are there, but mentally, they all have drifted somewhere else. Could it be that they are visiting their past perhaps? Yes, definitely yes!

Each one of the five women is visualizing the events of her own past when her breast cancer was diagnosed. It seems those days are unfolding before each woman's mental eyes like a movie. Each one of those five women; Anita, Ritu, Maya, Virani, and Shaina sitting there today, is a breast cancer survivor, each one with her own distinct story, each one with her own journey through breast cancer!

Anita

Nainum Chhindanti Shastrani
Nainum Dahati Pavaka...[9]

Atman can not be destroyed by a weapon, nor can it be burnt. It has no end. It is immortal!

Vasansi Jeernani Yatha Vihaya
Navani Grunhyati Naroprani...[10]

Just as a human being changes his or her clothes, so does the Atman change the attire; and the attire is the physical body of human beings. What is mortal in this world is this physical body!

Dr. Deven Dixit is reading aloud his favorite book on the Hindu philosophy, and the sound of his reading is ringing in the veranda. Day and night, he is seen sitting in his armchair, reading aloud, sometimes even in the wee hours of the morning. This has been going on for the last almost two years. It is almost his routine now-a-days; get up in the morning, read for a few hours, take a shower, have something to eat and read again, take a nap in the afternoon and then after having a cup of tea, read aloud a few lines from this book again, evenings are almost always occupied by reading some similar books on Hindu philosophy, and that continues till he is tired and ready to sleep at night. There is absolutely no room for anyone or any thing else in his routine. He has made this routine very rigid and unfriendly. No entertainment. No social life where he could meet some other people and have some fun. Not even a conversation with his wife Anita, who is actually a very friendly and smart woman.

Anita was almost staring at him while he was reading the philosophy book. Sitting on an armchair in that position, holding the book that way with both hands and looking into it, he seemed like a stranger to her. 'Who is this man?' she thought to herself. 'It wasn't so just a couple of years ago. He was an enthusiastic member of the society then. He was a loving husband, a very romantic at that; a caring father to our only

9. These are lines from the *Bhagvad Geeta*, a holy book on Hindu philosophy.
10. These are also lines from the *Bhagvad Geeta*.

daughter, Devnita. We three used to have so much fun together...' Anita's thoughts started flowing, and she was right actually.

Until recently, Deven loved playing badminton and was a member of a near-by sport club. He was a very popular professor of English literature in the college. The English course he taught was regarded as one of the best courses in the college. Students lined up for his classes. Those who couldn't get admitted to it, felt disappointed.

Even at his home, there used to be a continuous flow of people. Their house was a place where everyone was welcome with open arms. When his students and friends visited him, he would spend hours with them talking and laughing. When Anita's friends and colleagues would come, it was Deven who would spend more time with them. Devnita's friends loved him too. Many among them would say to her, 'you are so lucky Devnita; your dad is like a friend to you. Ours is so strict...' Devnita would laugh at their comment.

Anita looked at him again. He was still reading his book aloud. She wasn't sure if his mind was really in it, or he was reading it for the sake of reading. His voice, the passionate one that she loved so much and grown familiar to over the years when he read the poetry, was long gone. This was a totally unfamiliar voice, very dry and arid with no life in it.

"What happened? Why did he change so suddenly? Why did he stop talking to people, mixing with the people, going to places, even going to the sports-club? He hasn't played badminton, a sport that he likes so much, in months. He hasn't touched his badminton racket; he hasn't even touched *me* in the last two years. For some unknown reason, he picked up those philosophy books and since then, he hardly talks to me, his dear wife, Annie..."

Anita looked at him again. Sitting on that armchair, he was looking like an old man, who had lost interest in everything in life. She just shook her head lightly with mild frustration and went into the kitchen. From the kitchen window, she could clearly hear that dry, life-less voice of his. She tried to imagine that familiar, passionate tone in it. As she heard his voice longer with her imagination, she felt the familiar tone reverberating in the atmosphere. She was hearing the same passionate voice, except it had a touch of melancholy in it. She sat on the kitchen chair and started listening to it intently. The sounds of his passionate voice took her straight back into her beautiful past.

A young man by name Deven Dixit had recently joined the community college staff as an instructor in the department of English. It was the month of June and the semester had just begun after the summer holidays. This young instructor entered the class with his briefcase. It was his first time teaching a class. The students looked at him with a keen eye and after assessing this young man cruelly, started leaving the class room. He didn't seem to care though. He opened his briefcase and pulled out a book. It was a poetry book. The very first poem was a sonnet by John Milton, titled 'Paradise Lost'.

When I consider how
My light is spent...

Deven Dixit, after introducing himself to the class, started reading aloud from the book. His deep, passionate voice filled with emotions expressed in the poem captured some ears and the students stopped going outside. One by one, they all came back and took their seats and started listening to him. In a few minutes, he got them fully engrossed in the emotion and passion of that sonnet.

...They also serve
Who only stand and wait...

He finished the last line of that sonnet and looked around. Students were motionless, listening to his superb teaching without a word, as though they themselves were 'lost' in Milton's 'Paradise'! He closed the book and with a smile on his face, reminded them about the period being over. The students almost applauded his teaching. They all went towards him and started talking to him. The way he taught that sonnet that day made some students feel as though their instructor himself had been blind like John Milton. The immortal sweetness of Milton's poetry was delivered to them by Deven Dixit with no reservations that day. The students got hooked up to his teaching forever, and neither he nor the college administration staff ever looked back. Deven Dixit was a hit as an English professor, especially for English poetry, for the years to come.

Anita was in the class that day. She was a first year student taking English Literature as her optional subject. She was listening to his teaching, like everyone else, with an intent ear. Like everyone else, he had impressed her too, except he had done a little more to her than to others. He had touched her heart, she felt. She waited until everyone left the classroom. He was busy collecting his books and papers and putting them neatly in his briefcase.

"Are you new in this college?" She mustered her courage and walked towards him.

"Yes." He smiled at her and closed the briefcase.

"I liked your teaching very much."

"Thank you, thank you very much. This was my very first time teaching a class of this size in a college." He smiled again at her and started walking towards the door.

"I would say it was a total success..." Anita complimented him again. He just nodded with a smile and continued walking.

"I am a first year student here, planning to achieve a degree in Social Work ..." In an attempt to continue the talk with him, she also started walking with him and volunteered some information about herself.

"Oh? But then, you are here in English Lit..." He asked, exactly as per her expectation.

"I decided to try out English Lit. as an optional subject, so I attended this class today."

"So? What's the outcome now?"

"Well, it is definitely going to be my option now."

"Good. I am happy to hear that." He looked at her.

"Perhaps I might take it as my Secondary subject..." She said innocently.

"I never imagined English Lit. could be a secondary subject for anyone..." He emphasized the word 'secondary' and gave her a mischievous smile.

'God, he is funny...'! She thought when she saw his smile.

"Where did you go for your college education?" She asked him.
"I went to a community college in New Delhi for my undergraduate degree. Then, I finished my both Graduate and Doctorate programs at the Delhi University."

"Wow! You have a Ph.D. in English Lit." This was more of a question to him. He just nodded and said, "Please, do register in my class. I hope to see you there every day." He sounded quite earnest when he said this. He then gave her a long look, a look that seemed like an hour long to her, and then started walking rather fast. She stood still for a moment. A funny kind of tingling shiver went through her entire body in that second when she saw him look at her with that gaze. 'Yes, Dev, yes. Believe me; you'll see me every day from now onwards…', she said to herself and started walking towards the cafeteria. She had to share this beautiful incident with her dear friends, who were waiting for her there.

"I am so glad you are taking my course." Deven said to Anita the very next day after the class was dismissed.

"You don't even know my name." She said.

"I know. It's Anita, right?" He asked.

"How do you know that?" She was genuinely surprised.

"I have my own ways of finding out, especially about things or people I like." He said with his typical mischievous looking smile. She blushed at which he gave out a loud laughter.

And the rest was history. She didn't have to learn Milton's 'Paradise Gained' anymore for, she had gained it already.

Deven and Anita started meeting frequently outside the college environment. The more they met each other, the more they fell in love with each other. Anita finished her Bachelor's degree in Social Work and started working in a nearby rehabilitation centre as a councilor. Deven was very nicely settled in the college, extremely popular with both the students and the teaching staff. On one fine day, they both tied the knot. The entire college staff was invited for the wedding. They set up their home in a very close vicinity of the college.

Many of his senior students would come to his home for guidance. At times, even at home, it would seem as if he was conducting a college class for English right there. He had no problem helping anyone at any time, especially if the questions were about something in English poetry. That was his love and passion. Robert Frost, William Wordsworth, H.W. Longfellow, John Milton, were Deven's favorite poets. And Lord Byron! When he taught Byron, one would feel as though the Goddess of poetry had blessed Deven with her whole heart. Anita had no qualms about his students coming to their abode either. Many of them would come frequently, feeling quite free in their house. Many times, if she had some time, she herself would sit through Deven's teaching. She would really enjoy it. Many times, she would entertain them with hot steaming coffee. They all would then discuss jointly about some poet over a hot cup of coffee. On such occasions, there was never any time limit, nor there remained any distance between the teacher and his students.

Deven loved his wife and her healthy attitude of supporting his passion of teaching. To show his appreciation, many times, he would go outside late in the night and get her a string of fresh Jasmine flowers that she so dearly loved. Many of his students had noticed this. They had also noticed that huge mirror hung on a wall adjacent to their double bed in their bedroom, when they visited their home for the first time.

'There is a huge mirror besides his double bed, did you notice it?' Someone would start the topic.

'No wonder he can explain Lord Byron's poetry so well…' some other student would answer.

'The guy is a romantic soul…' a third student would say.

'Not just him. You need two to tango…' a girl would say.

'What do you mean?'

'His wife must be a romantic soul too. Know what I mean…' the girl would give her opinion like an expert.

'Did you see anything else interesting in the bedroom?' some one would inquire.

'Who do you think I am an intruder or a spy or something…?'

'No, no. just asked. You are a senior and go there frequently, that's why I asked…'

'Hum, let me think…'

'I noticed many dried up strings of jasmine flowers hung on one side of the bed…' some one would report.

'Really?' the girls' eyes would become saucer sized after hearing that.

'Oh, what a romantic couple…' All the girls unanimously muse over the idea and release a big sigh. Their gasp would be very clearly audible.

A discussion such as this one was quite common among Deven's students. And it was true. Deven and Anita had a wonderful relationship and a very romantic one too. Once in a while, when she would stand in front of her huge mirror to get ready for work, he would come from behind and embrace her; then looking at her image in the mirror, he would say to her, 'you are really the sunshine of my life, Annie!' That was his pet name for her. She loved it too. Looking at her, he would recite a few lines of one of his favorite poets,

'...Shall I compare thee
To a Summer's day
Thou art more lovely
And more temperate...'

His recitation of some such remarkable, classic poem in his voice that was full of passion, she would be totally lost in it too. But then, "okay, Dr. Deven Dixit. Enough of Shakespeare now, I've got to go to work..." She would come out of her own Trans. Trying to free herself from his strong hold. However, she would give up her attempt rather quickly and very much willingly.

The birth of their daughter was almost like a cherry on the top! They named her Devnita, a beautiful and imaginative combination of their own two names. Anita left her work altogether to care for their daughter and Deven's teaching at the college continued. He flourished in his career, gradually assuming the Dean's position of the Arts faculty at the college. After Devnita started full time school, Anita joined workforce on a part time basis and started going to a nearby hospital in a patient-rehabilitation program.

Devnita grew up to be a well-groomed, bright young woman. She completed her high school successfully and was ready to go the college. Everyone thought that she would choose her father's college but she chose the one a little far away from their city and got an admission there. It was time for her to leave home. The Dixit couple had organized a big party for her send-off to the college. Many of their colleagues from work as well as most of her own friends were invited to the party. The party was arranged in one of the halls on the college campus. Deven left a little early to oversee all the arrangements. Devnita was getting ready in her room with a few of her friends around. A lot of laughing and giggling was going on in her room. Anita was getting ready in her room next door. Just then Deven walked in.

"What happened? Did you forget something?" Anita asked him, she was busy tying her hair in a bun.

"Yes, a very important thing." He said, looking at her intently.

"What?" Anita was standing in front of her huge mirror trying to finish tying her hair. She was wearing a beautiful blue silk sari and a long pearl necklace that was dangling on her bosom freely. With her both hands raised above her head, she looked like she had assumed one of those famous dancing poses of the old Ajanta sculptures.

Deven came from behind and hugged her tightly and started kissing her passionately.

"This, this is what I had forgotten." He said and continued kissing her beautiful neck.

"Deven, Deven stop it. The girls are right next door getting ready..." Anita resisted a bit.

"I know that. But I wanted to do this, one last time before we send our daughter to the college, Annie, before we become empty-nesters. That's why I rushed home." He said.

"Why, wouldn't an empty nest be completely free?" She teased him.

"Yes, but that's no fun. Playing hooky to our grown up daughter and caressing you has been more fun to me. There is a different kind of thrill in it."

"Silly you, that's so childish..."

"May be, but so what? And that's exactly what I want to do right now, one last time..." He gave her that all too familiar mischievous smile.

"You are one crazy man, I tell you." She laughed.

He held her face and turned it towards him. He looked at her again very intently. Clad in a deep-blue silk sari and a pearl necklace, she looked like a star studded night to him. He started reciting,

"She walks in beauty, like the night
Of cloudless chimes and starry skies;
And all that's best of dark and bright
Meet in her aspect and her eyes..."

For a brief moment, she also got carried away, especially with that passionate voice of his and the way he recited those lines to her. But she didn't let him finish the poem. Instead, she shook him gently holding his shoulders. "Dev, wake up buddy, wake up from your childish antics. We have planned a huge party for our daughter, and we are the hosts, remember?"

He laughed and left the room murmuring softly a line from Lord Byron's poems.

Lately, this had become Anita's favorite pastime. When Deven read passages from those philosophy books aloud in his dry voice, she would imagine the sound of his passionate, familiar voice in its place and that would invariably take her into their past, a lovely past that she had enjoyed together with him, for more than twenty years. Alas; that past had become her treasured past now for, there were no guarantees for future any more!

Why not? What changed that? What happened, really? Even when she was diagnosed with breast cancer, he kept his 'self' intact. He was scared at the beginning when it was newly diagnosed, no doubt, but then he soon collected himself and took care of everything. He was her friend, her consoler, even her nurse looking after her wonderfully. Then what did happen suddenly, that he changed so much, to this extent? Anita drifted into the past again. She could clearly picture the days when her disease was diagnosed.

"Annie, you look quite tired these days..." Deven said to her one day after she got back from work.

"Hum. May be I'm entering menopause, or may be I'm missing our daughter very much ...." Anita warded off his comment with a shrug. Devnita had left home for college in another city for quite some time now.

"May be so. But just to be sure that there is no other problem, get yourself checked by a doctor, dear." He said.

With her increasing feeling of tiredness, Deven insisted her to see a doctor. One day, Anita returned from work with a tremendous fear and worry on her face.

"Why do you look like this Annie?" Deven inquired the moment he saw her.

"Just back from a doctor's clinic." She said.

"And?"

"He has ordered a whole bunch of blood tests for me and, and ..."she couldn't complete her sentence.

"And, and what?"

"He is sending me to a breast cancer specialist." She broke down crying.

"What, a breast cancer specialist?"

She just nodded.

"Why, why does he suspect that?" Deven's body developed a mild tremor on hearing that. "Did he examine your breasts?"

She nodded again.

"And?"

"And he said he felt a few lumps in my left breast. Since they are rooted deep inside, I couldn't feel them at all. But the doctor did." She said after the first crying spell was over.

"May be, he just wants to rule out anything extreme like cancer, that's all. I'm sure those lumps are just some benign lumps, some fibroids or some such things. We'll take the appointment of the specialist right away. Don't worry my sweet Annie ..." He collected himself right away and consoled her. He then dialed the telephone number and took the first available appointment of Dr. Vimal.

The day of her appointment dawned.

"Dev, my left eye is twitching since this morning." Anita said to him as she was getting ready for the appointment.

"So, what does that mean?" He was also getting ready.

"That means something really bad is going to happen today. I am feeling scared."

"Don't be silly. These are all stupid superstitions, only the uneducated and irrational people believe in all that. Nothing bad is going to happen today, okay? There is nothing to fear." He assured her and started reciting,

"Fear no more the heat O' the Sun,
Nor the furious winter's rages..."

"Dev, for crying out loud, will you stop this? Will you keep your Shakespeare aside for a few moments?" She seriously yelled at him and he stopped right away. She was truly upset and also scared, he could see that.

The examination by Dr. Vimal was over. So were the blood tests and other relevant tests. The test results were back. Unfortunately, the lumps that were detected in Anita's left breast were found to be malignant.

"It is a little unusual that a woman has more than one malignant lump in her breast at the same time, Mrs. Dixit. Very rarely I have found that in my medical practice." Dr. Vimal was talking to Anita and Deven in her office. Anita was almost frozen after listening to the diagnosis; and Deven, he just blurted out foolishly, "Oh my God, that means her days are numbered, isn't it?" and then he himself went in a shock. Listening to this sudden exclamation from him, Anita froze completely.

"What are you talking Mr. Dixit?" Dr Vimal stopped him right away from making such erroneous comments. "You are saying this because you are in a shock and perhaps in a confused state of mind. But there is no such thing as her days being numbered, okay?" Dr, Vimal was very firm about what she said. She was not pleased at all with his remark.

"Mrs. Dixit, we will have to remove your left breast immediately. This procedure is called 'mastectomy'. I would go one step further and remove some of your lymph nodes as well from the armpit. That way we'll eradicate the cancer completely and give no chance for its further growth in other tissues of the body such as liver or lungs." After explaining the biopsy and blood reports to the couple, Dr. Vimal was giving them an idea about what she intended to do next. After the first shock, they both seemed fairly quiet while listening to her, which surprised her mildly.

"Mr. and Mrs. Dixit, quite honestly I am a bit surprised at your reaction to this diagnosis. After finding out that they have breast cancer, almost all my patients cry loudly or yell hysterically, a few of them faint; some husbands faint too, some freeze completely for a long time, and some start doubting my medical prowess and take their case elsewhere, a few have even challenged my diagnosis and threatened to filing a court case. You have done none of this. I really admire your strength and your 'sangfroid'!" Dr. Vimal must have barely finished her complementing those two for their bravado when Anita tried to stand up but started shaking with an intense tremor. Deven tried to hold her but his hands were shaking badly too.

"Let me help you both." Dr. Vimal got up from her chair and moved towards Anita to help her stand up. And she noticed that Anita was not only shaking violently but her sari was completely drenched in her own urine. She looked at Deven to say something, but she noticed that Deven's pants were just as much drenched in his own urine, as Anita's sari was in hers!

Ritu

A very small bungalow, like an English cottage, is built in the middle of a small sized lot. It has everything in small proportion; a small yard in the back, a small yard in the front and a small patio at the entrance to the bungalow. A beautiful flower garden blooms in the front yard and the back yard has a small vegetable garden. The patio has four earthen pots, each one containing a rose bush, in its four corners. A single seater swing hangs on four brass links in the centre of the patio. The swing has a bright red colored, velvet cushion placed in it. The four rose bushes, when in full bloom, brings a special decorative look to the patio and enhance the whole ambience of the entrance area.

The bungalow has two rooms in the front area and three in the back. Of the three rooms in the back, there is the master bedroom, another bedroom for the children, and the third room is a kitchen with a small dining table in one of the corners. All these rooms look quite simple with modest furniture and equipment.

Of the two rooms in the front, one room is a living room, which has four comfortable looking chairs with a coffee table in the centre, nothing special or an expensive look about this furniture. A small show case with a glass door displays many pictures of the family. The second room, which is by far the largest room in the house, is decorated artistically and shows beautiful taste of the owners of this bungalow. This room is the music room! Old, authentic and very expensive looking musical instruments, such as two Tamboras, three Tabla sets, three Harmoniums and one Sarangi, are neatly kept on an equally beautiful, thick Persian carpet that is laid on the floor of this music room.

All these instruments look shiny and spotless clean. That is because, it is a regular routine of the lady of this house to dust and clean all these instruments every single morning. She enters this room every morning only after taking her bath. After cleaning the instruments, she worships them and then lights an incense stick in the room. She then sits on the carpeted floor with her eyes closed and hands in a Namaste position until the incense stick burns out. On occasional mornings, if she can not follow this routine, for whatever reason, her husband completes the routine himself. One can feel an air of sanctity in that room.

As can be easily guessed, from the artistic décor and the beautiful music room with its valuable contents, this house belongs to two musicians, Ritu and Parth Bose. Ritu is one of the leading singers of the country and her husband, Parth, is a renowned Tabla player. They have custom made this house for their comfort and convenience, and for their two daughters, Sangita and Shruti.

Ritu and Parth have already started giving training to their two daughters in classical vocal music, although they are quite young in age. Sangita is just about twelve years old and Shruti, barely nine years. Ritu teaches them the notes and nuances of various Raga and Parth teaches them the intricacies of various Tala.

Right now, the whole family is in the music room and the girls' music training is in session. Ritu is teaching them the notes of Raga Bageshri, and Parth is accompanying them on his Tabla.

"Repeat after me now, girls, ... dha ni sa ma ..." Ritu starts singing.

"...dha ni sa ma ..." Sangita is playing the Tambora and both the girls try to copy her.

"... ma ga re sa..." Ritu sings and the girls repeat after her.

"... ga ma dha ni..." Ritu sings again and the girls repeat after her.

And, almost as a ritual, the notes of that Raga sung in Ritu's melodious flawless voice take Parth back into their past.

She had sung the very same Raga when he first laid his eyes on her and heard her singing. It was many, many years ago, in a conference in Kolkata.

A huge, prestigious conference on classical music of India is going on for three days in Kolkata. Most of the stalwarts of music have gathered for this conference. It is an honor to be invited for this conference and even more so, if requested to present your music in this conference.

One of the oldest and very-well recognized vocalists, Guru Mathurabai, is invited to present her classical music for the conference. She is sitting on the stage with all her paraphernalia, which includes her many senior disciples as well. They are all sitting behind her. Guru Mathurabai starts singing one of the most favorite Raga of all times, Raga Bageshri, and within minutes, the effect of her singing makes the whole atmosphere come to a standstill. The audience is completely spell-bound. Just then she gestures to one of her senior disciples to join her in singing. The senior disciple joins her in singing and after a few minutes, the entire audience is swinging at the beat of her singing. This disciple is a young woman barely in her late twenties, named Ritu. Her pleasant face, demure look and the way she is dressed up for this occasion, all impress the audience. Her Guru gives her a look of pride and appreciation for her singing and gestures her to complete the musical piece. Ritu captures the attention of the entire conference.

A young man named Parth, is also attending the same music conference. He is extremely fond of playing Tabla and has been taking lessons from a renowned Guru of Tabla. Just as everyone, he is also taken aback by Ritu's singing and her melodious voice.

Guru Mathurabai's performance comes to an end and in a thunder of applause she takes a bow from her connoisseurs. As she descends the stage, she is surrounded by the audience and is completely hidden in their gathering. All her disciples also descend the stage after their Guru, each one carrying something, like a musical instrument or bouquets of flowers or candles, in their hands. Ritu descends down carefully with a delicate musical instrument, a Tambora in one hand. Seeing her, Parth hurries towards her, offers to take the Tambora in his hand and starts complimenting her for her singing.

"What a voice, simply heavenly." He says.

"It's God's grace." She says politely and declines his offer of carrying the instrument.

"And what a singing caliber? Simply amazing..." He persists.

"It's my Guru's grace." She says again very politely and starts walking towards a room that is specially assigned to her Guru for the evening.

"And that song you presented in it, oh simply heavenly!"

"It's called *Bandish,* not song..." She corrects him and smiles at him.

"May I know your name please?" He feels amused by her brevity.

"Ritu." She just utters her name and continues walking.

"Mine is Parth." He tries to introduce himself to her but she just smiles at him and enters the room disappearing completely from his sight. He feels frustrated. He stands there for a few minutes with a hope that she might come outside but instead, he sees her Guru enter the room. He gives up and turns back to leave. Just then, his own Guru of Tabla comes there and asks him, "Have you met Guru Mathurabai in person?" Parth shakes his head.

"In that case, come inside with me, I'll introduce you to her." Parth is about to decline his invitation, when he remembers who Guru Mathurabai's disciple is. He readily agrees, and follows his Guru to Guru Mathurabai's room.

"Oh, please come in, come in..." Mathurabai welcomes Parth's Guru with a big smile.

"What a performance? Mathurabai, I say you created history today, really. That Raga you presented, as though it was created only for you. Simply fantastic." Parth's Guru is showering compliments on Mathurabai liberally.

"Thank you, thank you, ji! It's after all Him who gets me singing..." Mathurabai looks up to the sky, indicating God and gives a hearty laugh.

"And you are training your disciples also very well, I must say. That young woman, who joined you later in the singing, she very expertly complimented your singing with hers. That's wonderful." Mathurabai thanks him again and calls Ritu outside. She then tells her to bow down and touch his feet with respect. As she does so, he says, "my heartfelt blessings to you my dear girl. Mathurabai, she will carry your torch much further. And this is my disciple, Parth. He has been learning playing Tabla from me for quite a few years now. A very dedicated disciple, quite promising too. " It is Parth's turn now to bow down and touch Mathurabai's feet. She blesses him and the two Gurus start talking with each other about music and also many other things besides music.

"Thank you, my dear God!" Parth looks at the ceiling and purposely says it a little loudly while smiling at Ritu.

"What's that for?"

"Well, you were avoiding me earlier, but God brought me straight to you, right here inside this private room." They both laugh and a link is established between them.

This incident took place a good fifteen years ago. What started as a simple relationship between a singer and her connoisseur transpired into 'love' and within a year, Ritu and Parth tied a knot.

Parth's prowess in Tabla was also getting recognized by the listeners and that complimented Ritu's singing career. In the last ten years or so, not a single performance took place where she didn't take Parth's accompaniment on Tabla. A special chemistry was created between Ritu's singing and Parth's playing Tabla and people just loved this chemistry. This 'duo' had become immensely popular with all the music connoisseurs, especially with the younger crowd, in the entire country. They were performing in most of the major and prestigious music conferences and music gatherings of the country. People would buy expensive tickets and go to the concerts mainly to hear this 'duo' perform; and would get back more than their money's worth for these concerts. Every music concert of Ritu and Parth was a success. Their performances would seem like a miracle to the listeners. Their musical prowess was considered to be one of a kind, their concert an unbelievable event, every time. 'Two stars are born', people would say. The stars above were smiling on them and so was the Goddess of music!

Three years into the marriage, Ritu and Parth gave birth to a beautiful baby girl. They named her Sangita, a name that stands for music itself in Sanskrit. Three more years, and they received another beautiful gift from God, their younger daughter. They named her Shruti, a term in Sanskrit, on which the entire classical music of India is based. Ritu and Parth took their daughters to every place they performed. The girls, although quite young in age, would sit quietly through the concerts, intently listening to their parents perform, which in turn, became a topic for admiration for the connoisseurs. Their music, together with their family life, flourished over the years, as though everything was made in heaven. Ritu and Parth were riding a high tide!

"Parth, are you ready to start playing Tabla for the girls now?" Ritu looked at Parth and saw that with his eyes closed, he was totally lost in something. She could guess what it was.

"Parth, Parth where are you honey? 'Earth calling Parth' 'Earth calling Parth..." Parth heard Ritu's voice calling his name and the girls giggling. He came out of his 'trance'. Giving Ritu a sheepish smile, he pulled the Tabla set in front of him and got ready for playing. Ritu just smiled at him and turned her attention towards her daughters.

"Now I will start teaching you a *Khyal*[11] in Raga Bageshri, Okay?" Ritu told her daughters and gestured Parth to start playing Tabla.

11. *Khyal* is the prime genre of Indian Classical vocal music.

"In vocal music, a Khyal of any given Raga is sung with the base of a song composed in that Raga." Ritu was teaching them the basics of Khyal singing.

"What do we call a song in Raga music?" She quizzed her daughters before starting the song.

"*Bandish.*" The girls simultaneously answered.

Feeling satisfied with their answer, she started singing a Bandish in Raga Bageshri,

"*...kaun karat tori binati piyarava...*"

"*...kaun karat tori binati piyarava...*" The girls started repeating after her and Parth slowly joined them by playing his Tabla. That was his favorite Bandish.

"*... Jabasay gaye moray...*" Just as Ritu tried to reach the lines of the Bandish in the higher octave, she started to cough mildly.

"Mummy I will get a glass of water for you." Little Shruti quickly got up and ran into the kitchen to get her mother a glass of water. Ritu closed her eyes, bent her head down and cupped her mouth with her hand; while Parth moved closer to her and started stroking her back gently. Every stroke was reminding him again and again of that black day he has been trying so hard to forget all these days. How many days has it been now; or has it been a year already?

It was almost after a decade that the same prestigious conference of classical music for three days was organized. This time it was going to be in Mumbai. There was only a week remaining before its commencement date. Ritu and Parth had the invitation to perform in it. Since it was a prestigious place to perform, they were very happy to receive the invitation to perform in it. Thousands of music lovers were expected to attend this conference. Ritu was preparing for her performance and so was Parth since he was accompanying her on Tabla. She was going to present a pentatonic scale named Raga Malkauns. As she was deeply engrossed in improvising the Raga, she felt a funny twitch in her throat and she busted out in a coughing spell. It didn't sound like a simple cough. A cough like this for a vocalist? She asked for a glass of water to Parth. After taking a few sips, she felt a bit better, so they ignored it and she went ahead with her singing practices. Nothing extraordinary, nothing unusual either, they thought. It was forgotten already.

The day of the performance approached and the whole family got ready for travel. They arrived at the Mumbai airport and headed straight to the conference hall. Just as they reached there, many people surrounded them with a lot of enthusiasm. The organizers escorted Ritu and Parth to the stage and were seated among the music dignitaries. Their daughters were seated in front of the stage along with the audience, from where they could conveniently see their parents.

It was Ritu's turn to present her music. She was seated down respectfully by one of the organizers on a thick carpet in the centre of the stage. Parth joined her with his Tabla in front of him. All the accompanying instruments were fine-tuned and the 'miracle music-duo', as they were so fondly called by their connoisseurs, started their performance. Ritu started singing the Raga pieces that she had prepared for this conference so diligently. The way she was improvising, the listeners felt as though the notes of the Raga were brought straight from the heavens. The intricate designs and the fine ornamentation she created with those notes were as if she was unfolding one treasure after another, each one priceless before the next. It was simply a fantastic presentation.

There were long periods of applause intermittently that were exciting to the organizers of the conference. She came almost towards the end of her performance when she felt the same kind of twitch in her throat that she had encountered earlier in the week at home. That twitch was followed by a spell of cough. She stopped momentarily and gestured Parth to pass a glass of water to her. He did. She sipped some water but it didn't help. She coughed again. She took a few more sips of water. Still it didn't help. She finished the whole glass of water and yet her coughing continued with increased intensity. One of the organizers rushed to get more water for the singer. Just then she coughed really loudly and with that coughing spell, fell down on the stage, totally unconscious, with her mouth open. A tiny stream of blood started oozing out of her mouth.

"Oh my good God!" Parth said loudly, pushed away the Tabla from the front and rushed to his wife's side. He picked up his wife's body delicately and started walking to the exit door. His exclamation was clearly heard through the microphone. Therefore, people started running towards the stage. Seeing him carry his wife's body like this, they became curious and wanted to know, 'what was going on?'

Their two daughters saw the whole thing and started crying. There was immense fear spread on their faces. In those few moments, many of the organizers rushed to the stage. Someone called an ambulance for Ritu. Some of them wanted to help Parth carry her, but Parth was not in this world. He was too engrossed in his grief and extreme worry, and totally confused about his wife's medical condition. What happened there in those few moments to his wife was a puzzle to him.

Just then the ambulance arrived. With its siren going at full blast, there was one big chaos. Someone advised Parth to make use of the ambulance. He darted towards the ambulance. All this time he held Ritu's body in his arms without letting anyone, even the ambulance drivers, touch her.

The ambulance rushed to a nearby hospital. Series of medical examinations, blood tests and X-ray tests took place. What came out of all that was a dark, shattering Truth!

"Cancer? My wife has cancer?" Parth was sounding too excited. He could not believe what the young doctor in the emergency room was telling him.

"Yes, Sir. I'm sorry to inform you but all the tests we did for your wife strongly point only to one disease, and that is cancer. I am not a cancer specialist, so I can't really tell you what kind of cancer it is. It could be lung cancer too, since she coughed a lot as you informed us, and vomited blood. But after examining her thoroughly, I felt tiny lumps in her both breasts, perhaps they could be malignant and that cancer could have gone to her lungs. I really can't say anything definitely right now, but my guess is that she could be suffering from breast cancer..." The doctor was almost apologetic to inform him about Ritu's disease.

"B r e..., B r e..., B r e a s t C a n c e r?" Parth had a very hard time repeating it. The doctor just nodded.

"And the blo...blo..blood, why did she vo...vo...vomit blood?" The words could barely come out of Parth. He started stammering badly.

"Again, it is my strong suspicion that she has breast cancer. We need to do the fine needle biopsy to confirm that, of course. The tiny stream of blood that oozed out of her mouth could be the result of the same now spreading in her lungs. " The doctor reiterated what he had informed Parth earlier. Parth stared at the doctor with a blank gaze.

'Ritu could have breast cancer! Really?'

'Really, Ritu does have breast cancer!'

Parth froze at the thought. His whole body became stiff. The doctor slowly walked him to a nearby chair, seated him and left the room, leaving him alone with his wife lying on a table, covered in a hospital gown, still partly unconscious.

There was some noise in the corridors outside. A senior doctor, the hospital administrator and a couple of nurses walked in the room.

"Mr. Bose, you heard what our doctor in the emergency room suspected, right?" The senior doctor walked towards Parth and almost startled him in his frozen state. "He is a very bright young doctor of our hospital and therefore we feel that his suspicion could be right. However, we have contacted one of the finest and renowned breast cancer specialists of the country and she is on her way here." He assured him. Parth just gave him a cold look. His mind was still in a frozen state.

"How are you doing, Mr. Bose?" The doctor seemed genuine. Parth just shook his head. "Please don't worry. Our hospital administrator will book a private room for your wife, and we will do everything within our capacity to make sure she is taken care of absolutely wonderfully. After all, she is the nightingale of our country, isn't she?" Parth nodded. The doctor was obviously aware of Ritu's profession and musical prowess. He then told the hospital administrator who came in with him, to arrange a private room for Ritu and instructed the nurses to move her there immediately. Then he gently put his hand on Parth's back and said, "Have courage, Mr. Bose, everything will be alright," and left the room.

As Parth's mind started coming out of its frozen state and as he started overcoming the original shock slowly, he started thinking of not just Ritu but also about his young daughters. Those few hours had passed in extreme agony and worry for him. Where were the girls? Who was with them in this new city? They must be scared to see their mother faint like that in the middle of her concert, and to see their father carry her in his arms and leave them in such a rush in an ambulance. They must be scared to see people make one big clamor like that.

He looked at Ritu. She was lying on the table in front of him, still partly unconscious. He walked towards her and gently caressed her face with his hand. A tiny line of dried up blood was still visible on one side of her mouth. He touched that line of dried up blood with his finger and just as he did so, he could not control his emotions any more. He broke down completely and started crying profusely. He was still crying when the hospital administrator and a nurse came into the room, ready to wheel away Ritu to another room. A private room had been arranged to start proper medical treatment for her. The nightingale of the country was a victim of cancer, possibly breast cancer!

Maya

"Ma, please come with me, at least see how you feel..." Kirti nagged and implored her mother; she was not going to listen to any of her mother's excuses today.

"Don't be silly Kirti, there is no way I'm ever going to see a psychotherapist, Okay?" The mother retorted.

"Ma please, just once, let us visit her. I heard she is really very good." Kirti begged her mother again.

"That's not going to help me Kirti. You know that, nothing is going to ever help me..."

"Ma, please don't talk like that. Why don't we go out somewhere, anywhere you like, perhaps just for coffee, and then on our way home, drop in to see this psychotherapist, literally for fifteen minutes. No more..." Kirti was relentless.

"Well, okay... we'll do that since you insist so much." The mother gave in.

Kirti immediately ran inside to book an appointment on the telephone with the psychotherapist for her mother, only for fifteen minutes as the mother agreed. Kirti and her mother, Maya Patel, were sitting on the patio in the backyard of their huge bungalow having their morning tea.

It was a daily routine for Maya and her husband Praful, for almost thirty years, to have their morning tea on the patio. There was a beautiful set of four wicker chairs and a table neatly arranged on the patio. The maid would bring a tray holding two fine China tea cups and plates, spoons and forks and lay them on the table. Just as Maya would come outside and sit on her favorite wicker chair facing the lawns of the huge backyard, the maid would bring another tray with a tea pot filled with hot tea, some biscuits and cut-up fruits. Shortly after that, Praful, still in his pajamas and an elegant gown over it, would join Maya on the patio. Maya would pour some tea in his cup and hand it to him. She would then pour some tea in another cup for herself. They both would slowly sip the hot tea, enjoying its flavor in each other's company and getting ready to start their busy day.

However, Maya's routine of having her morning tea on the patio had stopped altogether. Not only that, she gave up her morning tea altogether and hardly went on the patio that she so loved. It was at Kirti's insistence that Maya had agreed to join her on the patio for the morning tea that day.

"Oh my, some of the trees have grown so much taller since I was a child." Kirti exclaimed while looking at the well manicured lawns and the bushes and trees while sipping her tea. "Ma, it's so beautiful here in the mornings, isn't it?

"Hum." Maya said absent mindedly.

"In Mumbai, you hardly see a tree. We call it a concrete jungle, hardly any tree in sight." Kirti said.

"Hum." Maya said. She looked like her attention was drifted somewhere else.

"And such lawns and beautiful bushes, you have to drive for hours, to some far away park to see them." Kirti said.

"Hum." Maya responded while staring in a blank space.

"Even the air smells so fresh. And the peace, oh, it's so quiet and peaceful here Ma, there is hardly any sound heard here." Kirti went on chirping about how she felt at the moment, but all Maya responded to everything she said was with just a 'Hum'.

"Go to my Mumbai apartment and there's a constant noise of some kind or other, coming from some where, round the clock." Kirti turned to talk about her apartment, on which her mother's response was just a 'Hum', again.

"Ma, you are not talking at all. Why aren't you saying something, anything?" Kirti complained about her mother's lack of response.

"I know you are sitting with me for the morning tea because I forced you. I know you stopped having your morning tea altogether. I also know that you hardly come on the patio; but Ma, how long are you going to mourn Bapuji's death? How long are you going to feel sorry? I know his was a sudden demise but..." As Kirti started talking about her Bapuji, Maya turned her face towards her, but with a blank look. Slowly the sound of Kirti's talking started becoming fainter and fainter, as if Maya was slowly moving away from her daughter, away from all the surrounding, away from it all, into the past; her own past with Praful, her dear and loving husband of almost thirty five years.

She glanced at the bungalow that was dead silent since Praful's passing away. But, as Kirti's voice became fainter, there were sounds emerging from the bungalow, slowly becoming louder. She started hearing those sounds, sounds of life, her life when the bungalow was full with people. She felt the bungalow becoming alive again, with those all too familiar voices and sounds.

"Maya, where's my towel…"she heard Praful yelling from the shower.

"Here it is dear." she rushed to the shower to hand him a towel.

"Maya, have you finished all the preparations for my *pooja*?[12]" She heard her mother-in-law asking her. It was her routine to do a two-hour long pooja every morning and needed a lot of things prepared for it.

"Yes, yes, *Ba*, it will be ready in a couple of minutes, okay?" she gently told her.

"Ma, may I wear your blue sari today?" she heard Kirti yelling from her bedroom. She wanted to wear her mother's sari for the college day celebration.

"Yes, but make sure you don't put too many pins on the sari." she told her.

"Ma, I can't find my tennis racket?" she heard Anand, her youngest child and son, hollering all the way from the front door. His birth had brought a lot of joy to the family as he was the one to carry the family name,

"Anand, its right there, look carefully." She told her son lovingly.

"Ma, can I skip school today? I have got really bad stomach cramps." She heard Arti complain about her stomach cramps. Arti never had any liking for school and gave every reason possible to skip it. After entering puberty, *pms* was one more addition to her list of excuses for skipping school.

"Arti honey, you need not skip school for the whole day. I'll give you a pill and that should take care of your stomach cramps in a couple of hours, okay?" she rushed to get a pill for Arti's pms problem.

"Madam, there is a call for you…" she saw her servant standing in the doorway, politely holding a hand telephone receiver.

---

12. Pooja, a word in Hindi, means worshipping the deities. It entails some rituals that need many things such as fresh flowers, milk, sugar, oil lamps, etc.

"Who is it from?" she asked him.

"A lady from your Ladies Club, madam..."

"Okay, let me talk to her." Maya took the receiver from the servant's hand and started talking.

"Hello, yes, I do remember the Ladies club meeting this afternoon. What time is it at? Yes, yes, I'll be there. Oh, by the way, do you need a ride? Okay then, I'll pick you up, I'll ring you up just before leaving my house, be ready..." Maya hung up the telephone.

"Madam, the cook says she doesn't have enough vegetables to cook for the dinner ..." she saw her maid approaching her with the cook's complaint.

"Then you go to the market and get them soon. You know I make sure everyone eats plenty of veggies at dinner time, right?" Maya took some money out of her purse and gave it to the maid to get vegetables from the market.

"Ma, how do I look in your sari? I took some matching jewelry from your closet too" Kirti was modeling her attire to her mother. Maya looked at her daughter; Kirti's face was beaming with happiness.

"You look lovely dear..." Maya said while admiring her daughter in her sari. Kirti said 'bye bye' to her mother as she left for the college celebration.

And as Maya saw Kirti leave the house, so did she see that reverie of her past vanish away into the thin air. All those voices and sounds of life were also silenced completely. Instead, she heard Kirti calling her name.

"Ma, Ma, are you okay? Are you listening to me?" Kirti was gently holding her shoulders and shaking her. Maya gave her a blank look.

"Ma, I took an appointment with Meeraben for you early this afternoon." Kirti told her mother.

"Meeraben? Who's she?" Maya came out of her blank state of mind and asked in confusion.

"That's the name of this psychotherapist. Perhaps that's her professional name, I don't know that." Kirti told her. "You were getting that illusion again, weren't you Ma? You were thinking of Bapuji, and all of us still living at home, isn't it Ma?" Maya just nodded and kept quiet.

"We have to go and see that psychotherapist; it will be really good for you. Now, let us go inside, enough of sitting out here on the patio. You always think of Bapuji too much when we sit here." Kirti led her mother inside to her own bedroom.

Kirti was right actually. Every time Maya sat outside at Kirti's insistence, she was lost in that illusion of her past. What Kirti didn't know was that she got the glimpses of that illusion even when she was inside the house, anywhere, in the living room, dining room, family room, her bedroom, especially in her bedroom. Her life had been totally entwined with her husband's life for more than thirty five years, and with his sudden demise, it had become completely vacant. It seemed impossible for her to live without him, to live in his absence. It was as if he had taken the very essence of her life with him. She had no interest in living anymore.

Kirti took her mother to Meeraben, the psychotherapist, as per the appointment that afternoon. Her clinic was in a little brick house with a small garden and a white fence all around it. There was a little gate in the front portion of the fence and a walkway that led to a few steps in the front.

Kirti and Maya climbed up the steps to the front door and rang the doorbell. The receptionist opened the door, requested them to take off their footwear in the front area and led them to a sitting room. After seating there with a polite gesture, she went inside to inform Meeraben. In spite of the afternoon Sun, the room seemed a little dark. The walls and ceiling were all painted in bottle green color, and drapes of thick material of the same color were hanging at the windows. There was no furniture in the room, just a thick Persian rug with a few bulky looking cushions neatly laid on it. People were expected to use those cushions for sitting. There was a beautiful statue of Buddha on a tall pedestal in one corner of the room with a spot light focusing on Buddha's face. That was the only light in the room, the rest of the room was fairly dark. Maya and Kirti, in stead of sitting on the rug and waiting, walked closer to the statue and started looking at it intently. With the spot light, the divine expressions of Buddha's face had become even more prominent.

"The statue looks so peaceful, isn't it?" Meeraben entered the room.

"Yes, it certainly does..." Kirti flustered a bit but collected herself very quickly. She and Maya looked at Meeraben. She was a tall woman with a nice brown complexion. Her long hair were let lose on her back.

She was wearing a light yellow sari and a matching yellow blouse with long sleeves. 'She looks like a daffodil...' Maya thought to herself. Meeraben had a very pleasant countenance that was encouraging to both Maya and Kirti.

"Can you sit on the floor? Otherwise I can get a couple of chairs for you." Meeraben's voice was quite deep, its depth sounding very sweet.

"Yes, we can sit on the floor, no need to get chairs." Kirti said and all three of them sat on the rug using cushions. Meeraben sat in a lotus position and looked very comfortable in that pose.

"I understand your father is one of the leading astrologers of the country." Kirti tried to start the conversation with Meeraben.

"Yes, he is." Meeraben said.

"Do you practice astrology?" Kirti asked her.

"No, I don't, but my father has passed some of his knowledge to me over the years. So I do know a little bit of that science too." Meeraben responded pleasantly.

"Would you like to talk to my mother?" Kirti asked.

"Is it for astrology?" Meeraben asked Kirti.

"Uhhh...not exactly." Kirti was not explicit about their intentions for seeing Meeraben.

"As I said earlier, I do not practice astrology. I am a psychotherapist by profession. Would you like to see me for psychotherapy?" Meeraben made it quite clear about what she does, and what she *does not* do.

"My mother is feeling too depressed lately, so I thought I should bring her here to meet you." Kirti said.

"I hope, not for some entertainment with her astrology reading..." Meeraben stressed the word 'entertainment' and sounded slightly irritated.

"Oh no, no. Please, I didn't mean it that way at all..." Kirti felt embarrassed.

"That's okay, don't worry about it. A lot of people assume that being a daughter of a famous astrologer, I'm also an astrologer. Many people look at the science of astrology more as an activity for a good 'pastime'. They don't realize that it is a totally separate branch of science. My father always tells me, it can be a powerful tool that can be used in many areas of psychology, but I don't apply it in my psychology consultation. In my many years of practice as a psychotherapist, I have come to believe that astrology can provide a good base for starting some valuable conversations with the patients. Personally, it helps me connect with my patients quickly and positively. But I do not conduct my medical and scientific techniques of psychotherapy based on that science. Would that be okay with you ladies?" Meeraben intently looked at both the ladies. She wanted to know if after hearing this, they would still be interested in her professional services.

'This lady is quite forthright, and firmly believes in her own profession and convictions…' Maya was looking at Meeraben all the while she was talking, and thinking to herself, 'she is a trained psychotherapist. She must be quite good at it; otherwise she could have easily ridden on her famous father's name for her gains. ' Maya became interested in her.

As Maya was assessing Meeraben, Meeraben was assessing Maya. 'She looks lost in her thoughts, as if she is somewhere else. She seems to believe in astrology more than anything else right now. Perhaps, I should start with astrology, to get her attention and to connect with her…'

"I am going to draw an astrological chart for you first, before I start any of the medical techniques for therapy. Can you please tell me your date and time of birth?" Meeraben looked at Maya and asked her.

"It's August 31st, 1940, time is um …" It was Kirti who answered instead of Maya.

"And the time of birth?" Meeraben asked again. She was almost sure that the daughter may not have this answer. As guessed correctly, Kirti looked at her mother for answering this question.

"…it's 4.am …" Maya gave the information in a very nervous sounding voice.

Meeraben smiled, feeling happy that her strategy to get Maya say something, anything, worked for the time being. She jotted Maya's time of birth and then quickly and skillfully drew some kind of a horoscope chart on a pad of papers.

"You are a woman of tremendous energy. You try to achieve forty eight hours of work in twenty four hours, isn't it?" Meeraben looked at Maya and asked her. Her hand writing and her skillful drawing of chart impressed Kirti and Maya. They looked at her while she looked like she was studying the chart intently for a minute or so. Her conclusion of Maya's personality impressed Maya even more.

"Meeraben, you are one hundred percent right. Ma does do a lot of work in a short time. What she achieves in mere half a day, many women can't even think of doing it in two days." Kirti said.

"You mean, I *did do* a lot of work..." Maya corrected Kirti that gave a mild surprise to both Kirti and Meeraben.

"What do you mean, Ma?" Kirti asked.

"I mean, I *did, as in the past,* do a lot of work.. I used to be busy all twenty four hours back then, but not any more. Now, my all twenty four hours are free. No, not just free, they are *empty*! They are completely empty. I have nothing to do, no one to look after. My life is totally hollow, just plain meaningless. Nobody needs me any more..." Maya stressed the word 'empty' over and over again.

"Why do you call your life *empty*?" Meeraben asked her gently.

"Because it is so. My girls got married and moved away. My only son wanted to go to the foreign land, so I let him. He is so well settled there, there's no chance of him ever coming back to India now. And my dear Praful..." With those words, Maya started getting that blank look on her face again. 'She is slipping into somewhere else...' Meeraben knew right away. And so did Kirti.

"I can very clearly see that you have been suffering from some depressing situation for the past few years. Is it true?" Meeraben asked Maya but she didn't say anything. She had already dipped into the past, her own 'la la' land.

"Actually it's the last two years that she has lost complete interest in everything, I mean everything. She doesn't want to go anywhere or meet anyone, to wear any nice clothes or anything. All she wants to do is sit in her own bedroom and stare at the ceiling. She doesn't even as much go in the yard or the garden or even onto the patio that she loved so much. We have a beautiful house, and a beautiful garden around the house but she doesn't care anymore." Kirti answered on Maya's behalf.

"Kirti, did your father pass away suddenly and unexpectedly?" Meeraben asked Kirti, and Kirti just nodded to her.

"And what was his name?"

"Praful, Praful Patel. People called him '*motabhai*' with love and respect." Kirti said.

With the mention of that special name, Maya felt a slight jerk that brought her back to the present instantly.

"Yes, my Praful left me suddenly, and so unexpectedly, you have no idea. How I felt then and how I feel now, God only knows." Maya looked at the sky once and then looking at Meeraben, started talking directly to her. And that's exactly what Meeraben wanted; Maya to open up and talk!

"It was almost midnight." Maya was telling Meeraben, "Praful came into the bedroom after finishing his work. He was a renowned lawyer of the town and was very busy. We started our life together with nothing, you know. When we met, he was still doing his articling. Nobody called him motabhai then. But he was bright, he wanted to start his own practice and I supported him completely, mentally and financially too. I was working in a small office as a clerk. After marriage, we moved into a very small apartment, with hardly any furniture or other luxury things. But we worked hard, especially my Praful worked his way through the Law firm and in just twenty years, we built a huge bungalow on acreage. We had many servants and a social status that anyone would envy. He helped a lot of people who had no money to pay their fees, you know. That's when people started referring to my Praful as 'motabhai', out of love and respect." Meeraben looked at Maya as she was telling her about her own past. There was definitely an expression of pride in Maya's eyes about her husband.

Maya continued talking, "we had three beautiful children, all bright and lovely like my Praful. As Praful became more and more successful in his law practice, I left my work, and started concentrating totally on my children. His old mother was also living with us. Our house was full, my *life* was full! Just taking care of all of them, and especially my Praful, was a twenty four hour job for me. I had to actually squeeze out time for getting involved socially in the ladies club and all that. Can you imagine? Life was simply fantastic then..." Maya gave out a long sigh. Meeraben was listening quietly, and so was Kirti.

"Slowly one after another, all my children left home. Kirti and Arti got married and settled far away from here. Anand left for Canada, only to visit us once in every two or three years. Praful's mother passed away. All of a sudden, there was no one in the house..." Maya took a big breath and continued, "...but I had my Praful. I started focusing completely on him and believe me; he alone kept me quite busy. As it was, he was dependent on me; after our children left home, he became totally dependent on me. He just couldn't do anything without me. He relied on me for literally every thing, so much so, you have no idea. Right from putting paste on his toothbrush and giving him towel after his shower in the morning to laying his night pajamas on our bed, I took care of him. Taking the morning tea on the patio, sending hot lunch to his office, planning and serving a beautiful four course meal in the evening, I personally looked after everything. So many times, he brought his colleagues and sometimes even his clients for dinner to our home at a short notice, but that didn't make me nervous or angry or flustered, I would have the dinner ready with no problem."

Maya took a few seconds break and continued again, "and then that black night fell. It was almost midnight when Praful walked into the bedroom after finishing his work. He was working on some complicated case, he told me. He hadn't had his dinner yet, so I prepared a light dish and took it to our bedroom for him to eat before he goes to sleep. I was serving him the food when he felt he was sweating. He requested me to turn the fan on full strength. I did. But he was still sweating…" Maya gasped a bit but continued, "…he asked for a glass of water, so I poured some water in a glass and tried to hold the glass to his mouth. He was breathing very heavily. I tried to open the buttons of his shirt. He looked very, very uncomfortable. I tried to force some water in his mouth, with the hope that that would make him feel better, but that water didn't enter his mouth, it just rolled down his chin. That's because, Meeraben, the messenger of death had taken my Praful away from me at that moment on that black night..." Maya cupped her face partially and started crying. Kirti quickly pulled out a handkerchief from her purse and gave it to her mother.

Maya could not speak at all, so Kirti started telling Meeraben about what had happened on that night. "I got a call in the middle of that night by our maid. She was screaming and crying on the telephone. I couldn't understand what she was saying; all I could get was that she wanted me to come home immediately. I knew something was drastically wrong there 'where is Ma?' I asked her but she just kept on crying. I knew I needed to go there as soon as possible. I picked up my purse, my husband and I got into the car and we drove there as fast as we could. The drive from Mumbai is good two hours long, but honestly, I don't even remember now how we drove that night. When we reached home, we were told by the servants that they heard a very loud scream from the bedroom upstairs, so they all ran towards it. They described to me what they saw, Meeraben. According to their description, the ceiling fan was on at full strength, water and food was spilt all over the floor of the bedroom, Bapuji was lying on the bed with his mouth open, dribbling some foam from one side, and Ma was lying on him, unconscious." Kirti looked like she was about to cry too, but she managed to continue.

"One of the servants called the ambulance to take both of them to the hospital. We rushed to the hospital. All I remember now is that Bapuji was in one room, covered from head to toe in a white sheet, and Ma in the adjacent room, looking unconscious. She was under heavy sedation, I was told. 'How is my father?' I asked the nurses, they just shook their heads and looked at the sky. Meeraben, our Bapuji was gone. I was told that a massive heart attack of barely a few seconds took his life. All I did was to scream and bury myself in my husband's arms and cry my heart out." Kirti broke down.

Meeraben got up, got two glasses of water and passed them to the two ladies. Sipping some water made them feel a little refreshed. "Are you okay now, ladies?" She asked them.

Maya finished her glass of water. She sniffled a few times and started talking again. "Ever since then, my life has become one big empty hole. Kids came, stayed with me for a few days, then left. I realized that they have their own lives to live. But then, it's also true that no one needs me any more. And that huge empty house, it looks like it is going to swallow me one day." Maya started shedding some more tears.

"As you said, Mrs. Patel, you have suffered a big shock two years ago, right?"

"Yes, it was about my Praful…" Maya said.

"Mrs. Patel, is there anything else you are suffering from recently? Anything that you are suffering from *today?*" Meeraben asked Maya gently.

"Today?" Maya said with a slight surprise in her voice.

"Yes."

"Well, that's what it is, Meeraben, Ma's extreme boredom with life is what the suffering she is having today." Kirti said.

"Okay then. If there is nothing else, I will start working on her case to cater to her needs of feeling 'empty' and depressed. Now, before I start working on your case, I must ask you, how is your general health?"

"My g e n e r a l   h e a l t h ..." Maya faltered and kept quiet suddenly. Her stammering almost gave it away that she was not well.

"You are obviously having some health issues, isn't it?" Meeraben asked her.

"Did my chart tell you that?" Maya asked her.

"Perhaps yes, perhaps no. I told you earlier, I do not read peoples' horoscopes or birth charts although I am good at drawing them skillfully. But I am extremely good in my own profession, which is psychology; and that tells me clearly that you definitely have a health problem right now." Meeraben was serious.

"But, I don't want to live anyway, so why bother going to a doctor? I have no purpose in life; nobody needs me any more, so where is the point in checking my health issues?"

"In that case, you don't need to see a psychotherapist either. Psychotherapy is for people who want to get better and live well." Meeraben closed her chart and started getting up slowly.

"No, no, please sit. I have not been frank with you Meeraben." Maya said.

Meeraben sat again in her lotus position and started listening to her.

"I went in excessive depression after my Praful left me." Maya said.

"It was hard to recognize Ma just a year after Bapuji died. She was looking so ghastly, my beautiful mother looking almost like a ghost. I couldn't see that. So my sister and I insisted Ma see our family doctor soon, before she goes in some permanent kind of depression stage." Kirti said.

"And then?"

"We took her to our doctor. After examining her thoroughly, our family doctor advised us to take her to see Dr. Vimal..."

"Dr. Vimal? Isn't she the renowned breast cancer specialist?" Meeraben looked surprised and worried.

"Yes. Meeraben, she's the breast cancer specialist. I couldn't believe my ears first, 'did I hear correctly?' I had doubts. But when our family doctor insisted Ma sees a good breast cancer specialist, that's when I knew she meant it. So I took her to Dr. Vimal. To our total dismay, Ma has been diagnosed with breast cancer. Our family doctor had found a small lump in her left breast. After the fine needle biopsy, Dr. Vimal confirmed that the lump is malignant..."

"Oh God, no, and...?" Meeraben said

"And what? Ma does not want to do anything about it." Kirti said with total despair. She and Meeraben both looked at Maya to see her reaction, but Maya looked like she was already lost in her own thoughts again. This time she was thinking of her visit to Dr. Vimal.

"Soon after all my children left home, Praful, that's my husband, and I became the empty nesters. Just about that time, Ba, that's Praful's mother, also passed away. My children and Ba kept me very, very busy, for almost twenty hours of the day, you see." Maya was lying down on the examination table in Dr. Vimal's office.

Kirti was with her too. It was at the insistence of Kirti and her family doctor that Maya had agreed to go and see Dr. Vimal, the breast cancer specialist.

"I see." Dr. Vimal was carefully examining Maya and keeping her mind engaged by asking questions about her lifestyle. "Why were you so busy when they were around?"

"Oh, that's because they were totally dependent on me for practically everything and for all their needs. My children needed me in their studies too. Kirti, that's my daughter sitting outside in the waiting room, had a habit of reading her schoolbooks aloud and would insist that I sit in her vicinity somewhere. She needed me for doing all her studies. Arti, that's my younger daughter, didn't like schoolwork at all, so I had to literally push her to complete the high school graduation. So, she needed me for pushing her like this. Anand, that's our youngest child and son, he is very bright like his father, but seemed bored with his studies. So I had to nag and nag him constantly to study. He needed me even to complete his schoolwork and homework. And Ba, oh she was quite old and she needed me literally every step of the way..."

"Hum, and what about your husband?" Dr. Vimal was examining Maya's right breast.

"Oh my Praful, doctor, he was a very successful lawyer, all self made, you see."

"You must have helped him a lot in his early years then?" Dr. Vimal had moved on to Maya's left breast.

"Yes, doctor. Financially too."

"Oh?" Dr. Vimal was examining Maya's left breast very carefully.

"Yes. I had to work full time to support my family income in those early years of our life. Afterwards, of course my Praful's law practice flourished so much that there was no need for my full time work, so I gave it up, but by then, my three children were there, they kept me on my toes with their constant needs."

"Hummmm…" Dr. Vimal's face looked a bit serious as she pulled the gown over Maya's bare chest.

"What? What is it doctor?" Maya got up and sat on the table, looking worried.

"Mrs. Patel, you know why you are referred to me by your family doctor, right?" Dr. Vimal was washing her hands.

"Yes, yes I know."

"Your family doctor felt a tiny but significant lump in your left breast and wants me to give you a thorough examination on that lump."
"What's that?" Maya's face was almost warped with worry.

"Call your daughter inside. I'll explain that to both of you together." Dr. Vimal said.

Kirti came inside and sat on a chair. She also looked extremely worried.

"Mrs. Patel, I am going to do a fine needle biopsy on the tiny lump I felt in your left breast. We need to do this small procedure to rule out or confirm…"

"To rule out or confirm what?" Kirti and Maya both asked simultaneously.

"That the lump is not malignant." Dr. Vimal looked at them and said it in a serious voice.

"What's that?" Maya asked innocently as Kirti just looked at her in horror.

"That's cancer, Mrs. Patel. We just want to rule out or confirm Cancer in your left breast…" Dr. Vimal said.

"Cancer? I could have cancer? That can't be true doctor, no, that can't be…" Maya said. Kirti was still in a shock.

"Well, I hope so, that's exactly why I want to do a quick biopsy on that lump, okay?" Dr. Vimal said.

"Is that a complicated procedure doctor?" Kirti finally pulled her courage and asked.

"No, not really. I usually do it right here in my clinic. It's done under local anesthesia. The advantage is that the results help us rule out all the doubts and suspicions of any complications such as cancer." Then Dr. Vimal explained what a fine needle biopsy entailed to both the ladies and immediately carried it out.

"Come and see me after a couple of days to discuss the results." Dr. Vimal said as Maya left the clinic in total confusion.

And the confusion was over very shortly after that day, within forty eight hours!

"Well, all the doubts and suspicions are over now." Maya and Kirti were sitting in Dr. Vimal's clinic exactly forty eight hours after their first visit to her.

"Mrs. Patel, I am sorry to tell you that the lump in your left breast is found to be malignant. The result of the tests confirmed that." Dr. Vimal informed Maya and Kirti.

Maya had developed breast cancer!

"So, mother has cancer?" Kirti managed to utter those words, her throat had gone completely dry.

"Yes dear, I'm sorry. But don't worry about it. Your mother has a tiny lump that can be removed relatively easily, without losing her breast. She is very lucky that it was detected so early in the stage. I'll carry out what we call the breast conserving surgery on her. It is usually referred to as lumpectomy. It's called BCT, a short form, by all doctors. Breast conservation therapy is used for patients, such as your mother, who are a little older and diagnosed with early-stage invasive breast cancer. Also, it is usually of stage I or stage II in the classification system. It is a safe method in patients with small cancer of the breast and is being used more and more in the treatment of breast cancer..."

"I have breast cancer?" Maya finally seemed to get what was being discussed between Kirti and Dr. Vimal. They both looked at her questioningly.

"But mother is so very healthy, and she has no family history, then how is it possible mother developing this disease, doctor?" Kirti pulled herself from the deep shock and collected herself.

"What you said about your mother's health or lack of family history must all be true. I can't deny it, but then it could also be possible that she got this disease due to some other reasons..." Dr. Vimal said.

"Such as what, doctor?"

"Such as stress."

"Really?"

"Yes, really. As a matter of fact, it's my strong suspicion that developing this disease in your mother's case could be because of her mental stress. It's a long-standing belief among doctors that there could be a link between stress and breast cancer. If someone is excessively stressed, they could suppress their immune system with stress, and that may affect the hormonal balance in the breast. That may be the link between stress and breast cancer. Recently, scientists have found that excessive stress doubles a woman's risk of developing breast cancer."

"And why did you think mother has a lot of stress?" Kirti asked the doctor.

"Her one word 'need', resounding in her conversation, gave it away. The entire time I was examining her, she was telling me how everyone 'needed' her constantly. And now, how her 'being needed' state is completely over, especially after your father expired. According to her, this 'not being needed by anybody' has culminated into her thinking that her life is totally meaningless; and that feeling obviously has caused excessive depression in her mind. This depression could be the root cause of stress in your mother's case, which in turn has affected the hormonal balance in her breasts, resulting in her getting breast cancer." Kirti was listening to the doctor and so was Maya, very intently.

"But doctor..." Maya was about to say something but suddenly kept quiet.

"Of course, let me also tell you that breast cancer is an extremely complex disease and it's very difficult to pin-point any one single risk factor, such as stress, responsible for developing the disease. In your mother's case, it is a well-founded guess, that's all." Dr. Vimal said.

"But doctor..." Maya tried again to interrupt the doctor but Dr. Vimal continued her explanation to Kirti.

"There is nothing to worry. BCT, as we discussed, is very safe and at the same time, a very effective treatment for non-hereditary or sporadic forms of early breast cancer. That's what your mother seems to have." Just as Dr. Vimal finished her explanation to Kirti, Maya stood up from her chair and said to Dr. Vimal, "But doctor, it really doesn't matter now. As I told you, nobody needs me, and since nobody needs me, I don't want to live this meaningless life anyway."

And before even the doctor or her daughter could say anything to her, Maya had already gone out the door towards the car, ready to leave.

"Mrs. Patel, Mrs. Patel..." Maya heard someone calling her name. She opened her eyes. Meeraben was calling her name and Kirti was standing besides her, staring at her.

"Mrs. Patel, you must get that malignant lump out immediately. Don't you understand that? You are a smart woman, and surely you understand that the sooner it is out..." Meeraben couldn't complete what she intended to say because Maya interrupted her.

"...better are the chances of surviving, I know that. But Meeraben, like I said earlier, no one needs me. And since nobody needs me, why bother living? I don't want to live a meaningless life." As if resolved to a final decision, Maya got up and started getting ready to leave.

"Ma, wait." Kirti said in a firm voice. "This is exactly what you said when we visited Dr. Vimal's clinic, and without a moment's wait, you just left. Now you are doing the very same thing again, but this time, I'm not going to let you just leave like that..." Kirti got up, held Maya's hand firmly and rooting firmly her own two feet in the thick carpet, started talking to Meeraben.

"Meeraben, the doctor has told us that Ma's breast cancer is a result of her excessive stress and depression that has arisen from this miserable attitude of hers. She is continuously weaving this ridiculous idea in her mind that nobody needs her and she keeps calling her life a futile existence. Fortunately, right now there is only one tiny lump in her left breast, and it is at what the doctor called a stage I. If she gets that lump out by doing immediate lumpectomy procedure, and then followed by a good and regular medical treatment for only a few days, she should be just fine. Meeraben, I have been nagging Ma to go through this surgery. It's not a big, complicated one, but she just does not listen to me at all." Kirti sounded frustrated.

"Meeraben..." Kirti continued, "Dr. Vimal has also suggested a regular treatment by a psychotherapist after the surgery, that's when she suggested your name to us. Then I thought, why not come here immediately, *before* the surgery? Perhaps Ma would listen to you, a professional psychotherapist. Actually, that's why we are here today." Kirti took a deep breath.

"I am so glad you both finally told me honestly and frankly what the real problem is, and why you are here today. There is a serious health problem with you Mrs. Patel, and that is, you having breast cancer." Meeraben got up too.

She put her hand on Maya's shoulders and said in a very gentle voice,

"Maya, may I call you by your given name?"

Maya just nodded.

Meeraben said, "Maya, you are not the only one in this situation; as in, where you feel nobody needs you, or your life is one big empty hole. I have come across many, many women who go through such situations and have the very same feelings, especially after menopause. Their children grow and leave home, husbands are still quite busy and tied up in their work, and older people who live with them and depend on their help are dead and gone. Life suddenly seems hollow. The days seem longer with not much to do. Naturally these women start to feel that no one needs them any more. Around the same time, menopause sets in. It creates a doubt in their minds about their 'womanhood' and that becomes an additional stress. All this culminates into excessive stress or excessive depression or a combination of both. I see that's exactly what has happened to you, my dear." Meeraben sounded so loving, her deep, sweet voice was touching Maya's heart.

"We all very well know that our body is very closely associated with our mind. All the feelings, problems, stresses that occur in our mind affect the body directly. That is not good for the body. It gets affected, and when the body gets affected, sometimes, a deadly disease such as breast cancer, can originate from it and overpower our health."

Meeraben took a few breaths and continued.

"In the case of breast cancer, along with medicines and other medical treatment, women should also consider psychotherapy for controlling it. It can soothe them and it can also release some stress. It can help them get over the fear of this disease as well. Psychotherapy is an excellent tool that focuses on mind, which in turn, helps the body. Maya, do you get it now?" Meeraben had a very sweet smile on her face. With that smile, she looked so kind.

"Maya, come and see me regularly after you see Dr. Vimal. Do not postpone your visit to her any more." Meeraben gave a light hug to Maya. With that gentle and almost loving hug, Maya did feel a little relaxed and a little relieved.

"Meeraben, could she come to you a few times before she sees Dr. Vimal please?" Kirti asked Meeraben.

"Oh sure, if you think that might be necessary. Take my appointment next week again and make it for two hours. I have a feeling that we will need that much time." Kirti and Maya both nodded.

"And I repeat, go and see Dr. Vimal as soon as possible. Don't postpone that anymore..." Meeraben smiled at Maya.

Kirti and Maya left Meeraben's place after expressing their heartfelt gratitude.

"Kirti, I'm glad you insisted on me seeing this lady. I think she'll be a big help to me in many ways; and not just for dealing with my breast cancer, but for *everything else*." Maya gave her daughter a meaningful look when she said, 'everything else'. Her eyes were filled with tears of some relief!

Virani

"Kittu, Kittu, look at the sky, sweetheart..." Kittu started looking at the sky.

"Say now, 'twinkle twinkle little star'..." Kittu started clapping his tiny hands with joy.

Virani was standing by the window, trying to entertain Kittu perched in her arms. Little Kittu had become the sole purpose in this world for his mother, Virani. Though he was ceremoniously named Krishnadev, Virani lovingly shortened it to Kittu.

"Virani, we have given him such a fine name, Krishnadev, that of a great king, and you have corrupted it by shortening it to Kittu. What a pity!" Amma, Virani's mother-in-law, often joined Virani with a smile during such moments.

"Let it be so, Amma! Kittu is not such a bad name either. I like it."

"But, the poor child will for ever be known by that silly name."

"That's okay, Amma" Virani was still playing with her son.

"Look at me. I always address Dasprakash as Dasprakash. Never Das or Dasu or any such corrupted form."

"That was fine in a small village like yours Amma. But now we live in a metropolis like Mumbai. We have to be among all sorts of people here. Krishnadev is too long a name. I don't think children in the school would be able to properly pronounce that name. Kittu is a nice, convenient short form." Virani said and then added, "Amma, you know that everyone here calls Dasprakash, Das, even at the bank, right? It's the very same thing with Kittu's name, too." Amma quietly nodded at her explanation.

"Amma, do you think Kittu was Lord Krishna's pet name?" Virani thought Amma was a bit disappointed after this conversation.

"Yes, yes, Lord Krishna was also 'Kittu' to his mother Yashoda..." Amma laughed and nodding heartily concurred with her. That made Virani feel better. Such was the relationship between those two ladies, a very friendly and loving one.

With his dark complexion and big round eyes, Kittu was indeed like Lord Krishna to Virani. His thick mop of dark hair was a real stealer. He was a chubby baby. And that made him very attractive. Anyone would just want to hold him in arms and hug him tight. He was the crowning bloom of Virani and Das's family tree.

Dasprakash Rao, Virani's husband, was employed as an accountant at the local bank and was recently transferred to Mumbai on a senior post. He moved to the city with his mother and made Mumbai his home place. Virani was working as a Cashier in the same branch of the bank where Das got his transfer. When those two met at some bank function, some 'strange' chemistry developed between them.

Das took Virani home to meet Amma one day, after the bank closed. Amma liked Virani, especially her coyness and decent manners. And shortly afterwards, on one auspicious day, they tied the knot in an impressive ceremony and began their married life. They made quite a couple. How the first two or three dreamy years flew by, neither of them realized. And then they thought of starting a family. Amma had been long waiting for such a welcome decision.

One day, she was surprised to see Virani return home from the bank rather early.

"What's the matter, Virani? You are home early, did you get half a day off?" Amma asked.

"I had an appointment with the doctor this afternoon. From there I came straight home."

"Appointment with a doctor?" There was a twinkle in Amma's eyes. She was hoping to hear what she had been wanting to hear for quite some time.

"I missed my period last month..." Virani said hesitatingly.

"Oh my, oh my, bless you, my dear." Amma was too excited to hear that. "You are expecting a baby, I know. Does Das know?" She was so very happy, both for her daughter-in-law and her son and perhaps more for herself.

"Yes. He is on his way to the doctor right now to pick up my reports. He should be home too shortly."

"Oh, that's wonderful. Will you please call him on his cell phone and ask him to get lots of sweets before he comes home? Ask him to get both, the *pedha* for a boy and *burfee* for a girl, okay?" Amma then returned to the little temple she had set up in the kitchen and started conducting a small ritual, rather symbolically, to ward off the evil from her dear daughter-in-law. She was waiting for this day ever since her son got married. She then rushed to the stove to prepare something that her daughter-in-law loved to eat. So great was her excitement that she didn't know what to make first, she wanted to satisfy every craving of Virani.

"Virani dear, should I make rice pilaf that you like so much or curried potatoes that are quite hot and spicy and some lemon rice with extra dash of fresh lemon juice to go with it?" Amma couldn't contain her excitement. Just then, Das walked in with sweets in his hands.

"*Rani*[13], open your mouth," Das called Virani by his special pet name on all such occasions. By just taking the last four letters of her name, he had made her his queen! When she approached him while opening her mouth but with a little bit of shyness since she knew Amma would come out to the front hall any minute, he started putting a handful of sweets in her mouth.

"No, no. Dasu…" that was her private pet name for him, "not so many pieces of sweets at once…"

"These are only two pieces, you have to eat both pieces at the same time Rani, one for a boy and one for girl..." and lovingly, he forced two pieces of sweets into her mouth. It was just then that Amma came in from the kitchen.

"Amma, here is the report. You are soon going to be a grand mother. He put two pieces of sweets in her mouth too. 'One for a grand daughter and another for a grand son' as he explained to her. It was such an amusing sight to see those two ladies struggling to chew and swallow their mouthfuls of sweets. That made Das burst out in laughter. He too was pretty excited by the happy news of Virani's conception.

"Amma" Das rushed into the house, loudly calling his mother. It was still dark but the morning was round the corner." Amma, Rani delivered a baby boy! I got a son. You now have a grandson Amma." It was the news too exciting for everybody. After a moment of excessive joy coupled with some confusion, Amma rushed to the prayer room. She devotedly bowed before the three idols of three deities[14] that she

13. Rani means Queen in Hindi.
14. Brahma, Vishnu and Mahesh, together called the *Trinity*, are the three main deities, according to Hinduism.

so faithfully worshipped everyday of her life. She offered her utmost thanks and then returned to Das.

"How is Rani? No complications I hope." This was the very first time ever that Amma had called Virani by that endearing pet name, Rani. Virani was indeed a queen to her too, for a prince was born into their family!

"Rani is fine. She is very happy. She wants you to visit her in the hospital right away."

"Then, let's go. What are we waiting for?" Amma was too eager.

"Amma, have a heart. I have been in the hospital since last evening. The baby was born at sharp 12, midnight. I am terribly tired now. I need some rest. You also need it. I am sure you too must have been awake the whole night waiting for the news, right?"

"That's right." Amma was clearly seeing that her son was very tired but at the same time, she could not hold her desire to see her newborn grandson for too long.

"Are you going to take a shower first or have a nap first?" She had to contain her eagerness to see the baby.

"I will first take a nap, just an hour or so, and then do my shower and shave. We'll go right after that, okay?" He said, hoping she would agree.

She did, with a nod.

Das took Amma to the hospital. Virani had been waiting for them. The baby was blissfully asleep by her side. "Let me see, let me see my grandson." Amma lifted that little bundle of joy in her arms and streams of tears began to flow down her cheeks. A few of them were for Das's father. After his untimely passing, Amma had raised her son all by herself. It was a trying time for her, especially in that town where she had nobody to help. Das was a good son, he graduated from the high school and then from the local community college with good grades and landed on a job with the local bank as a teller. After appearing for and successfully passing the bank examinations, he got promoted to be an accountant. This was a moment of triumph and joy for Amma. She distributed sweets among all the people who had helped her raise the boy. Another equally joyful moment was when Virani and Das got married. This moment of becoming a grandmother to Das's baby boy proved to be the epitome of her joy. This little prince, with his recent arrival into this world, marked the continuity of Das's father in her mind.

Das and Virani were intently looking at Amma who looked so very engrossed in the baby and had tears running down her cheeks. The first flood of tears receded and now there was sheer joy in her eyes.

"Rani" Virani was a bit amused to hear Amma call her Rani.

"What a handsome boy! Doesn't he look like Lord Krishna?" Amma had not taken her eyes off the boy.

"And like Lord Krishna, he was also born at midnight." Virani added.

"Let us name him after Lord Krishna then." Das suggested.

"Why, that's a wonderful idea. Krishna it will be indeed!" Virani said.

"Let him be known as Krishnadev." Amma was still looking at the baby without even blinking.

"Krishnadev? Doesn't it sound a bit too long?" Virani wondered.

"My grandfather's name was Krishnadev, right Amma?" Amma nodded, her gaze still fixed on the baby in her arms.

"Amma probably wants to keep his memory alive. That is why she prefers Krishnadev. Rani, you address him the way you want but the formal name will be whatever Amma wants. Is it alright with you?" Das compromised.

After spending three days at the hospital, the young parents brought the little baby home. If it were the small town that they had come from, Amma would have invited the whole town to a feast. But it was different in Mumbai. Even then nearly every young and old resident of the building, where they lived, gathered to welcome the new arrival. Amma once again conducted a very short ritual that entailed 'removal of an evil eye' to ward off the evil before the prince entered his castle. Virani had Krishnadev all wrapped up in beautiful blue colored blankets and had held him close to her heart.

As Virani entered the home, she noticed the whole place beautifully done up. The cradle was tastefully decorated as if to make it worthy for the prince to sleep in it. It was not only the baby for whom the special arrangements were made but there were special things prepared for her too. There were special food supplements, cooked in pure butter, especially prepared by Amma for her daughter-in-law. Even a beautifully woven string of fresh jasmine flowers was kept ready to adorn her hair.

Amma had gone out of the way to prepare many special sweets that Virani liked to eat.

"What a welcome! And how very thoughtful of you Amma, for all this arrangement! You have taken so much trouble to arrange all this. It's incredible." The meticulous arrangements had impressed Virani a lot.

"To tell you honestly, in these past three days I doubt if Amma slept even for three hours. She has been continuously working. Do you know she has arranged a masseur for you on a regular basis?" Das said very proudly of his mother.

"This is too much Dasu. Let us engage a cook or a full time maid for a few weeks now..." Virani said.

"Oh no, no. No need at all. It will be my pleasure to do all the work during your maternity leave, Rani. I am capable of taking care of you and the baby." Amma insisted.

"But Amma, you will be burnt out by the time my maternity leave comes to an end."

"Rani, why don't we hire a cook after you join back your work after the maternity leave? Right now, you two can manage I suppose." Das intervened and that was finally agreed upon by both the ladies.

"A cook would enable you to spend all your time with Kittu after you came back from work right?"

"Did I hear you say 'Kittu'?" The question was clearly intended to divert the topic of discussion.

"Amma, I thought the name Krishnadev was rather too long. And also a bit difficult to pronounce. When my colleagues from the bank had come to the hospital to see the baby, they suggested this cute name, Kittu. It is also a short form of the same name. I liked it too. Of course, you can continue to call him Krishnadev!"

Amma didn't say anything. She left the room just muttering something to herself. Das and Virani looked at each other and laughed away.

Day by day, Kittu was making progress and his every new step was so very gleefully being noted. 'Kittu balances his head, Kittu recognizes this and recognizes that, now Kittu can turn on his sides, now Kittu can sit up without a support, and so on'. It was Kittu, Kittu and Kittu all along. Kittu was the one around whom the whole world revolved. That is how at least his mother and grandmother thought and behaved.

The period of six months flew by as if it was only a brief moment. Virani rejoined her duty at the bank. Amma, who loved the child more than she loved her own self, was available at home to take care of Kittu. Therefore, Virani took the decision of joining her work at the bank, She weaned her baby boy immediately, and fortunately, her son got used to it quite easily.

Kittu was soon going to be a one year old. It was unbelievable how fast the months had passed. Virani had been working at the bank already for almost six months since her maternity leave ended. Lately, and strangely, she started feeling some lumps that seemed like milk-accumulations she had experienced during her weaning times in her breasts. 'It has been over six months now? Why do I feel these lumps in my breast?' She wondered.

The observations and the thought began to worry Virani. It even showed on her face; Amma was the first one to notice it.

"You don't look so cheerful nowadays, Virani. What's the matter?" Amma asked Virani one evening after her return from work.

"Oh nothing, nothing at all. I think it must be the work pressure at the bank. It gets very tiring. I am also feeling a bit stressed out these days due to work, that is all."

"No. I don't agree. You are not the same old Virani any longer. What's the matter?"

"Nothing at all, Amma. Honestly." Virani's dry and cold response did not satisfy Amma. 'There must be more to it', she thought. She moved closer to Virani and patting gently on her back, said, "Virani, look into my eyes. I am Das's mother. And since your marriage, I am your mother too. Mothers know intuitively what the daughters feel. Tell me the truth. Tell me what bothers you?"

Amma's words, drenched with love and concern and even more so, her loving touch made Virani breakdown. She started sobbing uncontrollably.

'This is not the time to ask her what was wrong,' Amma knew. Things were to be just felt from the heart. She let the reassuring touch of her hands on Virani's shoulders do the talking. Virani sobbed and cried and Amma stood there by her side in silence that seemed like an endless period of time. When the eyes had run dry, Virani dried her nose with her sari and asked, "Where is Kittu? Is he sleeping?"

"Yes. I put him to bed before you returned home. He would not wake up at least for a couple of hours now."

"Amma..." Amma was standing right there next to her. "Amma. I am soon going to die.." Virani said.

"Oh my, oh no! What an evil thought." Amma was shocked beyond imagination on hearing those scary words. How would she ward off this evil thought, she quickly joined her hands in a prayer to the Lord.

"It is true. I am going to die. Really! Very Soon..."

"Speak no evil, my girl. Think of good and speak of good. I beseech you in the name of Lord Krishna. Tell me what's on your mind, Rani." Amma had hard time controlling herself, but she managed it.

Virani held her by the hand and led her to an inner room. Seating her there in a chair and herself sitting at her feet on the ground, Virani said, "Amma, listen to me carefully. I am saying this for the very first time to anybody. A woman would tell this perhaps only to her mother, but you are my mother, in fact even more than that. You have given me immense love all through my married life, and that is why, I want to tell you what's on my mind before I tell anyone else. Amma, Amma..." She stumbled at the words a little bit. Amma looked confused and very tense.

"Amma, I feel some small lumps in my right breast. I feel them every time I take my bath. I am very scared of them. In the beginning, I thought they must be lumps of un-suckled milk like those infamous milk-accumulations some women get after weaning the baby. But now it is nearly six months since I stopped breast feeding Kittu and those lumps are still there. Amma, I am terribly scared. Would these lumps be that of cancer?" The word 'cancer' sent a shiver through Amma's spine. She did not hear a word after that one.

Cancer! The deadly disease. And breast cancer at that. That was even worse. She lost all her courage and finally, she broke down too. With no strength in her legs, she kept sitting there helplessly and crying along with Virani. For how long they had been sitting like that could not be guessed. When Das returned home from work late in the evening, and saw them seated motionless like statues, he got truly scared.

"Rani, Amma, what's the matter? Is Kittu alright? Is everything else alright?" His questions shook them out of their trance. Virani once again burst into tears. That scared Das even more. He rushed to their room. Kittu was sleeping soundly in the cradle. He felt relieved.

What could be the matter then? He had no clue whatsoever. He was speechless. It was Amma who broke the silence." Das, Rani is unwell. Take her to a doctor. Right now..."

Amma sounded like she was giving orders. It was unusual. And that confused him even more.

"What's the matter?"

"Take her now. Take her to a women's specialist. A good lady doctor. I have heard someone mention the name of Dr. Vimal. She is known to be some specialist. Take Virani to her. Go to this doctor right now, without wasting any time." Amma said in the same, a bit of an authoritative, tone again.

"I will. I will. Right away, Amma, but please, will some body tell me, what's the matter with Rani, what's all this rush?" Das got into a real panic.

"You first take her to Dr. Vimal's clinic, get her examined and come home only after the doctor has examined her thoroughly." Amma's authoritative voice continued.

Das did not stretch the issue. Virani got up and readied herself to go and Das took her straight to that famous lady doctor, Dr. Vimal without wasting even a minute, as his mother *ordered.*

In the outer room the receptionist was making the patients comfortable and taking down the details of each one systematically.

It was Virani's turn.

"Name?"

"Virani Rao." Das responded for Virani.

"Age?"

"Twenty eight."

"Other details please."

"She is my wife. I am Dasprakash Rao. Virani works as a cashier with the bank. We have a son. Krishnadev is his name. He will be one year old in another fifteen days."

"Other family members?"

"One. Besides we three, there is my mother living with us."

The receptionist took it down pretty fast and neatly.

"Please be seated. You may have to wait for a while as there is no appointment in your name." She said.

"That's alright, we knew that." Das said.

"It could be just half an hour or as late as two or three hours."

"That's okay. Actually, I realize we are here without a prior appointment, and yet you have accommodated us. Thanks. Thanks a lot..."

"You are welcome! Please take seats in the waiting room. Be comfortable. I will call you as soon as there is an opening." The receptionist said with a smile and started attending to another patient.

It was the tradition of the clinic to examine, as far as possible, all the patients. Although this was not a walk-in clinic, Dr. Vimal did not like any of her patients being turned away just because he or she didn't have an appointment, especially if the patient looked like being in an urgent need of help. When the receptionist came and told them it was Virani's turn, Das gently held her hand and led her in to the doctor's room.

This was Dr. Vimal's patient examination room. The atmosphere there was purposely made pleasant. In one corner stood a large bronze idol of eight armed Hindu deity named Goddess Durga. There was a garland of fresh flowers hanging from the idol's neck. A soothing, melodic tune was being played on the stereo in the background. The lighting in the room was just adequate, not too bright nor too dim. The fragrance of the flowers, the quiet music and mild lighting in the room all together would make the patient feel at ease. In the centre of the room, there was a red mahogany table with a huge leather chair on one side and four smaller chairs on the other side. After examining the patients, Dr. Vimal would always request them to be seated on these chairs with her on the huge chair. Away from the table and adjacent to the far wall was the examination table. Neatly hanging on that wall were charts and pictures of female anatomy. It was quite a queer sight that one wall displayed charts of delicate female organs and across the room, the wall facing the charts supported a huge idol of Goddess Durga, a symbol of human strength!

"Now, what can I do for you, Virani Rao?" Dr. Vimal asked Das and Virani while signaling them to take seats. She started looking up the history sheets that the receptionist had filled up for Virani.

Sensing the reassurance that showed on the loving countenance of Dr. Vimal, Virani in spite of the fear of possibly being a candidate of cancer victim, felt a bit relaxed. She joined her hands in a greeting to the doctor and sat down in one of the chairs opposite to her. After she sat down, Das greeted the doctor and sat down too.

"To tell you honestly, I don't know why we are here. It may seem stupid but it is true. When I returned from my office, I found my mother and Virani both crying uncontrollably. I have brought her here because my mother bid me to do so. Other than that, I really have no idea why we are here. My wife hasn't told me anything either." Dr. Vimal seemed quite amused at the honest reply of the husband.

"That's fine. What I would like to do is a thorough physical examination of your wife. Would you please go outside and take a seat in the next room?"

"Oh, Yes." Das said and left the place dutifully. Dr. Vimal asked Virani to take off all her clothes and wear just a thin cotton gown to facilitate a thorough examination.

"Virani, please cooperate with me. Will you please answer my questions honestly? Without hiding anything?"

Virani nodded.

"You had a baby recently, right?"

"Yes."

"Any complication? Any problems?"

"No. Nothing whatsoever."

"Did you breast feed the baby?"

"Yes. I did."

"For how long?"

"About sixteen weeks during my maternity leave. There was no option after I joined work."

"How long since you stopped breast feeding?"

"Say about six months,"

"Do you have your periods now?"

"Yes"

"Any complications in that?" Virani just shook her head. Dr. Vimal was not just asking questions but was also examining Virani's ears, nose, throat and also taking the measurement of her pulse rate, blood pressure, body temperature and all that.

"Did you have any fever any time?"

" No. Not at all"

"Any Infection?"

"No."

"Any problems in your sexual activity?"

Virani shook her head to indicate a big no.

"Good! Now take the gown off so that I can examine your stomach, chest and the back."

The words 'examination of chest' almost brought tears in her eyes. Dr. Vimal's experienced eyes did not miss that detail.

She said, "Come on young girl, tell me the whole thing."

"Doctor, I stopped breast feeding my baby a good six months ago. I find some lumps in my right breast. I don't really know if they are of unsuckled milk or of some thing different, something more dangerous..." Every part of her body trembled as she said this.

"Oh, I see..." Dr. Vimal had finished examining Virani's abdomen and the back and was about to turn to her breasts.

"Does it pain?" Dr. Vimal asked Virani while gently pressing her left breast.

"No."

"Here?" It was the right breast this time.

"No. Here neither."

"I do feel two lumps in your right breast. I see the reddishness on the skin there. Since when has it been so.?"

"Reddish skin? I never noticed that."

"Did you not see yourself in the mirror?"

"No."

Dr. Vimal once again examined the right breast very carefully.

"I feel two lumps in this breast. Good that you discovered them now. I think it is early enough. Now let us do it this way, let us get the biopsy done here itself, in my clinic."

"My God! What is a biopsy, Doctor? Doctor please, please get Das here. I need him."

Virani was terribly frightened. The nurse called Das and led him into the room.

"Mr. Rao. Please listen to this very carefully. I feel two lumps in your wife's right breast. I have also observed that the skin around it is reddish. That is not a good sign. I have a doubt that these lumps may not be ordinary. We'll have to confirm what it is. Therefore, I recommend immediate biopsy. We will do it right here in my clinic. Technically, it is called a 'fine needle aspiration.' In this procedure, I will draw out some cells from the lumps in her breast. Of course, that will be done under local anesthesia, and send the sample to the pathologist. The advantage of this kind of biopsy is that the results will be available soon and we can rule out all the doubts and suspicions of any complications such as cancer."

"Cancer...? Did you say cancer?" Das broke into heavy sweating. When he left the house to take Virani to this doctor, he did not even have a clue as to why he was bringing her here. It was clearly at the insistence of his mother that he had brought Virani to this clinic. And what was this horrible thing he was hearing now? It was then that it dawned upon him why he saw Virani and Amma crying uncontrollably on his return from office.

"Doctor, why do you suspect that this could be cancer?"

"I said 'suspicions of any complications such as cancer'. I will not be able to tell you anything definitely unless I have the biopsy report in hand. My suspicion arose because those lumps are not painful, and she said she did not suffer from high fever in past six months after she stopped breastfeeding her child. Obviously, there had been no infection of any kind. That rules out what we call lactation mastitis. And still we see those lumps present. Also the skin surrounding them is reddish. These indications make me suspect something like that." As Dr. Vimal was talking, Das was getting more and more nervous.

"Yet, as I said, unless I have the biopsy report in hand, I can not tell any which way about this. Don't worry, your wife is only twenty eight years of age, so in my judgment, there is nothing to worry. It would be an exceptional case if her report tells something different. Only in very rare cases that women under thirty become cancer affected. That is why I am recommending a biopsy immediately." After hearing this, Das looked slightly calmer than before.

"Incidentally, was your wife on birth control pills any time?" Dr. Vimal asked.

"Yes. She was. The first three years of our marriage." Das said.

"Why do you ask that, doctor?" Virani asked.

"In one school of thought, some researchers are of the opinion that the hormone, called estrogen, in those pills could cause breast cancer. Of course, there is no conclusive evidence to prove the association. Not yet anyway. Besides, 'the pill' today has evolved into really a very refined chemical to have any such adverse effects on women. I have also noted Virani's family history; and there seems to be no case of cancer in her family. A woman of only twenty eight years of age suffering from breast cancer? Unimaginable! That is why there is no way to prove or disprove my assessment." Dr. Vimal was forthright about what she said.

"Doctor, is it possible that you do the biopsy tomorrow? Tomorrow afternoon? I must see my mother and my son before anything else…Please." Virani requested the doctor.

The earnestness in her voice made Dr. Vimal give the suggestion another thought.

"Virani, biopsy is not a major operation or any such thing as you might fear. It is done right here. Within minutes. Almost like taking a sample of blood. The advantage is, we can have those results in hand in a couple of days or so. Once the results are out, you both can have some peace of mind. We can then give a good thought as to what could be done with those lumps. But this confirmation is a must for me to have, to advice you in the right way. You need not take the decision in a hurry because you have been fortunate in detecting the lumps quite early..." Dr. Vimal sounded quite reassuring to both of them.

"Fortunately for you, your mother-in-law told your husband to bring you to me, a breast cancer specialist. There is something of suspicion, obviously, even to her, don't you see it? An early biopsy will settle the issue right away. It is in your interest Virani."

Both, Virani and Das saw the point, so they agreed.

"Mr. Rao, I always recommend a husband or a close relative of the patient be present during this procedure. It helps the patient feel secured and better prepared for the test." The doctor then requested the nurse to keep all the equipment ready for a fine needle biopsy.

Accordingly the nurse brought all the equipment systematically arranged in a tray. Virani laid down on the examination table. Dr. Vimal let Virani's gown slide down the chest, picked up a red marker from the tray and marked circle on the right breast where she had felt the lumps. That was the area where the local anesthesia was administered.

After a little while she lightly tapped the spot with the back of her fingers and asked," Any sensation?"

"Nothing."

"Good! Nurse, Give me the needle please."

She pierced a sharp hollow needle into one of the lumps, withdrew some fluid into it, spread it onto a couple of glass slides for microscope examination, and put back into tray the slides to perform further procedure.

"Stain the slides and send them to the pathologist immediately." She told the nurse who immediately took away the tray.

"That's it. It was pretty fast, wasn't it? Virani, put on your clothes now, and book an appointment with my receptionist to see me in a couple of days. By then the pathologist's report would be here. We will discuss everything then, alright?" Dr. Vimal said.

Virani and Das returned home after sincerely thanking the doctor.

Amma was standing at the door waiting for Virani and Das to return, with Kittu in her arms. As soon as he saw his mother come to the door, the little boy nearly jumped at her.

"Oh my darling son" Virani said. As she caught him in the mid-air, his head struck her right breast. Virani faintly sighed on the impact.

"What's the matter? Did it hurt?" Das asked her.

"Not much. May be the effect of anesthesia is receding." Virani answered.

"What is receding, you said?" Amma was shocked at the utterance of the word, anesthesia.

"I will tell you everything, Amma..." And then Das described in detail all that had taken place in the clinic.

The wait of next forty eight hours was of nothing but full of anxiety, making all three of them extremely uneasy. Only Kittu was blissfully unaware of the tension prevailing there. Virani had taken a couple of days off from work, so he was happy to have his mother home with him the whole time.

"Come in please. Be seated." The nurse led Virani, Das and Amma into the doctor's room and indicated towards the chairs. Dr. Vimal was studying Virani's file. The pathologist's report was in the file.

"Good morning Doctor." Das greeted the doctor as he took his seat. "I have got my mother also with me. She insisted on joining us."

"Very good. She is welcome. That way, she will be able to get all the information first hand. I encourage family members to be present with the patient." Dr. Vimal looked quite serious as she spoke. It alarmed Das a bit but he did not let it show on his face. Virani and Amma were looking quite nervous.

Dr. Vimal held a sheet of paper in hand, cleared her throat and began to speak, "Virani, I have your biopsy report here."

"And ?" Virani could not hide her anxiousness.

"As I told you the other day, a Fine needle biopsy report is considered to be conclusive. Particularly when it is positive..."

"Oh my God! Do you mean..." Das looked pale as a paper.

"I am very sorry to tell you Virani, the report indicates that the lump that was tested from your breast is flooded with cancer cells. I'm very, very sorry. You have developed breast cancer. It is confirmed." Dr. Vimal could not look into Virani's eyes while talking. It must have pained her also to break the news to this family.

"O my God! Cancer! That means I am going to die. No escape from it. It's a sure thing. No. Oh No. My little Kittu... Kittu..." Virani let out a weak cry and fell unconscious in the chair.

Das and Amma froze completely. Without any movement, they stayed still and stiff in their chairs. The doctor called in a nurse in a hurry. The nurse rushed in.

"Get me some ammonia, cotton balls and a glass of water." Nurse quickly got everything and held a cotton ball soaked in ammonia near Virani's nose to regain her consciousness. With that strong smell, she soon regained her consciousness. The nurse handed Virani a glass of water and gestured her to drink it. The nurse, then, went near Das and Amma and gave them a light jerk on their shoulders and wrists. The jerk helped them come out of their frozen state, but they seemed as if they had lost all the strength from their bodies.

"Would you please lie down on that table for a while?" The nurse took the empty glass from Virani's hands and asked her most courteously.

"No." was Virani's curt response. The nurse just looked at the doctor and left the room.

"Doctor, did you say Virani has breast cancer?" Das had somehow managed to gather strength to ask Dr. Vimal; Amma was still in a semi-frozen state, not able to respond in anyway.

"Yes. I am sorry."

"That means I am going to die. Isn't it doctor?" Virani asked. Dr. Vimal gave a fleeting glance in her direction. Before she could respond to her question, Virani fired away, "and before I die, you would chop off my right breast. Isn't it?"

Again, before even Dr. Vimal could respond to her question, Virani said, "and Doctor, you will cut my breast off; de-shape me and then leave me to rot and die. Is it not?" Virani had almost become hysterical and Dr. Vimal, who only a couple of days ago looked so cheerful, kept staring at Virani vacantly. She was shocked to see this young, fragile woman yell and talk like this.

"Rani..." Das lovingly pulled Virani in his arms. Resting her head on his chest, Virani started sobbing hard. "Rani, calm down. Calm down honey..."

Then he turned to the doctor and said, "Doctor, doctor please explain to us everything in detail. Please don't give us this shocking news and then stay quiet." Das himself sounded like he was on the verge of crying. Amma was holding Virani's one hand tightly, partly to give her some support and partly; to have some for herself.

"Mr. Rao, quite frankly, I was taken aback by your wife's reaction. I'm sorry but I didn't mean to stay quite as you thought. When I saw your wife's biopsy report last evening, even I was quite upset. Quite honestly, I did not know how I would explain this to you this morning. I have been in this profession long enough to see such cases. I thought I knew everything that is required for me to know in this profession. But ever since I read your wife's report, I have become quite restless myself." Dr. Vimal looked genuinely upset.

"Why so, Madam? It is nothing new for you in your medical practice."

"You are right. It is not. I'm a breast cancer specialist and my practice is treating breast cancer. But what I have seen with your wife still made me restless."

"Why doctor, what do you mean exactly?" Das was visibly nervous.

"Mr. Rao, your wife is suffering from a relatively rare kind of breast cancer. It is a special kind of advanced cancer and regarded as a serious one. It is called Inflammatory Breast cancer."

Whatever control Das had exercised over himself up until this moment, was lost at the mention of the words 'advanced cancer'. His darling wife had fallen prey to one of the most dreaded diseases; and he had absolutely no defense against it. He did not have even the slightest idea of any such disease just two days earlier, and today? The news was being hammered into his head so suddenly out of nowhere. The deadly disease was going to kill his wife and ruin his family life. And that bright little son of his? The death of his mother could devastate him permanently, who knows?

'Oh my Lord!' Das uttered these words, drew Virani even closer to his chest and began to cry profusely. The uncontrollable flow of tears down his cheeks was dampening her thick hair. Though Amma could not understand much of what the doctor had said, she could sense the seriousness of the situation. She too started crying ceaselessly and drying her tears with her sari from time to time. Dr. Vimal left the room for giving them some privacy.

How long those three were sitting there in that state of mind could not be guessed. All three had their eyes red and swollen due to incessant crying. Dr. Vimal returned shortly afterwards and requested the receptionist to get cups of hot coffee for all of them. She also told her to reschedule all other appointments for the morning.

"Amma, Mr. and Mrs. Rao, let us have some coffee. I know it is a very trying time for you, but what can we do about it? It has happened already and we have to face the situation. Please have some hot coffee, it might help ease your tension. You will feel a bit better. Let us see what can be done from here on. Let us plan."

The nurse brought in four cups of coffee and put them on the table. Dr. Vimal passed the cups to Das, Virani and Amma. They mechanically took the cups from the doctor's hand and raised them to their lips. Dr. Vimal then picked up one cup for herself and looked at them. They looked as if there were three robots sitting in front of her, drinking coffee.

"To summarize what I told you all earlier, Virani, you are suffering from inflammatory breast cancer. The lumps you found in your breast after you stopped breastfeeding your child were not the lumps of un-drawn milk as you believed but they were lumps of cancer. It is unfortunate that you did not notice the skin of your breast around the lumps that had become reddish. The exact sequence would be that it was your breast-skin that was the first to be affected by the cancer. Over a period of time, it invaded the cells in your breast and formed a couple of lumps there. You detected the lumps, but unfortunately, the redness of the skin slipped your notice completely."

Dr. Vimal stopped for a while to see their reaction to what she was saying. They looked like they were soaking in every word she was saying.

"Believe it or not, it is seldom that one comes across this kind of cancer. It is very rare. May be only about one percent among the breast cancer patients!"

"And it was only our Virani who was chosen to be the one. What justice of the Lord is this?" Amma said and once again burst into tears.

"What next? What's the way out?" Das somehow managed to ask the doctor.

"What do you mean, 'what next'? The procedure of mastectomy of course! The removal of the affected breast! We must go for the surgery immediately. No time left now. Immediately after the operation, we must opt for the radiation and then the chemotherapy will follow."

"Removal of what?" Suddenly Virani stopped crying and blurted out loudly.

"Removal of your affected breast, the right breast, of course!" Dr. Vimal was a bit shocked to hear Virani's loud voice.

"Doctor, what are you trying to tell us, that there isn't any other option? No option at all?" Virani was really loud.

The doctor shook her head.

"No. No. Doctor, I don't want that." Virani said in a dry voice that was filled with utter conviction. Dr. Vimal, including Das and Amma, wondered if this was the same woman who was crying endlessly only moments ago.

"By the way doctor, what's the survival rate among those who have this rare disease, after surgery and all that?" Virani asked again. It was really a daring question. There was a certain determination in her voice. It startled all of them.

"I can comment on it only on the available statistics." Dr. Vimal said.

"Let us have it. Doctor, I can take it." Virani assured the doctor.

"This type of cancer is known to be the 'aggressive' type. The survivor of this cancer lasts for about a year or two, occasionally three years!" Dr. Vimal was almost apologetic when she informed Virani.

"And for those two or three years, the patient's life would be filled with all kinds of treatments and chemo and what have you, isn't it?" Virani confronted the doctor without mincing the words.

"Well, yes, you can say that. However, the present technology does suggest that the survival can be extended to more than one year." Dr. Vimal tried to put all the information in perspective.

"Is it guaranteed?" Virani's voice had gone up by one more level.

"Well, no. There are no such guarantees, my dear, but..."Dr. Vimal was about to say something when Virani interrupted her, saying, 'let's go then,' and abruptly got up from her chair.

"Let us go Das. Get up Amma. Let us go. Whatever we were required to do here is done already. Thank you very much, doctor. Honestly, I cannot thank you enough for all that you did for us." Virani said with total dryness that was clearly evident in her voice and on her face.

"When do we start the treatment?" Dr. Vimal asked. The unexpected change of stance by Virani had caught her quite unaware.

"Never. It's all over." Virani picked up her purse, ready for leaving the place.

"Please listen. Virani, listen to me..." Dr. Vimal tried to say something but Virani interrupted her again.

"No, I won't listen to you. First you will remove my breast. May be both breasts to avoid any future problems, who knows? Then with radiation, you will subject my body to another kind of harshness. Then you will subject me to drink doses of that horrible poison under the treatment called 'chemo therapy', in the hope that something better might evolve and keep me alive for a few more months. And all this for what? Just to live for an additional year or two? May be three years, tops! No thanks. I do not wish to live like this. I have no desire to present my body to you for its dissection or to de-shape it permanently."

"Don't take such an extreme view about your treatment, Virani." Dr. Vimal was trying to calm her down.

"It is not an extreme view. I am saying all this, based on what you just told me. Doctor, I love my breasts tremendously. I am proud of them. They have given immense pleasure to my husband all along. They have fed milk to my child for six whole months. I would say my milk is still flowing in his veins. I do not want to lose my breast under the name of 'treatment', okay?"

Virani got up to go. Amma and Das got up too.

"Doctor, you have been very kind to me. I have seen the expressions on your face when you explained to us the pathologist's report. You seemed genuinely disturbed by it. That look on your face alone told me a lot about you. You are a very kind person and I thank you genuinely for your compassion. But Doctor, whatever time is left of my life now, I would like to spend that with my family, in *my style,* and in the way *I* want to lead it. In that little time I do not want to make innumerable visits to various doctors and hospitals, and suffer the nauseating smells of the medicines. This is my final decision. Let me spend these last few months of my life with dignity. And more importantly, in the way *I* want."

"Mr. Rao, please talk to your wife, put some sense in her head. Advise her. Discuss with her the benefits of my treatment after she has calmed down from this extreme emotional shock. I see her outburst as a natural reaction to finding out about her disease. Mr. Rao, I have seen many patients turning hysteric on being told that they are cancer positive. But later, when they calm down, they do realize the gravity of the situation and take a rational decision with my advice. Your wife's reaction is quite understandable. Don't be disturbed by it. Don't worry about it, but do call me when you have taken the right decision, decision of immediate treatment, that is, without wasting any precious time. We can start it right away. There is no point in trying to convince her now." Dr. Vimal gave a heartfelt advice to Das. She could see that this young family had just suffered a thousand volts jolt with the news.

Das didn't know what to say to the doctor or how to react to Virani's sudden outburst. He was even more confused than before. He barely managed to thank Dr. Vimal for her help and advice, and the three of them left her room.

No one uttered a single word in the taxi on their way home. One could have easily taken them all to be deaf and mute.

Shaina

"Shaina ji, just a couple more photos..."

"Ohff oh! No, no. I am really tired. Please, let us do that tomorrow."

"Oh pretty please, just two more photos and the whole session would be complete, I promise."

"Oh well, okay..." With reluctance Shaina agreed to the photographer's requests. He took a couple of her shots and then started wrapping up his equipment.

This incident took place one afternoon in a huge and an elegant photo studio. The photographer was one of the top and one of the most coveted photographers of the country. But then, Shaina was also one of the most desired and coveted models of the country. For lingerie, she was the top model, she *still* is, and wanted by all photographers, including the important ones as this photographer.

Shaina, a young woman with a gorgeous body and an absolutely perfect figure, also has a sweet looking, oval shaped face with two beautiful big eyes to go with that body! No wonder she has captured the entire Lounge Wear industry as a model. No matter how the clothes are, when she wears them, they look just perfect. And that helps the clothes industry sell their products in millions all across the country. Shaina as a model has become their trump card for selling their clothes, especially for their lingerie.

A tall body with long, slender limbs and a very narrow waist line, Shaina really can boast about her perfect figure. And the epitome of her figure is her beautiful, shapely and big breasts! As if a skillful sculptor has poured his heart and soul in carving them and then placed them precisely, with a perfect angle, above her slender waist.

The truth is that a skillful sculptor did carve them and place them neatly on her slender torso, almost fifteen years ago. Those breasts were the reason she got into a modeling career; and just as she entered the modeling career, she almost immediately shot up to being one of the most sought after models of the country. That career gave her a life of luxury she couldn't even dream of before. Whenever there were new and aspiring young women entering the field of modeling, Shaina very easily overtook them, mainly because of her figure with those 'out of this world' breasts!

Shaina need not worry about her modeling career and thereby, a life of plenty of money and luxury, as long as her breasts remain the same beautiful way. And they will remain so, because they have been 'man-made' and designed especially for her! Her beautiful breasts have given her security of a modeling career, and those breasts have given her security of life as well. Yes, those breasts have given Shaina a guarantee of cancer-free life too!

It all started almost fifteen years ago, in a tiny village near the town of Burrelpur in North India. Shaina was a schoolgirl of about twelve years of age. Her real name, as per the registration in the school, was Shailender Singh. Youngest of the three daughters in the family, her older two sisters, Baljeet and Daljeet, were much too older. They were in their late twenties.

"Shailu, get me my kurta..." Baljeet would yell from the bathroom and little Shailu, as Shailender was called at home, had to run and get it for her.

"Shailu, go in the kitchen and make me a cup of tea, I am very tired now..." Daljeet would order her as soon as she would come home from work, and of course, Shailu had to go to the kitchen and make her a fresh cup of tea. Both the sisters would give a lot of small chores to their younger sister and Shailu had no choice but to do the chores.

"Shailu, get me a glass of water, I am thirsty...' her father, Papaji, would ask for a glass of water almost every hour of the day and she had to run and get it for him. Papaji would keep asking for many different things to be done for him practically for the whole day, and as she was the only one around, she had no choice but to get them done for him. She many times felt that he was constantly bossing her around without uttering a single loving word. What she detested even more was, when the Sun would come up and the day would get hotter, Papaji would take off his shirt and continuously scratch his hairy stomach and chest, his equally hairy back, and sometimes with one hand raised, scratch the armpit with the other. At such times, she would avoid to even go near him. A young girl of pre-puberty years, she had developed a nausea for him. When no one was watching, she would sit in her favorite place in the backyard and cry silently for hours, wishing every moment her mother was alive, although Shailender didn't remember how she was, or even, how she looked.

Her mother was known to be a very good looking woman with light complexion and beautiful big, eyes. She was dead for a few years now, when Shaina was barely out of her toddler years. Nobody figured out how and why she died. Ever since her death, Papaji became almost insane. He owned a small shop of miscellaneous articles where his wife would help him sell the articles. She was a good woman with good social skills needed for the business. With her help in the shop, Papaji could manage their livelihood from that shop. But after her sudden death, Papaji went bankrupt and the shop closed down. He started staying at home just sitting in one corner the whole time, doing absolutely nothing and looking at the ceiling for hours together. People would say, 'he is in a shock due to sudden death of his wife'. Shailender was too young to understand their comments. People would also say, 'Shailu has taken her mother's looks'. She didn't remember her mother, so she couldn't comprehend fully what they said. All she had seen ever since she was a very young girl of four or five years of age was her father sitting around the house whole day doing absolutely nothing except ordering her relentlessly; and her two older sisters leaving for work at the crack of the dawn, doing a lot of manual chores for people to bring home money for the livelihood of the family.

Shailender was sent to a nearby village school when she became almost eight years of age, but she had no interest in learning anything. The school was one of the most primitive schools with no facilities that would attract little girls and boys and encourage them to learn and study. She barely managed to finish four grades and was able to do some reading and writing, when one day she was sent home by the school head for family emergency.

Her eldest sister, Baljeet, while finishing her daily chores, was found to vomit some blood and after a few hours, died. The whole thing was so sudden that it gave no time for anyone to take her to the Burrelpur hospital that was about seventy miles away. Papaji was completely motionless, just staring at her dead body, and repeating, 'that's exactly how she died'. He meant his wife. Villagers took the dead body and cremated in the village crematorium. He didn't even go there. The family observed the mourning period and then everyone got back into their routine, everyone being Daljeet and Shailender. Papaji became even more depressed looking and much more difficult to handle since that day.

Shailender started going back to the school, a place that had become her solace, to free herself from the depressing environment of her home, especially from Papaji, at least for a few hours of the day. She was barely in the middle school when she was called by the school head one day to be sent home, when exactly the same calamity befell the family one more time. This time it was Daljeet's turn to get intensely sick. With the previous experience in memory, a few of the neighbors got together and admitted Daljeet to the hospital for treatment. But a few days later, Daljeet died with no cause known to the local doctors or nurses. She too, in short, had left the world suddenly and unexpectedly.

The family saw three deaths, one after another in such a short span of time. All three were women, two among them, quite young. Nobody knew why it happened. Was it a curse of some sort? Papaji became completely neurotic, and Shailender even more averse to go near him. She quit school altogether, but who would have noticed that? There was no one to question any of her actions, or take care of her, or show any interest in her well being. She started detesting every thing about her home, especially staying home during the day. A young girl, having just entered her teenage, she started wandering all over the village during school hours, occasionally going to her friends' homes with them and feeling intensely jealous of their homes, where their mothers made hot meals in the evenings, asked them about school and other things and took care of their needs, especially when their mothers helped them with their hair. Shailender had long, beautiful hair. She would get many compliments for her hair from her friends, but that didn't help the difficulty she faced in maintaining her long hair. She missed her mother terribly at such times, especially after her both sisters' deaths. She was alone in this vast world.

And one day, as Shailender was wandering on her usual route through the meadows and uncultivated farms of other people, she was located by the school peon and taken to the school office. Scared like anything, she was continuously shivering with fear. What had she done?

"Come in..." the school head said. An elderly lady was sitting and talking with the school head when Shailender was brought into the office room.

"Come, come, and sit down." The school head gestured her in a kind voice. Shailender got the mat from the corner, laid it on the floor and sat down. No student was allowed to sit on a chair in the school. Besides, both chairs in the office room were occupied.

"Meet our guest, Usha ji Pundit. She is new in town, and has come to our school all the way from New Delhi." The school head said.

Shailender looked at the guest. A lady in her fifties or so, she had a very kind face. She felt a little at ease.

"*Namaste*."[15] Shailender politely greeted the lady.

"Namaste. And what is your name?"

"Shailender, Shailender Singh." Shailender told her name in a very low and polite tone.

"Shailender, how old are you?" The lady asked with a smile. Her disarming smile made Shailender feel further relaxed.

"Thirteen years." Shailender answered politely to this 'kind-looking' lady with a faint smile on her face.

"Usha ji, please tell her yourself why you are here today." The school head said.

"Well, okay. Listen, the Central government of India, that's at New Delhi, you know that, right?"

Shailender just nodded.

"Good. They have made some kind of an arrangement with all the state governments of the country to inculcate literacy, and if possible, promoting education up to high school graduation, for every body, especially for girls and young women, free of cost. This is a major project and the government of your state is also participating in the project. With big cities and urban centres, we have had no problem. Most of the people are literate; many go to schools and complete their high school education. It is the small villages, such as this one, where the real problem, and a real challenge, lies. We are trying to meet that challenge by taking one village at a time. We are continuing with that project this time right here in your village, starting next month."

Shailender was listening to her, while nodding at times, to express that she was able to understand what she said.

"Usha ji has dedicated her whole life to this cause; inculcating literacy among the villagers, especially women, of India." The school head looked at Usha ji with great admiration and respect.

"Shailender, I am told that you were a bright student, and you were just a couple of years away from completing your middle school when you quit school a few months ago, for no obvious reason, is that right?"

Shailender nodded and looked down.

---

15. Namaste is the Indian way of greeting people politely.

"Would you join my project, then?" The lady asked.

Shailender looked up and nodded again.

"First, you will have to finish the middle school right here, and then judging from your progress, I will arrange for you to go to Burrelpur to complete your high school graduation. That means you will have to be away from your home for three years. Is that okay with you?"

She was listening to the lady intently. She nodded vigorously as a firm 'yes' to her question.

Perhaps, she was thinking, 'anything to get away from my wretched home, especially Papaji'.

"You said she has an old father at home. I think we need to take his permission for his daughter to be a part of this project, isn't it?" The lady turned to the school head and asked.

"No, no, you don't need his permission. Please don't talk to him, I do want to learn..." Shailender blurted out rather loudly that startled both those ladies in the room.

"Calm down Shailender, there's no need to get excited. I'll talk to your father and get his permission for you to enroll in this project, okay?" The school head assured her and then looked at Usha ji with meaningful eyes.

'These two women look like they will definitely help me', Shailender assessed the situation and felt relaxed.

"If I finish the middle school successfully, then I will get to go to Burrelpur, right?" She looked at the ladies and asked bravely.

"Yes." Both of them answered simultaneously. "You will go to Burrelpur."

There was again a faint smile, this time of satisfaction, on Shailender's face. And not surprisingly, even on the face of her school head.

"Okay, you can go now. But don't go back wandering on the meadows now, go to your old class room. I'll send a chit with the peon and the teacher will allow you in the class." The school head gestured her to leave.

Shailender picked up the mat, put it neatly in the corner and left the office room with a big smile on her face, darting straight to her old class room.

"Oh come in, come in..." Usha didi opened the door and she saw Shailender standing in the doorway. "Now, what are you doing here?"

"May I come in madam?"

"Yes, yes of course. And you can call me Usha didi, not madam." Usha didi led her into the living room. There were four chairs in the room, all alike, and a matching coffee table to go with the chairs. Shailender sat on one of the chairs very hesitantly. 'This must be the only place in this village with so many chairs looking alike' she thought. She glanced at the coffee table. A couple of modern magazines with glossy covers were neatly laid on the coffee table. One of them had a picture of a young woman with beautiful figure with shiny hair and white teeth, advertising some product. Can this really exist? She had never seen anyone having such a body, or such shiny hair and white teeth, in her village.

"I am so glad you joined the project. I understand you are a bright student, I want a couple of more bright girls like you and this project will take off very well here also." Usha didi's comment brought Shailender back from her deep thought to the present reality.

"Um, hum, hum! Uhhh madam..." she felt flustered.

"No, no, it's Usha didi, remember?" Usha didi had the same smile on her face that Shailender had seen for the first time in the school head's office room. She felt a little at ease.

"Sorry madam, I mean Usha didi. I came to ask you if I can come and study at your place after school?"

"Why, sure. But don't you want to go home and see your old father after school?"

"Yes, but..." Shailender lied. She had to take a deep breath before she continued, "But, I really want to study hard, and that wouldn't be possible at home..."

"Okay, I don't have any problem you studying here. What grade are you in right now?"

"Seventh grade." Shailender had her face down, for she should have been in the ninth grade at her age.

"Seventh?" Usha didi sounded quite surprised.

Shailender just nodded.

"In that case, would you like to do two years in one? I can help you with that."

"Yes, yes, very much so." Shailender looked happy.

"You will have to work very hard, not miss single day of school and appear for all examinations of all subjects and pass them. Agreed?"

"Yes, agreed."

"In that case, start right away, as in, tomorrow! I'll take care of the paper work that's needed for this process, okay?"

Shailender had no words to express her happiness. With her vigorous nod, Usha didi could see her genuine happiness for this arrangement.

"Thank you, thank you, oh my..." she barely managed to offer her heartfelt thanks to Usha didi and left with a heart full of hope.

Usha didi had grown to be fond of this young girl over the year. She had even started addressing her by her family pet name. Shailu would come to her house every single day after school for studying. Usha didi had seen that she had put in her heart in the studies, and worked very hard over the year, to complete the middle school.

Once in a while, during the year, Shailender would pick up some of the magazines that were regularly delivered to Usha didi's place, and look very intently at the advertisement inside, especially if they were done by young beautiful women's pictures, women with shiny hair and white teeth.

"Are these women real?" She would ask Usha didi sometimes.

"Yes, I guess so. Why?" Usha didi would ask her.

"They look so beautiful, with perfect bodies and all that. And their hair and teeth, they seem out of this world. Is that possible?" She would ask her Usha didi innocently.

"Yes. These women are called models." Usha didi would answer.
"What?"

"Models. I am sure these young women take extra care of their bodies and their hair and teeth too. As I understand, they eat very little and exercise a lot, to maintain their beautiful, shapely bodies." Usha didi would explain to her, amused a little with Shailender's innocence.

'I wish I could be a model' Shailender was fascinated by these models.

"I am so glad you finished your middle school successfully. Now we'll try to send you to Burrelpur. How's that?" Usha didi asked Shailender, but she didn't say anything.

"Shailu, what happened? Are you alright?" Shailender was still quiet.

"Hey, what's the matter? I thought you will be very happy to leave this village, especially Papaji." Usha didi had come to know about him and his ways of dealing with life, and also how Shailender felt about him, over the year.

"Usha didi, where will you go now?" Shailender asked her.

"Back to my home place, of course!"

"Where is that?"

"Mumbai."

"And your project, is it finished?"

"Yes. It's finished for this village. Now I'll go to New Delhi, give all the reports to the department, and head to my home town, which is Mumbai. I was on a loan from the provincial government to the Central one, which is in New Delhi. With you all girls, this project was successful. But, why do you ask?"

"Usha didi, I don't want to go to Burrelpur."

"What?" Shailender gave Usha didi a mild shock.

"I said, I don't want to go to Burrelpur."

"I heard that. Why not? I thought you always wanted to get away from here. Besides, you did very well in the middle school, so finishing high school education will be very good for you. I shall recommend appointing you as a school teacher when you come back here."

"I don't want to go to Burrelpur and I don't want to come back here after I finish high school."

"Then what do you want to do?"

"I want to come with you to Mumbai."

"What?" Shailender gave Usha didi another mild shock.

"That's silly, and you know that. What will you do there? And what about High school?" Usha didi collected herself from the shock.

"I can do it in Mumbai too. I'll stay with you and study very hard there."

"I'm not sure what you have in mind but taking you along with me will be very difficult for me."

"Oh please, please take me with you. I'll stay with you, and in return, I'll do all your household chores. I'll be like your 'live-in-maid'. And just like those models, I will eat very little, so you need not worry about my food either..."

"Shailu, Shailender, what are you saying? Do you think my difficulty is because I can't give you food?"

"Usha didi, in this last year, I hardly stayed at home. After school hours, I was at your place most of the evenings, barely going home to sleep, sometimes not even that. You made arrangements for me for many nights to sleep in your home, remember? The warmth I had in your home and the genuine affection and love I received from you, I have never ever experienced that in my entire life. I have absolutely no attachment to my home, or to that man who is only biologically my father."

Usha didi was listening to her and looking at her. She was taken aback by a mild surprise. Shailender's mannerism and bearing had improved manifold in this one year, not to mention her language and thought process. The girl had picked up many cultured habits from Usha didi, no doubt.

When Shailender saw that Usha didi was not staying anything, she took that as her indifference and felt dejected. With a sad voice, she just said, "I have no cne in this world, but who cares? I know if I stay here any longer, I am going to die ..." and started gathering her stuff from Usha didi's house, trying to control her crying.

"Hey, Shailu..." Usha didi called her, but Shailender continued whatever she was doing without a word.

"Stop that and listen to me now. Shailu, I said stop doing that and listen to me." Shailender momentarily stopped gathering her stuff and looked at her.

"Listen, I don't have any one in this world either, you know that. You also know that I live alone in Mumbai."

"Then why can't I be your 'some one'?" Shailender interrupted Usha didi "And if I can be your 'some one', then why can't I live with you there? You always told me you care for me, not a day passed in this year when you disliked my coming here. I felt that you were like a God sent messenger to me, then why are you abandoning me now?"

Usha didi was still feeling a little surprised at the conviction of this young girl of a small village. She laughed mildly at her warped logic and said, "...but for me, my work is my life..."

"I will never interfere your work Usha didi, I promise." Shailender was determined.

"Well, let me think about all this. This would be a major decision for you, leaving your home and coming with me to a far place like Mumbai; and it is a major decision for me too, believe me." Usha didi said.

"Does that mean, it's a 'no'?" Shailender asked her directly.

"No, it means 'I need to think about it'." Usha didi said. Shailender looked completely dejected and on the verge of crying..

"Listen, let me talk to your school head. She is familiar with your village customs and your family situation too. She may talk to your father, and then he may grant you permission to come with me, okay?" Usha didi could not see Shailender's sad face.

"Please do it soon. I can't wait to pack up and leave with you." Shailender said.

"Is that how strongly you feel about leaving this place, and about me and coming with me to Mumbai?" Usha didi asked her with a little surprise in her tone.

Shailender gave her a vigorous nod. Her face seemed like it was brightening up already.

"Okay, if that's the case, then let's decide on that. It's settled. You will come with me and live with me in Mumbai. I'll still talk to your school head though; to get an official permission from your father, okay?" Usha didi said.

The moment Shailender heard that, she dropped everything and ran towards Usha didi, embraced her tightly, and started shedding tears, tears of excessive joy, of course!

'The world is soooo beeeaaauuutiful...la...la...la...'

Shailender was humming her favorite song one day while she was preparing meals for Usha didi. She was about to return from a conference held in some other city, and Shailender was sure she would be very tired from the journey. She was planning on serving her hot food as soon as she arrives.

As was decided, Shailender left her village and moved with Usha didi to Mumbai. It was almost five years now that she was living with Usha didi in her Mumbai apartment. In these years, she never even once visited her village, or inquired about anyone, especially her father. It was like she cut off her roots with that place altogether. Usha didi was her family, and she was completely devoted to her.

In Mumbai, she finished her High school education and also a two-year diploma in teaching kindergarten. An ordinary country girl from a very small village in North India, she very nicely settled herself in this huge urban place. The credit went to Usha didi. She had become her mother, her mentor, her confidante and her Guru. And Shailender had proved herself to be worthy of all that care and affection her Guru showered on her. There never was any regret, in either of their minds, about her leaving her own village and coming with Usha didi.

Shailender set up the table for two and was eagerly waiting for Usha didi to come home, when she saw her walking home with another person, a very smart looking woman in her early thirties or so. They both were talking and laughing, they seemed like they knew each other quite well.

"Shailu, meet my past student and now, a very dear friend, Dr. Vimal."

"Namaste" Shailender greeted her and then turned towards Usha didi and said, "Usha didi, the table is already set for two. Would you both like to have your meals now?"

"That would be wonderful." Usha didi said and then turning towards Dr. Vimal, said, "Get a quick wash and join me for dinner."

After a quick wash, both ladies took their seats at the table and started eating.

"This is really good..." Dr. Vimal said.

"Shailu is a very good cook. She is very bright too." Usha didi said.

"Where did you find her?"

"I had been to a remote village in North India on one of my projects..."

"Your wonderful project of starting schools for the local villagers, right?" Dr. Vimal said.

"That's right. I started middle school there, that's where I met Shailu. After the middle school years, she just wouldn't stay there with her family, so I brought her here."

"That's wonderful. Shailu, I would say you are one lucky person to live with Usha didi here. She is my mentor, my ..."

"Okay, enough already. Let us eat now." Usha didi interrupted Dr. Vimal. "Why don't you join us too, Shailu?"

"I'll eat a bit later." Shailender said and went inside to get some more food for them. They looked like they were really enjoying it.

"It's really something, we both had our conferences arranged in the same city at the same time, and our living arrangements made in the same hotel, isn't it?" Dr. Vimal said.

"That's because we were meant to meet each other, after so many years. How long has it been Vimal?" Usha didi asked.

"Oh I would say, at least fifteen years, Usha didi. I was barely out of high school at the time."

Dr. Vimal calling her Usha didi caught Shailender's ear. 'Is she also some one like me?' A doubt crossed her mind in that split second. 'May be, may be not' she ignored it.

"Shailu, Vimal was one of my brightest students when I was a school head in one of Mumbai's high schools. She is a doctor now, and a breast cancer specialist, right?" Dr. Vimal just nodded.

"And Shailu must also be bright. Just taste the food she has made…" Dr. Vimal said, while munching on the food.

"But tell me something Vimal; were you not studying the science of genetics a while ago? I remember reading about you getting the top national scholarship in that field."

"You are absolutely right. It's much later that I specialized in the field of Oncology."

"What's that?" Usha didi asked.

"That is science of cancer. I am trying to combine these two areas of bioscience and find a common thread in them."

"How do you mean?"

"It is postulated that there is a 'genetic factor' for breast cancer."

"What's a genetic factor?" Shailu unexpectedly showed interest in their conversation.

"Oh, that deals with the heredity characters of a human being. To explain in very, very simple terms, the science of genetics says that, since every human being is a product of a man and a woman, the genes of both parents are passed on to the offspring. This is a very simple definition. In one of the papers that I presented, I had quoted one renowned scientist stating that some women had developed breast cancer primarily due to their genetic lineage."

"What does that mean?" Shailender asked.

"That means, those women got this disease because their mothers had some kind of either ovarian cancer or breast cancer. Sometimes, it was their grand mothers or aunts or someone very close in their family, where the genes could be passed on to them, who had cancer. Luckily, the hereditary risk in the general female population is only about seven percent and the percentage of such occurrences is very low, but it still is existent unfortunately."

"Oh, my God!" Usha didi and Shailender both exclaimed at this information.

"You will be surprised to hear but I have read in a few international journals that many cancer centres are opting for 'preventative mastectomy' for a few breast cancer patients now-a-days." "What does that mean?" Shailender asked again.

"You know what Mastectomy means, right?" Dr. Vimal asked her.

But Shailender shook her head.

"It means removal of one or both breasts by surgery. Preventative mastectomy means removal of one or both breasts without the presence of cancer. This surgery is sometimes chosen as a preventative measure by women who have a strong history of familial breast cancer."

"And how do such women know that they may have breast cancer in future?" Shailender was getting curious about this conversation and that made Usha didi very happy.

"They don't know that. Nobody knows what the future holds, right? But, if there is a strong familial background, as I explained before, and especially if there are deaths of women in the families due to such cause, then such women opt for 'preventative mastectomy'. They don't want to take any chances."

"And what if there are sudden, unexpected deaths of women in the family, actually more than one woman's death in the same family, but nobody knows why these deaths happened, then what should the remaining women of the same family do?" Shailender was sounding a little excited when she asked this question. And her question almost alerted Usha didi.

"Then the remaining women of such family should get themselves checked thoroughly for cancer of female organs, especially breast cancer. And if possible, get the surgery done for 'preventative mastectomy' well ahead of time. It's not wise to take a risk and wait until the onset of the disease, is it?"

"Oh my God, Oh my good God..." Shailender shivered.

Dr. Vimal thought that Shailender was moved by her narration, so she continued.

"One of my colleagues, who is a surgeon, recently had a case where the patient came to him shortly after her mother died of ovarian cancer. After doing the family research, the patient had discovered that her numerous female relatives had died from breast or ovarian cancer. My surgeon friend suggested that this patient also considers getting tested to study her risk of breast cancer and also the risk of ovarian cancer. When she was tested, it was learned that in fact she did have a risk of developing breast cancer. She herself was shocked to learn that result."

"And then?"

"The surgeon told her that with screening tests, such as mammograms, when done regularly, they could find cancers at an early stage and lower the risk of the patients dying from breast cancer. He also told her that with Breast MRIs, which are shown to be better at detecting early-stage cancer in high-risk women, he could detect it much too early. However, detection of a cancer is not the same as prevention of a cancer, even if it is early enough, isn't it?"

"I guess not. So, what did that patient do finally?" Usha didi asked.

"Well, she opted for preventative mastectomy. You see, even if the detection methods have come a long way, preventive surgery is the only way to dramatically reduce the risk of developing breast cancer. Studies have shown that the procedure cuts the risk by nearly 95%. That's very encouraging."

"Did the surgeon cut both her breasts?" Shailender asked.

"Yes, both of them. That's called bilateral mastectomy."

"And how old was this patient, Vimal didi?" Shailender seemed to get emotionally involved in the story. Unknowingly, she had both her hands over her breasts.

"I think she was in her late twenties or so. I am not sure of her age." Dr. Vimal said.

Shailender was quiet like a mouse after hearing all that, but Usha didi and Dr. Vimal did not notice it. They had moved away from this topic to some other one.

"The dinner was simply fabulous Usha didi. It certainly was a treat." Dr. Vimal complimented Shailender too for cooking such good food.

"And the way you tell about your work and describe everything, one would feel as if you are telling a very interesting mystery story or something, Vimal." Usha didi was full of admiration for Dr. Vimal.

"Usha didi, this science is really like one big mystery of life. The more you unravel, the more complex it seems to become, and the more you search for the treasure, the farther it moves. It seems almost impossible at times to explore and study. Oh, I really get lost in it, as if I am holding a big mystery novel in my hand."

"For you, there is really no difference between the two, isn't it?" Usha didi said with genuine admiration for Dr. Vimal.

"Well, there is, actually. The difference between the two is, there is an end to a mystery novel and invariably, the mystery gets solved; as against that, unfortunately, the end in this mystery book remains ever-growing and there is no end to the hunt, if you will, and all this struggle!" Dr. Vimal said and they both laughed heartily.

"It was a lovely evening, indeed." Dr. Vimal got up from the chair and started getting ready to leave. "I think I should leave now."

"We should meet more often than this, don't you think?" Usha didi said.

Dr. Vimal concurred with her and after thanking both the ladies, she left.

Usha didi looked quite tired so she retired to bed. Shailender was still very quiet. Without uttering a single word, she started clearing the table and collecting the dirty dishes and putting them in the sink for washing. While doing that work, she was continuously thinking. Her mouth was shut but her thoughts were racing at a phenomenal speed in her mind.

'Could that be my case too? Ma died so suddenly when I was barely three years of age. Nobody knew exactly what happened to her and why she died. Could that be some kind of cancer? Baljeet and Daljeet also died so unexpectedly a few years after Ma, and they were so young. Was that due to some female cancer too? Would mine be the next turn to die?' Shailender shivered vigorously at this thought. She unknowingly increased the speed of her work in the kitchen. After cleaning up everything, she went to her room and lay down on her mattress. She tried to sleep but these thoughts wouldn't stop poking her brains. They had set in with deep roots by now in her mind.

'What if I have that heredity? Would I get breast cancer? Does that mean I will have to cut off my breasts too, like that patient Dr. Vimal was talking about?' She automatically put her hands over her breasts and started stroking them gently. With every stroke, her thoughts became more intense and more fearful. She tried hard to flick away those thoughts but they kept recurring, over and over again. She took her hands off her chest and put them in a Namaste pose, as if praying to God above. She lay awake the whole night in that pose, staring at the ceiling, stiff with fear, while Usha didi was snoring softly in the adjacent room.

•••

As the Journey Continues...

The meeting in the community centre is going on ...

"So, as I was saying, we may be able to establish a support group for breast cancer patients and their families. And once that is established, we may be able to build a beautiful Centre like the one I saw in Canada, right here in our home town. What do you all think about it, ladies?" Dr. Vimal is addressing the women in the meeting.

"Ladies..." Dr. Vimal looks around, anticipating some response from the women in attendance. However, they look like they are still lost in the world of their past.

"Ladies...ladies...Anita, Maya, what about you, Ritu? Any ideas?" Listening to their names being called out, the women look startled. And as though suddenly pulled out of their lost state, they give a confused look to Dr. Vimal.

"Centre?" A couple of them ask, trying to collect themselves.

"Build a Support Centre similar to the one I saw in Canada." Dr. Vimal reiterates with a smile. She seems to be fully aware that these women had just been on their journey into their past, that time of the past when their breast cancer was just diagnosed.

"Oh, I think it's a wonderful idea, doctor." Maya quickly collects herself and responds. "We can hold many educational sessions in the Centre for teaching about breast cancer."

"And not just for women with breast cancer. We can have some educational sessions for the husbands of the patients as well, doctor. Women with breast cancer need their husbands' support the most, and if the husbands don't know much about the disease, then everything else collapses too, I think..." Anita emphasizes awareness among the husbands of breast cancer patients. She knows why?

"Yes...yes..." all of them agree, except Virani. She is sitting quietly.

"Don't you agree, Virani?" Dr. Vimal asks her.

"Yes I agree, but you know what? My husband is quite aware. He has enough information about the disease. It is *me* who is still quite bitter and negative about my disease..." Virani says in a low voice.

"So, what do you think we should do for such problems?" Dr. Vimal throws a general question to all. She is fully aware of Virani's background.

"Doctor, perhaps holding a few educational sessions with an emphasis on positive and proactive thinking rather than just the disease itself would help such problem. Would that work?" Anita suggests.

"Something like that..." Virani says, again in a very low voice.

"Actually that would be wonderful. I don't mind attending such sessions myself." Maya says. "As a matter of fact, I know one such lady who would be ideal to conduct such sessions of positive thinking for us." Maya is obviously thinking of her own experience with such a lady, named Meeraben.

"We should encourage families of patients as well, especially the husbands, to attend these sessions, doctor." Anita is determined to have her husband face the reality of breast cancer. Everyone nods with agreement.

"Dr. Vimal, I have one more suggestion. I sincerely think that patient's children, especially young daughters, should be given some special training about how to handle their mothers' breast cancer." Ritu says.

"What do you mean Ritu?"

"I mean, along with awareness about breast cancer, teaching them about human bodies, and giving young women general information about some relevant topics, such as female development would also be a good idea." Ritu explains and everyone agrees to her statement full heartedly.

"I feel that along with awareness, a little education about science and current research in the field of this disease is also needed." Maya sees some nodding heads around as she completes her sentence.

Just then, "Disease...disease...disease...! I'm fed up of it." Everyone is stunned to hear Shaina shout at the top of her lungs. They stare at her. "Isn't there anything else we can discuss? Is that all that matters, the disease?" She stands up and expresses her disgust with everyone's attitude of focusing only on the disease.

"You are right, dear." Dr. Vimal concurs with Shaina. "We should have a few sessions on the post-disease care as well."

"Care and *beauty*, doctor, I mean beauty too" Shaina feels good that the doctor is on her side. "We are *women*, and women like to look beautiful. Women of all types. There is no exception to this rule." Shaina looks around but no one seems to agree with her.

"I bet you are all going to focus only on the disease even when we have that beautiful centre..." Shaina says with total frustration in her voice and sits down.

"You are absolutely right, Shaina." Dr. Vimal says calmly. "Ladies, Shaina is right. We are women and we like to look good, no matter whom or what we are facing?"

Then she turns towards Shaina and asks her, "Are you suggesting reconstructive surgery for those who have undergone mastectomy, Shaina?"

"Yes, but not just that, doctor," Shaina feels encouraged with the doctor's support. She stands up again and says, "Even during the treatment, we can take care of our looks by wearing some make-up, some lipstick, etc. Don't you want to look in the mirror anytime and see a presentable reflection of yourself? Having breast cancer doesn't mean there's an end to carrying yourself well. It doesn't mean you can live shabbily and look ugly..."

"Calm down dear, no one looks ugly." Dr. Vimal says to Shaina and then turns to the women and says, "Ladies, what Shaina is trying to say is that during the cancer treatment also, women must look after themselves cosmetically. Getting breast cancer or having mastectomy is not the end of being complete females, right Shaina?"

"That's absolutely right. Thank you doctor. Ladies, we are women, and we will remain women, even if we have to have our breasts cut off. Let's be proud of being women, and we women like beauty in everything we do, right?" Shaina looks around and sees a smile on every one's face in the room. She feels satisfied and sits down with a smile on her own face too.

"Now that we are all in complete agreement of establishing a support group, and conducting educational sessions for families and friends according to the needs, how shall we divide this work?" Dr. Vimal asks everyone. All the women look at each other questioningly and start speaking to each other in soft voices. Dr. Vimal, looking at the women so engrossed in their conversations, is feeling satisfied with the success of the meeting today. She is thinking, 'All these sessions for open communication and awareness for breast cancer must be built into the routine for all my patients and their families...'

"Dr. Vimal, you are a doctor, an oncologist, and a breast cancer specialist at that. We would really like you to teach sessions on science and research. So, can I put your name down for this volunteer service?" Anita asks Dr. Vimal. She has become quite friendly with the doctor in the last few years.

"That would be fine." Dr. Vimal agrees to Anita's suggestion with a smile. Anita pulls out her a small chart from her diary and scribbles something in it.

"And who else would like to volunteer?" Dr. Vimal asks everybody.

"You all know, I'm a social worker, by training as well as work experience. I shall gladly coordinate and manage all the sessions, including the doctor's." Anita tells all the ladies and then looks at the doctor with a smile, as if she is reciprocating to her.

"Someone said earlier that she knows of someone who can teach us about positive thinking..." Ritu says in her beautiful voice.

"That was me. Thanks for reminding me." Maya tells Ritu. Then she looks at every one else in the room and says, "I know of a lady who is professionally a psychotherapist. I can request her to conduct a few sessions for us here."

"Would she agree to come and talk to the patients of breast cancer though?" Someone doubts.

"Yes, most definitely." Maya has developed confidence in Meeraben.

"I have two teenager daughters. I can get their help in organizing sessions for children for the patient families, especially young women." Ritu volunteers too.

"Shaina, you would be the most suitable candidate to teach the basics of beauty and care, especially during the medical treatment, I think." Dr. Vimal looks at Shaina and suggests.

"Yes, I can arrange a few sessions for beauty tips for breast cancer patients." Shaina feels very happy to be of such a special service to the women.

"And money? We also need some money, ladies, for conducting these sessions." Dr. Vimal reminds them.

"That's no problem, Dr. Vimal." Maya and Shaina say simultaneously and look at each other and laugh. "We will personally look after that too." There is a round of applause in the room.

"Well, I haven't offered anything as yet. But I am good with handling money since I was a cashier in a bank. I can give help in that matter, if it's needed..." Virani says in a polite, but hesitant way.

"Of course, it's needed Virani. Thank you dear..." Dr. Vimal tells her and then turning towards everyone, asks, "Is there anything else we need to discuss today?" All the ladies look at each other and shake their heads.

"Ladies, you all have forgotten the very first problem we face. And that would be, where do we hold our meetings until we have our own place?"

"Yes, that's the first obstacle. We do need a place." Everyone agrees.

"A support Centre is a huge project which may take a long time, and obviously, it will need a lot of money too. However, we can discuss this issue at a later date. The immediate concern is a place where we can start all these activities." Dr. Vimal looks at everyone.

"Well, Dr. Vimal and ladies, place is not a problem at all." Maya says with a smile on her face.

When all of them, including Dr. Vimal, start looking at her with a question-mark displayed on their faces, she says, "I have a huge bungalow, and it is completely empty. I live alone with my two servants. I would like to offer my home as a starting place for our support group. We will hold all our sessions there." Maya says and there is another round of applause in the room.

A big obstacle is overcome by Maya's generosity, first that of her money and then her home. Everyone is happy. And so is Maya, very genuinely happy, for, she is slowly getting her desire fulfilled, that of *being in need*!

The meeting is adjourned. Although it's the very first one, it has been extremely successful and productive. The women come out of the room talking and laughing with each other. Establishing a support group for breast cancer patients itself is a marvelous idea that they have come up with; building a Cancer Support Centre would be an epitome of this idea, like a bright red cherry on the top, they tell themselves.

"Do you need a ride?" Maya and Shaina are asking the rest of the women. Their cars are parked in the parking lot with their drivers waiting outside.

"No, thank you, Das is picking me up on his way from the bank." Virani is telling them.

"I'm heading to the music concert to join Parth and our daughters. I will grab a cab, thank you." Ritu has already started walking out the door.

"I'm taking a ride with Dr. Vimal to her clinic. Thank you." Anita is seen walking away with Dr. Vimal.

The ladies are dispersed; Maya and Shaina in their own cars, Anita in Dr. Vimal's car, Ritu in a cab and Virani with her husband, Das, on his scooter.

As their vehicles pick up the speed, so do their minds, which are literally overflowing with thoughts of their post-diagnostic days. It seems that their thoughts are racing even faster than their vehicles.

Anita

Lost in her favorite pastime of thinking of those beautiful days that were gone by, Anita suddenly got up from her kitchen chair and gave a mild shake to her sari as if it was wet with urine, even now. She shook her head hard. The hard shaking of her head brought her to the present and she laughed at herself for the silly act of shaking her sari. She looked outside through the glass window. Deven was still sitting in his armchair reading the philosophy book. She decided something to herself and went outside towards where he was sitting.

"Dev, do you recall the day when Dr. Vimal diagnosed my breast cancer?" Anita's question almost startled him.

"What? Sorry, what did you ask?" He seemed a bit flustered.

"I said, do you remember the day when we were in Dr. Vimal's clinic for the first time and she told us about my breast cancer?" She repeated her question.

"Of course, I remember. How can you ask me this? That day is clear like a picture in my mind. Unfortunately it never gets wiped out, and actually that's the problem for me."

"What do you mean?" Anita was puzzled. That day, when her breast cancer was diagnosed, was clear like a picture in her mind too but she never tried to wipe it out. As a matter of fact, in her indulgence of revisiting the past, she herself had visualized that day many a time.

"What followed after the diagnosis of your cancer is even clearer in my mind and that's what has instilled this eternal fear in me." He closed the book and looked at her.

"What are you saying? What eternal fear? Fear of what?"

"Fear of that..." He looked at her chest.

"That what?" She sounded totally confused.

"That!" He looked at her chest again.

"My breast cancer?"

He just shook his head.

"Then, what?"

"That, that flat chest of yours on the left side, the absence of your left breast, and especially..." He couldn't finish his sentence and started shaking again.

"But all that happened two years ago. I lost my breast a good two years ago. The scars are barely visible now. We thought seriously about the plastic surgery once, remember? And we jointly took a decision against it, right? So what's the problem now?" Anita went closer to him and could see his entire body shaking with a mild tremor. She held him tightly to make him steady.

"That sight just does not seem to leave my mind at all, Annie..." he addressed her with that pet name after a very long time.

"What sight dear?" She gently seated him down on the armchair.

"That sight, sight of those ugly scars spread over your delicate chest, where there used to be your beautiful breast. Those scars running all the way to your armpit. With those scars as a neighbor, even your beautiful right breast looks lonely and abandoned to me Annie..." Deven's voice sounded very dry. He was also looking very pale.

Anita went inside and got a glass of water for him. Then she pulled another chair for herself near him and sat down. It was going to be a long talk, she figured. Deven emptied the glass within minutes and looked better.

"I get nightmares all the time and in my nightmares, I see those scars on your chest. When I see them, I wake up sweating and shaking like anything. Since that day I have not been able to sleep peacefully, Annie. Since that day, I go to sleep with a fear that that nightmare is going to appear again." Deven said.

"Since what day, Dev?" Anita asked him gently. He was slowly opening up to her. After so long. After two whole years.

"Since that day, when I saw those scars for the first time on your chest, and those ugly, black stitches. Annie, those stitches seemed to me like an army of devils that had captured the territory and forbidden me to come near you; and I, like a defeated soldier, had to walk stealthily away from them."

"Oh my God, Dev! I never knew this was how you felt when I had that surgery."

"No, not when you had the surgery. Not when you were in the hospital either. Do you remember how I was and how I felt after your surgery?"

"Of course, I remember. I was a mess, but you were an angel, you became my everything, mother, father, a friend and even a daughter.

We encouraged Devnita not to come because of her final exams. You played her role too for me. You were a dream husband, Dev." Anita was honest when she told Deven about how she felt.

"And then it happened one night..."

"What happened?" Anita interrupted with intense curiosity.

"That horrible encounter I had with my fear after I brought you home from the hospital." Deven said.

Anita just looked at him questioningly.

"And I was completely defeated by my own fear..."

"Can you be more explicit? I can't understand all these riddles." Anita was getting impatient.

"Okay, please listen. You had just come home from the hospital and finished talking with Devnita. You both had cried a lot on the telephone and I had to intervene and quiet down both of you, do you remember that?" Deven asked her.

Anita just nodded, she was waiting impatiently for his explanation.

"Annie, you were exhausted and were lying down on the bed. It was close to our dinner time. I went into the kitchen and prepared your favorite dish that evening. I got it nicely served on a plate, then I filled up a glass with tomato juice and took both those things on a tray. I was bringing the tray to the bedroom when I saw you standing in front of your, no our, favorite mirror looking at yourself with your back towards the door. You were wearing only a long skirt, and nothing from the waist up. I saw your bare shoulders and bare back, so I got a bit excited. I kept the tray on the side table and slowly walked behind you with full intention of embracing you from behind as I always did. You must be looking intently at your scars on your chest. You were so absorbed in observing yourself that you didn't realize I was behind you. I had all the intentions of hugging you, kissing you on your neck, and telling you softly in your ears, 'Annie my darling, I'm so glad you are back, back home, back in my arms from the jaws of Death, safe and sound with no fear of anything, anything at all.' I wanted to kiss every inch of your body. And then? Then I looked in the mirror at your reflection, and...and..." Deven couldn't finish what he intended to say. "And you just exclaimed, 'Oh my Good God' and fell down." Anita completed his narrating the experience as though she was re-living that moment.

"I remember that scene too clearly." Anita said. "I would never forget that evening either, that black evening of our life, Dev."

They both were quiet for a few moments.

"Annie, that was the nemesis of my everything, really. What I saw that evening in your reflection in the mirror, I just can't erase from my memory at all. You could be wearing beautiful clothes, but one look at you and the only thing I see is those scars. And that has become my major source of fear. I tried a lot to forget that sight, to overcome my fear, but to no avail. I tried to read many new books, tried to read Shakespeare again, but no use. Just can't get over it Annie." Deven started sobbing profusely, as though all the grief in the world was blocked in his stomach until this moment and he was letting it out in buckets.

Anita started stroking his back gently. 'This is why he never came closer to me, never even once touched me after the surgery,' she figured it out.

"Dev, is that why you are trying to read those philosophy books, to get over your fear?" When he seemed a little quiet, she asked him softly. He just nodded.

"And is that why you lock yourself out? From all the people, from everybody, even from me?" He nodded again.

"Do you know," He sniffled a bit and continued, "I tried so many times to come close to you, especially when you were sound asleep." Deven said.

"Uh...hum..."

"I felt that urge to be with you in total unison a few times, but then, nothing happened."

"Uh...hum..."

"Annie, even now, I face this situation. In the middle of the night, when you are sound asleep, I try to muster my courage and try to come close to you. I hold your hand and very softly try to recite some lines of my favorite poem. That is for my own encouragement mind you, not you, you are fast asleep anyway. I focus only on your face and whisper, 'my sweet Annie'. I feel my body getting excited, I even feel a mild erection. I am encouraged to wake you up for some 'intimacy'! But then alas, my eyes deceive me, they move from your face to your chest. One look at your chest and the picture of your scars and those black stitches comes before my eyes, like an ugly black doll teasing my masculinity. I get numb with fear. I lose my nerve completely. My entire body becomes completely limp, like an old stale vegetable leaf. I just get up and leave or sometimes start reading a philosophy book to do away with that fear." Deven was about to cry again.

"You know, I have seen you, *actually seen you*, do that a few times." Anita gave Deven a mild surprise.

"Really?"

"Uh…hum! And that made me feel even sadder. It made me feel that you don't find me attractive anymore. I lost my one breast and that took away the graceful symmetry of my figure. I lost all of my hair that you loved so much to chemotherapy, and that took away the glamour of my face altogether. I felt very unattractive because of all this. And as if to add to that, you stopped flirting with me, reciting poems to me, talking to me with an eye contact; what's more, Dev, you stopped even fighting or arguing with me. As if I don't exist anymore. That has made me feel that I have lost your love too."

"Oh my God, Annie, really?" Deven looked confused, but Anita's firm nod confirmed his confusion.

"How could you doubt my *love* for you? Annie how could you? Oh my good God, I never ever imagined you could ever have a doubt about my love for you, my sweet Annie." He was genuinely upset with her accusation, but that was not the time to argue with her.

She had started crying and sobbing with her face turned downwards.

"Annie, honey, please hear me out. All those thoughts you had, have nothing to do with our 'love making' or any of these things you just mentioned, dear…

"How do I love thee?
Let me count the ways…"

Deven started reciting a few lines from poetry in order to console her but she didn't stop sobbing. She momentarily looked up at his face and saw him looking at her and reciting a few lines from her favorite poem. 'Has he come back to his normal self?' she wondered, and hoped so for a fleeting moment, but continued crying.

"Look at me now, please look up and stop crying…" Deven was holding her chin with his one hand and holding her at her waist with the other, trying to pull her towards him.

"Annie, give me a smile now, please my dear girl, give me that lovely smile of yours..." Deven was desperately trying to erase her doubt about his love for her, from her head.

After her sobbing became much less intense, she said, "You know, Dev, you are a romantic soul, and we both know that. As a matter of fact, that is an important part of who you are, right?" She managed to smile for him through her sobbing.

Deven just nodded in agreement.

"Just imagine Dev," Anita tried to control her sobbing more and continued, "Since after the chemotherapy, I started tying a scarf around my head, do you remember? As it is, I was feeling very unattractive. That evening, the evening that you just mentioned, when I tried to look at myself, especially my chest, in the mirror, I almost fainted at my own reflection. I didn't look horrible just with a loss of hair on my head; I had become ugly and shapeless with my body too. Looking like that, my morale had gone down to the lowest level that you can imagine. I counted on you to give me a boost in my morale. But then, what did you do? One look at my reflection in the mirror and you almost fainted. It was me who had to quickly compose myself and help you. Dev, it was *me* who helped you. Instead of you giving me support, you needed *my* support..."

"Yes honey, yes..." Deven looked down, feeling a bit shameful.

"And after that day, you have practiced total celibacy! What does that tell me? It's as though, you just can not be bothered to make love to an ugly woman like me..." Anita started sobbing again.

"No, my love, it's not at all like what you say." Deven was still looking down, feeling a bit embarrassed too.

"It's been almost two years now, do you realize that? You haven't even as much *looked* at me with affection."

Deven couldn't say anything to her. He felt totally shameful and embarrassed after listening to her. However, unfortunately, that was a fact.

"And without that romantic part of you, you seem crippled to me Dev. Totally crippled. Crippled, disabled and *incomplete...*"

"Annie..."

"Yes, incomplete. I am sorry to say this but you take those books of philosophy just to camouflage your own drawback. And as if to shun me away, you read them aloud in that grotesque monotone of yours."

"Annie..."

"With that horrible monotone of yours, you are not shunning *me* away, you are shunning away yourself from the real *you.*"

"Annie..."

"In that camouflaging, you stopped socializing with people, you stopped meeting your students and other faculty members that you enjoyed so much, you even stopped doing everything that we two did together for fun. Alas! Our 'love making' was the first casualty of this camouflage of yours. In front of the world, you pretend that you have done total renunciation of life's pleasures, Dev, but I know you are faking it. It is a mere façade. It's one big façade, and a big lie!"

"Stop it Annie, stop it..."

"I am sorry. I am really sorry. Getting breast cancer was not my fault, looking ugly and unattractive like this was also not my fault. It was my fate and it was your fate too Dev. Why can't you understand that?" Anita was sobbing uncontrollably.

What could Deven say to her? He realized the helplessness of her situation, but he himself was feeling equally helpless. He didn't know what had gone wrong with *him*? He knew that along with her breast, *he* had also lost something very valuable and dear to him. Unfortunately, he didn't know what it was, he just was aware of the gravity of the situation.

Ritu

"Daddy, Mommy is feeling okay now, stop stroking her back..." Sangita was telling Parth that gave him a mild startle in his immersion into that ugly past.

"Uh, what, yes, yes, honey, I'll stop now..." He looked at Ritu. She was looking a little tired.

"Why don't we stop the tuition right now and continue it later in the evening or perhaps tomorrow?" He told his daughters and then gently helped Ritu get up.

"But Daddy, Mommy said she has to teach us everything as soon as possible." Shruti said.

"Why?"

"That's because, she is going to die soon, that's why..." Shruti said again innocently.

"No, she is not going to die soon..." Parth assured his younger daughter while slowly leading Ritu to their bedroom.

"You dummy, are you stupid or something?" Sangita started scolding Shruti as soon as the parents were out of their sight. Shruti looked at her innocently with a confused expression on her face.

"You don't talk of dying in front of Mommy, you stupid. She has cancer, don't you know that?" Sangita said.

Shruti shook her head and looked like she was about to cry.

"Yah, she has cancer. Uhhh..." Sangita raised her shoulders and with her eyes closed, shivered momentarily.

"Why does she tie that ugly, black scarf on her head?" Shruti asked Sangita.

"Because she has no hair..." Sangita informed her.

"What?"

"That's right. She doesn't have a single hair on her head." Sangita told her.

"How do you know that?" Shruti asked her older sister.

"I know that, I asked Mommy about it once when she took off the scarf and showed me her head."

"Really?"

"Um hum."

"Did you ask her why she has no hair?"

"Yes, I did actually."

"And?"

"She told me that she has no hair because she had to have some really horrible medicines to get rid of her cancer."

"How come she didn't tell me all this?"

"She told me all that because I am old and mature." Sangita boasted about herself.

"I don't like Mommy with that black scarf on her head Sangita, I like Mommy without it, like she looked before, remember?" Shruti was about to cry again.

"Of course, I remember. Hey, do you know something else?" Sangita was about to say something to Shruti when Parth returned to the music room.

"Sangita, Shruti, let us pick up all these instruments and clean up the room." Parth said.

"But what about our music training?" Sangita asked.

"I said we'll do that sometime later, didn't I? Now, let us all go to the kitchen and have some snacks. I'll pour some milk for you girls and make a cup of tea for myself." Parth said.

"I don't want milk. That's for kids. I want tea..." Sangita said a little curtly.

"Sangita..."

"You give milk to Shruti, not me. I am grown up now..." Sangita said again in the same voice.

"Okay." Parth didn't argue with her. He just started picking up the instruments. The girls also quietly joined him in cleaning up. There was a complete silence in the room, except the faint sound of Sangita's continuous mumbling while she was helping her father tidy up the room, 'this is how my music lesson ends up..., every single time..., I will never be a good singer like mommy...' everything will be over before I am trained...; Parth could hear some of it, but decided to ignore it completely.

"Coming honey..." Parth got up from the table and almost ran to the bedroom.

They were having snacks and tea at the kitchen table. Parth had made tea for Sangita, as she wanted.

"May I have some tea too?" Ritu asked him with a smile on her face.

"Yes, of course. Do you want it here or ...?"

"No, I'll come to the kitchen. I want to sit with you all." Ritu said and requested him to help her get up from the bed. They both slowly walked to the kitchen.

"Mommy, mommy is here..." Shruti said with joy. Sangita was quiet though; she just looked at her mother and continued sipping her tea.

"Girls, we'll continue our Raga Bageshri tomorrow first thing after school is over, okay?" Ritu said.

"I can't do it tomorrow, sorry." Sangita said and became abruptly quiet again.

"Why not dear?"

"I will be late from school tomorrow, a lot of schoolwork to catch up..."

"Well, we'll do it whenever you come home dear..."

"No, no can do!"

"What do you mean by saying, 'no can do', Sangita? Behave yourself, okay?" Parth was losing his patience but Ritu quieted him down with her look.

"No, I wouldn't behave myself. I hate you all, I hate this house, and I hate music too..." Sangita said in a loud voice that startled everybody, more so Ritu.

"Sangita..." Ritu said gently.

But that didn't make any difference to Sangita. She ignored her mother completely, pushed her chair back and stomping her feet, started walking towards her room.

"Sangita, come here. I said come here right away. Sangita..." Parth ordered her in an equally loud voice.

But she didn't listen to him, she ran to her room and slammed the door of her room hard behind her.

Shruti was looking at all this with a big wonderment. She had never ever seen anything like this in her entire life of nine years in this house.

'Daddy yelling like that? Never!'

'Sangita not listening to mommy she so much admired? Never!'

Her little head was full of very sweet memories. This house was a peaceful house of two fine musicians who loved each other and their daughters. What was wrong today?

She was confused. She just sat like a quiet mouse, trying to finish her snack.

"Have you finished your snack Shruti?" Ritu asked her lovingly.

Shruti just nodded to her.

"Alright then, go to the living room and watch some television, okay dear." Ritu said.

Shruti put away her plate quickly and went to the living room to turn on the television. She knew that it was her hint to leave the parents alone.

"I don't know what's wrong with Sangita? She has never behaved like this..." Parth said.

"I don't know that either but I can guess why she's behaving this way?" Ritu said.

"It's only lately she has started all this nonsense..." Parth said.

"Remember you were out of town a few times last month for playing Tabla with other musicians?"

"Hum, hum."

"Sangita took care of the entire household all by herself. She did the cooking, cleaning, taking care of her younger sister; and she managed to take care of me too. She had to stay away from school a lot last month because of all these responsibilities, Parth." Ritu was telling him.

"But we have a cook and a part time maid for all this work, isn't it?"
"Yes, but still the lady of the house has to be there to supervise the work, Parth. And Sangita assumed that role. I would say, she *is* the lady of the house right now, Parth, especially when you are out of town for your performances." Ritu said.

"Do you think that's causing her a lot of stress?" Parth asked Ritu.

"I think so. She had to bunk school a few times." Ritu answered.

"Hum, that's why she said she has to catch up with a lot of schoolwork" Parth said.

"And that's not the only reason why she sounds so stressful."

"Oh? What do you think it is then?" Parth was genuinely wondering about it.

"Did you talk to her when I got sick with this disease?"

"Yes, of course. When your disease was diagnosed and when you were to have a surgery, Ritu, I had very nicely explained to both our daughters everything." Parth said.

"Did you tell them I have cancer?"

"Yes, of course."

"Did you tell them I had breast cancer?"

"No, I didn't."

"And I had to have my breasts removed?"

"Um…no."

"And I had to go through the chemotherapy?"

"Um…no."

"And that would mean I would lose all my hair?"

Parth just shook his head.

"Then what did you tell them Parth?"

"I told them that you were sick, that you have cancer, and you had to have a surgery. You would become quite sick for a while, so they have to be really very supportive." Parth said.

Ritu just smiled at him.

"Did you notice Sangita lately?"

"What do you mean?"

"Did you look at Sangita carefully, as of late?"

"Well, yes."

"I don't think so dear. Sangita has two tiny bumps on her chest now-a-days."

Parth didn't say anything. He had not noticed anything like that.

"She has entered her puberty years now. She'll get her period any day now."

"But…"

"Parth, this age is a very confusing age for most of the girls. I was one confused young woman myself for a while when I was in that age. But my mother was around for me. Fortunately for me, she was healthy and she was there to explain everything to me. She even took me to the market and gave me a choice of which 'training bra' to buy and which brand of pad was better for me. In Sangita's case, I got sick precisely when she needed me, and my disease was so deadly that all the focus of our entire family, especially you, was on me, and me alone. I wasn't there for her, and neither were you dear. I didn't help her and neither did you."

Ritu waited for a few minutes to take a few breaths, and then she continued.

"In her pre-puberty and puberty years, I should have been there for her. But unfortunately, she is compelled to manage her confusion all by herself."

Parth was quietly listening to his wife. This was new! Something he had never imagined. He had two children, both *girls*. Obviously, they needed more their mother than their father for their specific needs.

"It is only in the last few days that I am noticing a change in Sangita's behavior." Ritu was talking again. "I'm home now, luckily coming out of my own shock of getting breast cancer. That is a very sweet and obedient daughter of ours Parth, but she is going through the change, and therefore she seems a little erratic at times."

"You could be right Ritu. Our Sangita is a very sweet girl. Especially, the way she managed everything when you were in the hospital, the way she looked after her younger sister, it was commendable. Actually, when I felt totally devastated, she was a big support to me too." Parth got a little emotional.

"I know, I know." Ritu gave a light pat on his shoulder. "What we can do is, next time when we go to Dr. Vimal for my check up, we will take our girls too with us, especially Sangita, and we'll have the doctor talk to them directly about anything and everything they want to know. How does that sound?" Ritu asked Parth.

They both agreed and finalized their plan of taking their daughters to Dr. Vimal at the time of Ritu's next visit.

"Dr. Vimal, these are our daughters, Sangita and Shruti. Sangita is the older one." Ritu and Parth entered Dr. Vimal's clinic. It was Ritu's check up time, and as they had decided earlier, they took their daughters with them to the clinic.

"Hello girls. Have a seat." Dr. Vimal pointed to two chairs near her table and asked them to sit. "How is it that you brought your girls today to the clinic?" Dr. Vimal asked.

"Well, doctor, we brought them, because we thought they should know a little more about their mother and her sickness." Parth said.

"That's good. You have told them that their mother has cancer, right?" Dr. Vimal asked while getting ready for Ritu's check up.

"Yes. They know that." Parth said.

"But they don't know that I have had breast cancer, doctor..." Ritu said.

"Oh, really?" Dr. Vimal stopped for a second what she was doing and looked at Ritu. Then she looked at the girls. They looked quite scared. "You mean to tell me that you kept your daughters in the dark all these days?" Dr. Vimal asked Parth.

"Well, yes, sort of. They feel extremely scared of cancer, doctor." Parth said.

"And that's because they have not been told what their mother had, Mr. Bose. How long has it been since you were diagnosed with breast cancer, Mrs. Bose?" Dr. Vimal turned to Ritu and asked her.

"It has been almost a year now."

"And all these days, months, the girls didn't know you had breast cancer."

"Uh...that's right."

"Do they know that both your breasts are removed?" Dr. Vimal asked.

"Uh...no" Ritu looked down.

"But I know. I know that mother does not have any breast..." Sangita inadvertently blurted out the truth; and all of them, including her younger sister, looked at her. There was a big surprise written on their faces.

"What else do you know Sangita?" Dr. Vimal asked Sangita in a very loving and soft voice.

"I know everything. I also know that mommy got breast cancer that means I am going to get it too, for sure." Sangita had a slight tremor in her voice. Listening to her, Ritu and Parth developed some concern about her but Dr. Vimal stayed calm.

"Sangita, what else do you know dear?" Dr. Vimal asked her again very lovingly.

"Mommy thinks that I don't know anything about her disease. Daddy also thinks so, but Doctor, I know everything. I have even seen the scars on mommy's chest after her surgery." When Sangita said this, Shruti was looking very scared.

"Um hum! Go on..." Dr. Vimal encouraged her to continue.

"I have even touched those scars on mommy's chest once, when she was fast asleep in her bedroom. She was wearing daddy's white tee-shirt. She used to wear those white tee-shirts all the time, not a sari and a blouse like she used to wear before she got sick. She had also started using that black scarf on her head."

"I don't like that black scarf at all; it scares me too much..." Shruti interrupted and abruptly became quiet.

Everyone looked at her.

Sangita started telling her experience again when everyone turned their heads towards her.

"Daddy told us that mommy is very sick and she is going to have a surgery. I remember the day when she went to the hospital. It was during her concert in Mumbai. One of Daddy's friends took us to his home. We were there for almost a whole week. During that time, we never saw Mommy, and saw Daddy only once. That's when he told us about Mommy's surgery. Afterwards we all came home, to our home. That's when we saw Mommy for the first time wearing Daddy's white tee-shirt. I asked Daddy about it, so he said,

'She's wearing that because that's more convenient to wear.'

I didn't like her in Daddy's tee-shirt but I just kept quiet. Over the next few months after the surgery, Mommy was visiting some hospital in our home town regularly. She used to come home very, very tired. She used to sleep most of the days. Slowly she started tying a black scarf around her head. That puzzled me. So one day, I asked Daddy about it. He said,

'Due to excessive sickness and surgery, she is very tired and have no time to wash or comb her hair, that's why she ties that black scarf around her head.'

I wasn't satisfied with his answer, so I decided to ask Mommy directly. She took off the scarf and showed me her head. There was not a single hair on her head. She looked so scary, I was horrified. When I asked her why there was no hair on her head, she said,

'Because of some strong medicines, she lost her hair.'

Nobody told me why my beautiful mother was looking so sick and why she had no hair on her head." Sangita looked like she was about to cry.

"Mr. Bose, did you tell your daughters that your wife had cancer?" Dr. Vimal asked Parth.

"Yes, I did actually." Parth said.

"But that was much too later Daddy, almost three months after Mommy had her surgery, when I was the one who asked you if Mommy had cancer, and you said, 'yes', isn't it?" Sangita said.

"Well, yes." Parth agreed.

"I heard our maid talking about it one day. She was continuously using the word cancer in her conversation with someone. I overheard her conversation, and when I asked her whom she was talking about, that's when she told me that Mommy had cancer. I was absolutely horrified with her answer. But I pulled my guts and asked her again, where did my mother have her cancer, she just pointed to her own chest and almost on the verge of crying, she left immediately. I was frozen stiff with that answer. It was my *mother* who had cancer, doctor, my own beautiful mother, and the cancer was somewhere on her chest." Sangita. started crying silently.

There was a pin drop silence in the room, and everyone in the room was listening to her story with full attention.

Dr. Vimal looked at Ritu and Parth. She was surprised that an educated couple like them had kept all this information hidden from their own daughters, especially Sangita, who was old enough to understand.

Sangita sniffled a couple of times, wiped her nose and eyes and continued narrating her experience.

"I had to take quite a few days off school because of housework. One afternoon, when Daddy was away and Shruti was in the school, I slowly went into Mommy's room. She was fast asleep. As usual, she was wearing Daddy's tee-shirt. I looked at her and then looked at her chest. I couldn't believe it. Her chest looked absolutely flat, just like Daddy's. I kept on staring at her chest and wondering what had happened to her, you know, her boobs? I just moved my hand gently on her chest, my doubt was correct, the chest was flat. So, slowly without disturbing her, I lifted her tee-shirt and oh my God, what I saw was unbelievable.

There were no boobs. Instead, there were a couple of dark lines around the area. I was confused for a minute. What were these dark lines for? Then I remembered, Shruti had a fall sometime ago when her chin had split open and the doctor had stitched it with dark thread. The dark lines on Mommy's chest were similar to that. Does that mean the doctor cut away Mommy's boobs and stitched the skin over it? I wondered. And the moment it became clear to me that that was the case, I quickly covered her chest and literally ran away from there." Sangita lost her courage altogether at that point and started sobbing.

"That's alright dear, you were scared like anything after seeing your mother's surgery area, isn't it?" Dr. Vimal consoled Sangita.

Ritu and Parth were stunned to hear Sangita's experience. They had absolutely no idea what kind of trauma their daughter had gone through, after Ritu's surgery. Ritu pulled Sangita in her arms and held her tightly to give her some comfort. Shruti was sitting stiff in her chair.

"It's sad that you didn't talk to your daughters frankly and honestly about your disease and your condition, Mrs. Bose." Dr. Vimal said. Then she turned to Sangita and said, "Sangita, do you have anything more to tell us dear?"

Sangita nodded.

After wiping her eyes and nose, she moved away from her mother and said, "I couldn't sleep at all that night and kept on seeing Mommy's chest. I felt like asking Mommy, 'why did the doctor cut off your boobs Mommy?' But I couldn't get any courage to do that. I was about to tell Shruti once but then decided against it, she was already too scared just seeing a black scarf on Mommy's head."

"Yah… I was so scared when I saw Mommy in that black scarf for the first time." Shruti said from where she was sitting.

"Oh, I remember. You used to come to my bed and sleep with me on my bed most of the night for a long time." Sangita said.

"And we both used to pull the blanket over our heads and sleep, remember?" Shruti said again.

"Uh…hum…" Sangita looked at her sister with meaningful eyes.

"Oh my good God! I had no idea, doctor, none whatsoever, what my girls were going through, especially Sangita." Parth said.

"And here I was, trying to protect them from the trauma. I thought by telling them openly about Ritu's sickness, I'll be unnecessarily causing a lot of stress and fear in them, therefore, I tried to avoid it, more like, hide it from them."

"This is exactly where we adults make a big mistake. What you just said, that you may cause unnecessary stress and fear in your children and therefore you hid it from them; that's how most of us adults think. We assume all that, and that's where we commit a blunder." Dr. Vimal said to Parth. "If there is unfortunately a case of cancer in the family, the family members must communicate openly with each other. Especially, if it is breast cancer diagnosed for the mother of young girls." Then she moved closer to Sangita, held her hand and looking at Ritu, said, "Mrs. Bose, you must communicate with your daughters openly. You should not hide it. No one should." Dr. Vimal was looking at the parents while continuing to hold Sangita's hand to give her some comfort.

"Mr. Bose, what you said about causing trauma to the children, you are right. But it is always better to get it out in the open. Once it is discussed openly and frankly, it takes away the fear of the disease. Do you get me?" Ritu and Parth both nodded at Dr. Vimal's question.

"Your daughter found out about your breast cancer from the maid. *From the maid.* That was bad. That proved to be much more traumatic than finding it out straight from either of you, isn't it? Had I known earlier that your daughters were not aware of your disease or your surgery, I myself would have asked you to bring them to me and I personally would have explained it to them. I would have even shown them your scars and explained them to your daughters in simple words. That's what I expected *you* both to do. I encourage all my patients to discuss this with their family members. I *expect* that from all my patients, actually. Remember, cancer is a family disease." Dr. Vimal was a strong believer in 'open communication'. She followed it herself with her patients, and strongly advised her patients to do so with their families.

"Mrs. Bose, your older daughter Sangita is standing on the threshold of puberty and adulthood. I clearly see her being on the way to developing a female figure. Surely she has some knowledge about it. And, when she saw you lying in bed most of the days, wearing her father's tee-shirts with no trace of any breast inside and having lost her hair completely, surely she could guess what was going on? Didn't you think that that would cause some curiosity within her? In addition to all that, when you have been coming to me regularly for your check up since the surgery and you are taking a lot of medication, she is the one who is managing your household most of the times, right? Didn't you think she deserved to be told the truth about her mother's sickness?" Dr. Vimal was forthright to Ritu about how she felt about this 'hush...hush...' attitude.

"We are very, very sorry doctor. Honestly we never realized any of this. Sangita and Shruti are our dear little girls, we love them very much, there never was any malicious intention of purposely hiding this disease from them. If anything, we thought we would be protecting them by *not* telling them anything." Ritu and Parth were feeling genuinely sorry for hiding Ritu's breast cancer and her surgery from their daughters.

"What's done is done now. It's still not too late. Let's start the 'open communication' now. I'll examine you and then we'll discuss everything, especially the female body, right here, in front of your daughters. How does that sound?" Ritu and Parth agreed with Dr. Vimal full heartedly.

"Should I stay or leave at that time?" Parth asked.

"Of course you will stay here Mr. Bose. It is *medical science* we'll be discussing, nothing else."

Dr. Vimal took out a few charts from her desk drawer and hung one of them on the wall. That chart had all the diagrams of a female reproductive system. Then she told both the girls to sit in front of the chart and said, "I feel that all you young girls must get this information since it is directly related to your body and health. The graphics make the learning process much more easy, and it helps clarify a lot of information, isn't it?" The girls nodded.

Then she asked them, "Have you seen and learnt all this in the school?" To their parent's utter surprise, *both* the girls nodded again.

"Good. Now all these organs you see in this chart, they can function only and only when there is secretion of necessary hormones in the body. It's called 'hormonal evolution' in medical terms. During puberty, the development of female body is promoted by the presence of a hormone called estrogen. The rate of development varies widely, from individual to individual."

"That means I develop differently even from my own sister here, right?" Sangita looked more cognizant of what the doctor was explaining to them.

"That's correct. We all have a gland in our heads called the pituitary gland which causes the ovaries to produce this estrogen." Dr. Vimal then hung another chart on the wall which showed the figures of females with their breast development.

"Here you see how women develop their breasts. Around age eleven or twelve years, the breasts start developing on the female chest." Everyone noticed Sangita unknowingly putting her one arm across her chest, as if to cover her breasts, which were not too visible as yet.

"Once developed, they become almost cone-shaped. Again, everyone's breasts grow at their own pace, and develop their own shape according to a woman's nutrition and genetic makeup. The round brown area around the nipple is called areola. As you can see, the nipples and areola both are much darker than the rest of the breast. It's very common for a woman's two breasts to develop at different rates making one larger than the other during puberty. Therefore, most adult women have one breast slightly larger than the other."

"Really?" It was Ritu who inadvertently exclaimed at this information.

"Yes."

"I never noticed that with mine. Of course, it's too late now, isn't it?" Ritu didn't mind joking, and that helped the atmosphere in the room become much more friendly and pleasant.

"That's because, their difference is only marginal and they seem approximately of the same size."

"But then, what about all those models and actors in movies? Theirs look perfect." Parth showed interest from a man's perspective, for which he got a look from his wife, since they were in their daughters' presence.

"Well, most of the supposedly perfect breasts you see on models and actors in films are illusions, made possible by the magic of padding. They just *appear* symmetrical in size." Dr. Vimal was smiling. She was happy to see that this exercise had stimulated a healthy conversation in the family.

"Back to our lesson, Sangita and Shruti. Breast development is a vital part of puberty in the human female. Unlike other mammal females though, human females are the only ones who develop full breasts long before they are needed to nurse the offspring."

"'That's '*dhudhu for the baby*', right?" Shruti whispered to Sangita.

"Yah, now shut up..." Sangita put on a serious face for, she was the 'old and mature' one.

"Once you turn eleven or twelve years of age, you weigh around one hundred pounds, and your breasts are relatively well developed, that's the time to prepare for your first menstruation. Sangita, have you had your first period?"

"Not yet." Sangita and Ritu answered simultaneously, then looked at each other and smiled. There was that all important mother-daughter bond that was getting established there.

"I would say that the time could be approaching pretty soon now for Sangita. Once it starts, the maturing of the breasts begins with the formation of secretory glands at the end of the milk ducts. The breasts and ducts continue to grow simultaneously." Dr. Vimal saw a faint smile on Sangita's face when she finished explaining this part of the female development. She right away recognized that like all the young girls in puberty, this explanation had made Sangita also feel 'come of age'. Dr. Vimal had yet to see an exception to this observation.

Dr. Vimal hung a third chart on the wall. In that chart, there was a series of multiple figures of a female body starting from young age to the full grown adult figure in a straight line. Pointing at the very first figure of the chart, she said, "Here is a very young girl who is yet to approach her puberty, just like our Shruti. She has the whole process in place but there is still some time." Shruti felt a little shy when Dr. Vimal took her name.

"Then we have Sangita here," Dr. Vimal pointed at a figure next to the previous one and said, "here, we see a girl who is approaching puberty, that is to say, to be a young woman in the making..." Sangita felt good and proud to be there at that stage.

"What is puberty? Can you tell me Sangita?" Dr. Vimal asked her.

"A girl becoming a woman..." Sangita said.

"Very good. Puberty refers to the process of physical changes by which a child's body becomes an adult body, as you said, a girl becoming a woman. It is also capable of having a baby. All this happens due to the function of what we call hormones. Earlier I mentioned the term 'hormonal evolution', remember?"

Sangita nodded. Shruti just gave a blank look to the doctor.

Dr. Vimal continued, "Puberty is initiated by hormone signals coming from the brain to the ovaries in a girl. In response to that, the ovaries produce a variety of hormones that stimulate growth, function and transformation of almost all the parts of our body, such as the brain, bones, muscles, skin, breasts and the reproductive system. This is indeed a very complicated process involving many hormones of the body. That's why it is termed as hormonal evolution." Then Dr. Vimal pointed to the next figure of the chart and asked the girls, "What do you see here?"

"Mommy..." Shruti quickly answered.

"Very good. Shruti you are here, Sangita you are here and your mother Ritu is here. You girls are slowly moving from here to here..." Dr. Vimal slowly moved her finger on the chart starting from figure one through all the figures in between, to the figure of a fully grown female with full breasts.

"You mean, Ritu *was* there, until... last... year..." Ritu mumbled softly but that was heard by Parth and Dr. Vimal. They both looked at her, and as expected, there was a sad and stressed outlook on her face. Fortunately, the girls were intently looking at the chart still. They didn't notice any of this.

That's when Dr. Vimal decided to go over the topic of breast cancer for the girls.

"This hormonal evolution is known to stop completely after the woman gets pregnant and has a baby. But during the hormonal evolution, as the breasts are still developing into fully grown mature ones, if there is some problem with the evolution itself, then a few cells of the breasts alter a little. In scientific terms, this process of alteration of the cells is called mutation. Mutated cells are different from the original ones. Some scientists consider these mutated cells to be faulty cells. Breast tissue is considered to be quite sensitive to carcinogens. What's carcinogen, anybody?" Dr. Vimal looked at the girls but they didn't know what it was. Parth just nodded and said softly, 'Cancer causing'.

"Some scientists believe that these mutated cells of the breasts are responsible to cause breast cancer in women. And if a woman gets breast cancer, normally, removal of the breast itself is the first remedy for controlling her cancer." Dr. Vimal said.

"But doctor..." Sangita looked confused.

"Don't be afraid and ask what you want to ask."

"Mommy had me and Shruti as her babies, right?"

"Right."

"That means the hormonal evolution had stopped in her body right after she got pregnant with me, right?"

"Right."

"You said hormonal evolution stops after a woman gets a baby and that altering of the cells…"

"Mutation."

"Yah, mutation. That happens only during the hormonal evolution. If the hormonal evolution had stopped in Mommy's body, then how come she had those mutated cells in her breasts to get breast cancer?"

"Very good question Sangita, you are a very bright girl, and very perceptive too. If more people think along the lines of what you just said in your question, then there will be hope for much more research with this theory in focus, isn't it?"

Dr. Vimal was full of compliments to Sangita for her way of thinking logically and being able to grasp such a complicated subject relatively fast. However, when she looked at Sangita, she saw Sangita's hands covering those tiny bumps on her chest, supposedly her breasts, and she had turned completely white with fear.

"Hey what happened? Sangita, what happened dear?" Dr. Vimal went close to her and put her hand on her shoulder. Sangita's parents also looked quite worried.

"Doctor, doctor my mother had no reason to get breast cancer, she had us, her babies. But still she got cancer. That means when I grow up and have my breasts, even if I get a baby, I can get breast cancer." Sangita started crying softly. Shruti joined her, in spite of not knowing exactly what made her sister cry.

"Hey, you silly girls, don't think like that. Don't be afraid. Your mother got breast cancer, that does not mean you will get it too. No, not at all. Let me ask you, did your grandma, that is your Mommy's mother, have this disease?"

"We don't know." The girls shook their heads.

"No doctor, my mother didn't have it, she never even heard of this disease until I got it." Ritu provided the answer.

"Girls, listen. Your grandma didn't have it, still your mother got it; that tells you that even if your mother got it, it's not necessary that you will get it. Right?"

The girls didn't say anything and kept on crying softly.

"Sangita, Shruti, listen to me. What you are thinking is along the lines of what we call 'a genetic factor'. And genetic factor is known to be responsible for carrying out this risk only in about ten percent of the cases of breast cancer patients. Listen to me, that's very, very low. So there's very little chance of you girls getting it just because your mother got it, okay?" Dr. Vimal put her other hand on Shruti's shoulder and said, "Hey, do you want to know a secret of your mother?"

The girls looked at the doctor and nodded.

"You know that your mother vomited blood right in the middle of her music concert, do you remember that Mr. Bose?"

"Yes, yes. That's one black day I can never forget doctor, that day and the following two days after that..." Parth wiped his face, suddenly he had developed some sweat on his forehead.

"After the doctor in the emergency room examined your mother and called me, and after your mother's breast cancer was confirmed, she kept on asking me one and only one question continuously. Do you remember that, Mrs. Bose?"

"Yes..." Ritu looked down, her eyes were full with tears.

"She asked me exactly about what you girls feel afraid of, except it was in the opposite direction." Dr. Vimal then looked in Ritu's direction and said, "Sangita, Shruti, your mother kept on asking me, 'doctor, I have two beautiful girls. Now that I got this disease, does that mean I have given the heredity of this disease to my girls too?' Do you remember that Mrs. Bose?" Dr. Vimal and the girls saw Ritu nodding at this question.

"Really, Mommy? You were more concerned about *us* than you or your singing career?" Sangita asked Ritu.

"Were you not afraid that you wouldn't be able to sing in your whole entire life, Mommy?" Shruti asked her mother too.

"That's right, girls. Your mother was more concerned about your health than her singing career. As a matter of fact, she didn't even ask me how sick she was or how long she would live. Her real fear was that she had given this hereditary gene to her daughters. Quite frankly, I was touched by her love for you two." Dr. Vimal's voice sounded a bit shaky. Ritu and Parth had tears running down their cheeks. Their daughters ran towards them and hugged them tight. They held their daughters tightly in their arms. For a few minutes, no one talked.

Dr. Vimal took away all the charts from the wall and rolled them and kept them away in the drawer. She went back to her chair and sat down.

"Mrs. Bose..." She called her patient. Ritu moved away from her family hug, wiped her eyes and slowly walked towards the doctor. "I think we should get on with your check up now. Do you want your family here as well?"

"I don't think so. All that information my girls got today from you, I think that should be enough for the day."

"Alright then, I'll request them to stay right here, you go to the examination room now." Ritu got up and headed to the examination room. Dr. Vimal followed her after a few minutes.

Maya

"My Praful meets me every night when I go to bed..." Maya was telling Meeraben in her clinic, where she treated all her patients with psychotherapy.

Maya was sitting comfortably on the carpeted floor using two large cushions in Meeraben's clinic. As decided in their previous meeting, Kirti had taken a two-hour long appointment for her with Meeraben.

"How does he look?" Meeraben decided to go along with Maya's fantasy for a while.

"He looks as fit as when he left me." Maya said, sounding quite earnest in her tone.

"Oh, so he did leave you..."

"Yes. But now he is calling me where he is. He is waiting for me, he says."

"I see. Quite honestly, I can see his point of calling you there." "What do you mean?" Maya sounded a bit confused with Meeraben's concurrence. No one had ever concurred with her fantasy up until now.

"I mean, your husband is calling you because he needs you. No one needs you here in this world, so why live here? That must be his reason too for calling you wherever he is, isn't it?" Meeraben asked Maya a bit sarcastically.

"Yah...yah...that is the reason." Maya did not quite get Meeraben's sarcasm. "My children left home, they don't need me. Praful is not there either, now there is no need for me being here in this world, so why live unnecessarily, right?" Maya said.

"You are absolutely right. No one needs you here, so why live unnecessarily. I agree with you completely."

"Yes, that's why my Praful is calling me." Maya felt very good about her firm belief of 'her life being un-needed', especially when she felt that Meeraben also believed in her.

"I'm not surprised to hear that. But then, to be with him, you have to die too, right?" Meeraben said quietly.

"Hum?" Maya was confused again.

"I said, you have to end your life too. You do feel like ending your life, isn't it? In order to join your husband, that is. That's the only way, isn't it?"

"Yes."

"So, did you try it anytime?" Meeraben asked her again in a very calm voice.

"Try what?"

"Committing suicide."

"What?" Maya was taken aback with what sounded like a bizarre question to her.

"I said, did you try to kill yourself to be with your husband?" Meeraben asked calmly.

"Uhhh..." Maya was even more confused.

"You said, your darling husband is meeting you every night and begging you to join him. After all, he is the only one who *needs* you badly, so shouldn't you end your life by killing yourself?" Meeraben sounded calm and collected.

"Yes. And I did feel like killing myself at least a million times, I still do, but..." Maya answered.

"But, what dear?"

"But...but, I didn't try to."

"Try to, what dear?"

"Commit suicide."

"Never?"

"That's right. Never."

"Why not?"

"I didn't have the guts to do it, I suppose." Maya said in a very low and soft voice.

"But Mrs. Patel, your husband *needs* you badly there, so you must end your life here, isn't it?" Maya didn't respond to Meeraben at all. She just looked down.

"Maya, this tells me clearly that your desire to *live* is much stronger than your desire to die, isn't it?" Meeraben tried to look at Maya's face but Maya had turned her face downward, almost like hiding it from Meeraben.

"Mrs. Patel, please, look up. Look at me and listen." Maya finally looked up and gave an eye contact to Meeraben.

"You keep feeling that nobody needs you anymore. And that could be the situation at this moment, I don't deny that. It's true that there is a sudden vacuum created in your life. But that vacuum is only *temporary.* It is completely transient. Can't you see that?" Meeraben asked Maya in a gentle voice, but Maya just stared at her with a blank face.

"Let me ask you a simple question, if your daughter Kirti decides to have a baby tomorrow, would you not help her with the new baby?"

"Yes, of course."

"And if your younger daughter also decides to have a baby, wouldn't you help her too?"

"Yes, I would, of course."

"Doesn't that mean that they will *need* you at that time, which may not be too far away in the future, Mrs. Patel?"

"Um...yes, I suppose."

"Your son would visit India sometime soon. He might want to get married. Won't you help him finding a suitable girl for him? When he would bring his bride with him, would he not expect you to welcome him and his bride in your home? You told me once that that's your only son and the light of your family. Would he not *need* your attention at that time?"

"Yes, yes of course." Maya's face was looking a little brighter and she was sounding a little elated too.

"All these lovely children of yours would feel extremely disappointed and sad if they find out that their mother wasn't there in their need, and their happy times, isn't it?

"Well, yes."

"And when they'll find out that their mother committed suicide because she had lost all her interest in life, that would tell them clearly that they didn't mean much to their mother, isn't it?"

"What do you mean, Meeraben?"

"What I mean is, if you purposefully end your life or if you are stubborn to ignore your health problem completely and die, then that would give them an impression that the only person their mother really cared for was herself. She didn't care for them; she left them in their *need*!"

"Yes, you may have a point there." Maya sounded even more convinced.

"Mrs. Patel, listen carefully. This feeling, of 'not being needed', that you are having about yourself is temporary. It is only a passing phase. Your feelings are overpowered right now by figments of your own false pretences and imagination. They are not real." Meeraben took a deep breath.

Then she looked at Maya and continued.

"Being needed is absolutely wonderful, you feel *useful* that way. And feeling useful forms the basis for our desire to live. You feel like ending your life because you feel you are unwanted and therefore useless. But always bear in mind that it's up to *you* to create that feeling, feeling of being useful, that is! Keeping yourself busy with what you like and in what you are good, can make you feel good about yourself. And more importantly, if, what you do is helpful to others in some way, that makes you feel being useful as well. Does this not entail a 'need'? You being needed, that is?" Maya was listening to Meeraben with full concentration. This was a new thought for her.

Meeraben continued.

"After your children left home and your loving husband passed away, your days came down from twenty four hours to practically zero hours. Unfortunately, all this happened in a very short time. No one was left at home so you were left with no work, no chores, no errands, no responsibilities, and therefore, you felt that there was no need of you being around anymore. But as I said, this phase is a short-lived one. It's temporary. Your children may need you tomorrow, they may depend on you for your help. You were obviously a very good home maker; your children have experienced that while they were living at home. Naturally, they will count on you in their times of need. So my dear lady, don't be so disconsolate or feel dejected. Instead, get busy now preparing for tomorrow."

Meeraben was smiling at Maya. Her deep, soothing voice coupled with such wise and consoling words gave a tremendous boost to Maya's morale.

"Well, what you just said makes a lot of sense to me, Meeraben." Maya had a faint smile on her face. The tone of her voice also had changed slightly, from that of despair to that of enthusiasm.

"Good. Now, you know what the first step for that preparation is, right?" Meeraben asked Maya.

"What's that?" Maya asked, with a bit of confused look.

"Going to Dr. Vimal and getting that malignant lump out of your breast, of course! That is the very first step to your health. It is the top priority of your life right now. You may need some rest after that, so that's also of high priority. During that time, if you wish, and I'm sure Dr. Vimal herself may recommend that for you, come and have a few psychotherapy sessions with me. That would definitely improve your health and ..."

"And my attitude." Maya completed Meeraben's sentence with a smile. Meeraben could clearly see a spark in Maya's eyes.

Virani

"Please come in Ratna, and meet my husband. Das, this is Ratna, she has just recently joined our bank as a cashier." Virani introduced her husband to Ratna. Ratna and Das exchanged a polite Namaste to each other. Ratna was new in the bank and new in the city too, she didn't know anyone there, so Virani showed a friendly gesture of inviting her to their house.

"I am in the same bank but I never saw your husband there." Ratna said to Virani.

"Well, he sits on the second floor Ratna, how can you see him? We cashiers are on the main floor and never have to go upstairs, isn't it?" Virani said.

"That's right. Besides, we are always behind a window, almost for the whole day. It's hard to notice people behind the bars." Ratna said with a pleasant smile.

"Amma, meet my friend from the bank, Ratna Gudi. Ratna, this is Das's mother, but she is like my own mother. Amma lives with us. And this is our prince, Krishnadev, but we call him Kittu. Say Namaste to aunty. He is about eighteen months old." Virani was excited to introduce her family to her new friend from the bank.

"Are you from Karnataka?" Amma asked Ratna.

"Yes, yes. How did you guess?" Ratna was pleasantly surprised with Amma's question. "Your last name and your accent gave it away. It is the same as mine. I am also from there." Amma said and they all laughed about it.

"Oh good. Now I feel I have someone very close to me. Karnataka is so far from here, I was feeling a little homesick anyway." "Now, you can come here whenever you want and stay here as long as you want. We would love it, wouldn't we, Das?" Virani said. Das nodded but he wasn't sure why she would bring home someone new from the bank, a total stranger, introduce her to all of them and then offer her to visit anytime, with a standing invitation to *stay* with them; but he kept quiet. Virani rushed into the kitchen and called Amma to join her in the kitchen. She wanted to make some fine dishes that were a specialty of Karnataka with Amma's help. Das and Ratna were left alone in the front room.

Although Virani was in the kitchen, her whole attention was out in the front room where Das and Ratna were sitting. She expected them to chat with each other. When she could not hear any voice coming from there, she came outside under some pretence and quickly glanced around the room. Kittu was quietly playing with his toys. Ratna was reading a magazine that she had picked up from the coffee table, and Das was nowhere to be seen.

"Where is Das?" She asked Ratna. Ratna just shrugged her shoulders.

"Das, Das where are you?" She hollered.

"I'm right here in the bedroom, changing my clothes." Das quietly answered her. She rushed into the bedroom.

"Why aren't you there in the living room? Ratna is sitting alone, do you realize that?" She sounded a little angry.

"Don't worry. I took her permission to leave the room. You know I like to change my clothes as soon as I get home from work." Das answered her again, very quietly and calmly. She accepted his answer grudgingly and went into the kitchen.

The special dishes were almost ready. Virani set up places for all of them on the table and called Ratna for dinner in their dining area. Kittu's special little high chair was placed right next to Ratna's, in between Das and Ratna, instead of his usual place between Das and Virani.

"Dinner is ready." Virani called Das to the table. When he saw the seating arrangement, he looked surprised and a bit perturbed too, but he didn't say anything. They all sat on their assigned places and started eating.

"The dinner is absolutely delicious. And this *Bishibali*[16] tastes exactly like my mother used to make." Ratna said.

"Amma made it." Virani provided the details.

"Can you teach me sometime, Amma?" Ratna asked her politely.

"Oh sure, she will be very happy to teach you Ratna. She taught me many special dishes from Karnataka that Das loves so much, right Amma?" Amma just nodded smilingly and felt good that her daughter-in-law was full of praise for her.

---

16. Bishibali is a specialty dish of a province named Karnataka. It is made with rice, lentils and a lot of regional vegetables, all simmered in tamarind juice.

"So, Ratna, how many are you at home?" Amma asked her.

"Just myself. I am sharing a room with somebody." Ratna said.

"Not here, I mean at home in Karnataka?" Amma asked again.

"Oh there? My father and my younger brother, Vishnu. My both younger sisters got married and moved away with their husbands. Vishnu just finished his commerce degree. I hope he'll get employment somewhere soon." Ratna said.

"Aren't you married?" Amma asked her frankly.

"No. Not yet." Ratna said with an unnecessary loud laugh, which caught Kittu's attention. He looked at her and gave a big smile to her. 'Oh you are so cute…' Ratna said looking at him. Virani saw all that and felt really good at heart.

"I wonder why you didn't get married, Ratna?" Virani asked her politely.

"You see, my mother died quite a few years ago when all of us were really young. My brother was barely four years old then. After my mother's death, *Appa*, that's my father, went almost berserk. I was barely in my teens, but I could understand his condition. I was the oldest child, so I decided to take care of him and my siblings. Just as I finished my high school graduation, I started working in a local bank and started earning some money. Slowly, the family came to be settled. My younger sister got married after her high school graduation and so did my youngest sister. I was still working, earning the money that my family needed. Now that my brother has finished his college degree and can take care of my father, I thought I can change my job from that local bank to this big, national bank. My brother is there to look after my father from now onwards." Ratna gave all the details of her life.

"Now you are free to get married too, right?" Virani asked her.

"Yes, but who will marry an old maid like me now?" Ratna again gave her typical loud laugh, and Kittu again looked at her with his cute smile.

They all ate their dinner, enjoying the new and tasty dishes from Karnataka, made especially for their guest, Ratna.

"I feel so good today, really. You all made me feel at home. The food is so good, your family environment is so warm, and dear little Kittu, he is so cute…" Ratna gave a light rap on Kittu's cheek and got up from the table.

"How will you go home Ratna?" Virani asked her out of concern.

"Don't worry. I am used to taking the city bus." Ratna said.

"But it's late and fairly dark…" Virani said.

"That's okay. The streets are very well lit, so there's no problem." Ratna didn't seem worried at all.

"Hey, I have an idea…" Virani looked at Das, ready to request him to give her a ride on his scooter, but when she saw his face, she dropped that idea altogether.

"Okay then, Ratna, if you feel confident, then there's no problem." Virani smoothly withdrew the introduction of her idea. After thanking everyone heartily, Ratna left.

"Ratna seems like such a sweet person, doesn't she?" Virani asked Das when they were in their bedroom at night.

"Hum." Das was putting Kittu to sleep.

"She is about the same age as I am, perhaps a couple of years older; and same height and complexion as mine too." Virani said.

"Hum."

"And did you see how Kittu liked her? He was giving her sweet smiles all the time." Virani continued.

"Hum." Das was focusing on putting Kittu to sleep.

"Can you believe she took care of her entire family since such a young age, it is commendable, isn't it?" Virani said.

"Hum."

"She must be a very compassionate person. Looking after her father after her mother's death, and her siblings too, is not a joke." Virani said while helping Das spread a blanket on Kittu.

"Hum."

"It's no small thing to work full time and look after three young siblings, when you yourself are barely out of your teenage, right?"

"Hum." Das went to his bed and lay down.

"Poor thing. She got her both younger sisters married, but she herself has yet to get the taste of married life, isn't it?" Virani followed Das and lay on the bed too.

"Why are you so quiet Das?" Virani moved towards him on the bed.

"Nothing..." Das said.

"You are so quiet all this time. I was noticing even in the evening, when we were having such a good time during our dinner, and we had such a charming visitor like Ratna, you were quiet like a lamp post. Why so, Das?" Virani complained about Das's behavior.

"Oh well..." Das was non-committal.

"And why did you give me that look when I was about to propose you dropping Ratna home on your scooter?" Virani asked him.

"Why did you bring that woman home for dinner in the first place, when you yourself barely knew her?" Das looked at Virani and asked her in a very dry voice.

"Why, to introduce my dear family to her, Amma, Kittu and..." Virani started answering him, when he interrupted her with a question, "...and especially me, your husband, right?"

Das said in a style that startled her a little.

"Why are you sounding so angry, my dear Das?" Virani moved closer to him and tried to console him.

"What else can I do anyway? I don't want to get angry at the guest and I can't get angry at you, but I want to ask you now, Rani, what the heck are you doing bringing all these single, young women at home? Not just that, this evening you were ready to actually propose me dropping her home. Alone on my scooter. What the heck is going on here? Ever since we are back from Dr. Vimal, you are behaving as if you are on the look out for a woman, a woman of your age and height and all that, for me; *for me*? You had brought one more woman before this one, some one who had lost a husband prematurely or something, right? What was your intention then, and what is it *now* in bringing a young female home and introducing her to all of us, especially *me*?'

"Well, Das..." Virani stumbled at the words.

"Well what? Don't you think I know what you are doing? You are trying to fix me up with someone, isn't it Rani, tell me the truth." Das sounded very angry.

Virani just nodded.

"You are a crazy woman, do you know that? Simply crazy. And insane." Das moved away from her.

"Ever since your diagnosis of breast cancer, you are behaving as though you are going to die very soon. Ever since we are back from the clinic, I have been literally begging you, 'let's take Dr. Vimal's advice, let's take her medical treatment Rani'; but you are adamant in rejecting that, you don't want to even listen to me, you don't want to take her advice. Not a single day has passed when I haven't tried to literally implore you for your medical treatment; and not even once have you considered that. Instead, you are more interested in the *aftermath of your death.* Your death would leave me alone in this world, and therefore, you want to take care of my loneliness in future. But what about *now*?" Das took a few long breaths to do away with his anger.

When his anger subsided slowly, it was replaced by a gentle and warm feeling that was clearly noted in his gentle voice when he started talking to her again.

"Rani, listen to me, for God's sake, listen to me. When I beg you, and you know it's literally every single day, to consider taking medical treatment for your cancer, you just flick it away with a big philosophical statement that, *'death is inevitable to me'*. Well, I know that. We all mortals know that. It's nothing new or unusual. We all know we are going to die someday for sure. That's a guarantee. But at the same time, when you are living and you get a disease, especially a disease like this one, you must take medical treatment immediately and fight the disease full-heartedly. You don't just start focusing on death alone and be totally complacent about the disease..." Das moved closer to her and looking at Virani intently, said, "Dr. Vimal said, you have two or three years, but the technology has gone ahead so much, who knows, it could be five or ten or fifteen years before you leave me..." Das's voice was cracking up and it sounded like it was filled with sadness.

Hearing his voice, Virani came to be on the verge of crying. And seeing her become so emotional, so did Das.

"Rani, don't consider the treatment for anyone's sake, not even for my sake, but consider it for the sake of our baby, our lovechild, for Kittu's sake, um?" Das barely finished his sentence when he saw Virani crying. He held her tightly in his arms.

A few moments passed before Virani could collect herself. She said, "Das, don't you realize why I'm doing all this? It's for you, for our baby, for our little Kittu? Look at me, please look at me and tell me that you do realize that too."

"What's all this? As in meeting new females and all that?" Das wiped his eyes and asked her.

"Yes."

"You are doing it for *me*? For our Kittu? What nonsense are you…"

"Das, don't call it senseless, please don't. Listen, after I leave you, I mean after I die, don't you think you need someone who would love you very much? And take care of our Kittu too? If I can find someone who would lovingly do that for my dear family before I die, then wouldn't that give me tremendous peace of mind to die peacefully?"

"This is the most senseless and erroneous explanation I am hearing Rani, and downright stupid too." Das was getting a bit ticked off with her argument.

"Please, my dear Dasu, I am not stupid and I am not talking nonsense either. I very well know how serious my disease is, and I'm fully aware of what I am talking about. When Dr. Vimal told us that what I have is a rare kind of breast cancer and I might have one year, at the most two years of life remaining, that's when I took this decision. I can not avoid death, which is in the near future. Death is unbeatable in my case but I can always beat it by *my way*. And this is my way of defeating death. Death wants to take away a loving wife from my Das and a loving and caring mother from my Kittu, right? Well, I wouldn't allow that. I personally will find a loving wife for you and a loving and caring mother for our baby *before* I die. That's my way of *winning* over death. I am going to win over death, Das, I'm." Virani started sobbing. Das pulled her near him and started wiping her eyes and gently caressing her face.

He let a few moments pass by in silence. Then he said, "What you are thinking is really foolish, Rani. Do you expect to fill your gap in my life by someone you find today? Um, do you? Do you actually believe that some other person can replace you? Um? Rani, listen to me now. No one, I mean no one can ever fill your gap or replace you. Not for me, not for Kittu either. This thought you have in your head about 'winning over death' by some ridiculous idea like finding a replacement is downright rubbish." Das was forthright about how he felt about her idea of 'winning over death'.

He continued, "If you really love us, then instead of wasting your precious time in these senseless activities, focus on your own treatment, in you getting well."

"Do you think I'm not focusing on that?" Virani asked him while sobbing.

"What do you mean?" Das was mildly surprised to hear that. "Do you know that I went to the library, read a few journals, borrowed a few books and read them too? I didn't understand all of it but whatever I could get from all this literature, it clearly pointed to one fact, and one fact alone; survival rate among the women with Inflammatory Breast cancer is very, very low. Once affected, they don't live for too long. No treatment can help them live longer. Then what do I do Das? I am left with no choice..." Virani was sobbing uncontrollably by now. Das was quiet for a few seconds, allowing her to get over her sobbing fit.

"Rani, you said you read a lot of literature on this subject, right?" Das asked her.

She nodded while still sobbing hard.

"And they must have quoted examples of a few women while describing the various methods of their treatment, right?" Das asked her.

Virani nodded again.

"Did each woman they described live exactly as long as the other?"

Virani shook her head.

"Their survival time was of varying lengths, right?"

Virani nodded again and looked at him.

"Some women must have lived for only a year, others for more than one year, and some for as long as five years, perhaps?" Das was looking at her.

"What are you saying Dasu?" She asked while still sobbing.

"What I'm saying honey, is that you may live for as long as even ten years, who knows? Although the treatment for the disease is the same, every patient responds to it differently, right?"

"Yes." Virani slowly wiped her tears. Her sobbing seemed like being in control.

"And again, who knows? You may respond to all their drugs and other treatments so well that you may live for twenty years and be quoted in the literature as a miracle survivor."

"A miracle survivor?"

"Hum, hum. And not just that, you will inculcate some hope in the minds of both patients and the doctors and scientists as well that, surviving this rare disease for a good twenty years could be a definite possibility." Das looked into her eyes and said with confidence,

"...but all that is attainable only and only if you think positively about the treatment and take it willingly as soon as possible, right?"

Virani stopped crying and looked like she was thinking about some thing.

"Rani, you heard Dr. Vimal say that we need to start your treatment as soon as possible, and removal of your right breast is necessary in that treatment. Please don't think how it's going to look, think of it as just a step in your treatment, that's all. Now put all your focus on the treatment for getting better; getting better for me and for our Kittu, okay?"

Virani nodded and looked at him.

Das started kissing her face gently.

"Oh God, why do you love me so much, Dasu?" She asked him, rubbing her nose on his cheek.

"Because you are so silly and childish, that's why." He kissed her face a few more times, and asked her, "So, will you see Dr. Vimal right away?"

She nodded while rubbing her nose on his cheek.

"And start her treatment right away?" He was asking her while still kissing her face gently.

"Yes, yes, yes..." She had a faint smile on her face.

"And while you are at it, can you do one more thing for me?" He stopped kissing her and asked.

"Now what?"

"Will you stop this nonsense of bringing home different women and introducing them to me with 'that absurd idea' of yours?"

She couldn't answer him, for he had his lips on hers.

Shaina

"Shailu, don't make any breakfast for me this morning, just tea will do." Usha didi told Shaina the next morning as she was getting ready for work in her room. "The dinner you served last night for Vimal and me was a bit too filling, but you eat your breakfast, okay?"

Usha didi couldn't hear Shailender's response as she just nodded quietly.

"I am leaving for out of town tour tomorrow, so pack some clothes in a small suitcase for me and keep it ready by the time I come home this evening. It's a brief one this time, so I should be back in a couple of days or so." Usha didi came out of her room and started gathering her papers.

"Why are you so quiet? Did you hear what I said?" Shailender nodded quietly again. Usha didi looked at her. Her face was looking almost ghastly with a sullen expression.

"Hey, what happened to you?" Usha didi asked.

Shailender just shook her head quietly.

"Say something. What's bothering you?"

Shailender again just shook her head.

"If it's nothing, then why are you so quiet? Are you feeling alright?" Usha didi put her hand on Shailender's shoulder and asked her kindly; and just hearing that kind voice of hers, Shailender started crying.

"Shailu, come, sit here on this chair and tell me everything. Are you feeling okay, was there any letter from your village about your father, or what?" Usha didi asked her while patting on her shoulder gently. And with that loving hand on her shoulder, Shailender started crying in bouts. Usha didi was a little confused but she let her cry it out, whatever it was, for a few minutes.

"Usha didi..." Shailender's crying lessened a little, and she could talk,

"Usha didi, I'm scared."

"Scared? Scared of what, dear?"

"Scared of what Dr. Vimal told us last night."

"What did Dr. Vimal tell us last night? She told us about her work. Can you be a little more specific?"

"Remember, she was telling about one case where that young woman had breast cancer because of family history and the patient had discovered that her numerous female relatives had died from breast cancer at a very young age."

"Yes, I remember. She was talking about some experience her colleague had in their work, but why is it scaring you?"

"Usha didi, I think I may have that very same family history." Shailender sniffled a little and tried to control her crying.

"What? You are talking rubbish. There is no such family history for you..."

"I don't know that but I feel strongly that I could have it." Shailender stopped crying completely and she looked at Usha didi looking very serious.

"Why do you think that you could have it?"

"Look at *my* own family background. Ma died suddenly, no known cause of her death. My two older sisters, Baljeet and Daljeet died very young, again no known cause of their deaths. Ma was less than forty years of age and my sisters even younger than that. No one knows why there were three deaths in the same family in such a short time. And only of women. Papaji is still around. Now, you tell me, doesn't my family history sound like the patient's that Dr. Vimal didi was talking about?"

"Well..." Usha didi couldn't say anything.

"Usha didi, I didn't sleep at all last night. Ever since I heard that story, I just can't get it out of my head. I think my mother and sisters died of cancer, possible breast cancer. They lived in a small village and didn't know anything about it. They couldn't receive any medical help either. I think my case is the same as that patient and I'm also going to die like my sisters, very young and due to breast cancer..." Shailender started crying again.

Usha didi was thinking for a few minutes, she walked to the telephone and dialed a number.

"Hello, it's me Usha didi talking ...

Yes, yes, can you see me sometime soon? ...

It's for Shailu. ...

Next week? Sounds good ...

See you then." Shailender could hear Usha didi taking an appointment of some doctor for herself.

"Shailu, we are going to see Dr. Vimal next week. She will examine you thoroughly. That way all your doubts and questions will be ruled out completely. Now, stop crying and until we see her, don't think of it." Usha didi gave a loving pat on Shailender's back and left for work.

"Remember the case of some young female you were talking about in my house that evening, Shailu here thinks that she *might* have the same family history as that patient. She is very upset since that day." Usha didi told Dr. Vimal when she took Shailender to Dr. Vimal's clinic as per decided in their telephone conversation.

"Oh, I see." Dr. Vimal looked at Shailender and smiled, "well, let us do all the relevant tests and find out for sure, but first the family history. Who are all there in your family, Shailender?" Dr. Vimal wrote down everything what Shailender told her about her family. "Didn't anyone find out what exactly killed your mother, or your sisters?" Dr. Vimal asked. Shailender just shook her head and kept quiet.

"She has a father at home, but since the death of his wife and two young daughters, he has become practically insane. That's why I could bring this girl with me." Usha didi started telling Shailender's family background to Dr. Vimal.

"Vimal, she comes from a remote village in North India. You know, even the simple school education is only up to the primary level. After that, education of all children comes to an end. How can there be any awareness about such diseases or any other things relating to medical science in such villages? Science, scientific advancements, medical technology, all these things are way outside the scope of those people. They don't understand it, nor do they *want* to know about it. When I started the middle school in her village, I had to literally beg a few of the parents to send their children to school. I did the same with Shailu's parents too..."

"Only my father. Ma was dead already." Shailender corrected Usha didi.

"That's right. Her sisters died at a very young age too. Both of them. No one knows why or how? And that's why she has developed this doubt, especially after listening to that specific case you told us about, that evening."

"Oh I see. Well, okay. Now let us think hypothetically..."

"What's that?" Shailender asked innocently.

"Well, let us assume that your mother or sisters died of either ovarian or breast cancer. The genetic science states that the greatest risk factor for breast cancer is heredity, that is having a mother, aunt, sister, or daughter who has breast cancer. A woman is at even greater risk if her relative developed breast cancer before age, forty years of age. Breast cancer is a prime example of this higher risk."

Dr. Vimal then walked closer to Shailender and said,

"Let me explain to you in simple terms Shailu. If a woman, let's call her Miss X. If this Miss X has a first degree relative, which means a mother, a daughter, or a sister who is diagnosed of breast cancer, then the risk of Miss X developing breast cancer is two times higher compared to the general population. If that first degree relative of Miss X had developed breast cancer prior to the menopause, the risk for Miss X would be three times as much. If that relative had developed bilateral breast cancer, that is cancer in both her breasts, then the relative risk for Miss X would be five times higher. Again if that relative who developed bilateral breast cancer had developed the breast cancer prior to menopause, the relative risk for Miss X would be nine times higher. Now you can see the genetic factor playing a major role to increase the risk of breast cancer for Miss X, right?"

"Yes, but…"

"Now, do you remember the genetic science that we talked about in Usha didi's house that evening? It is based on genes. Each cell in your body carries about a hundred thousand genes. Genes control how the cell functions, such as telling the cells when to divide and grow, right?"

Shailender nodded.

"Among all these genes, there are two known genes, the *breast cancer genes,* called *BRCA1* and *BRCA2.*"

"Oh, really?"

"Yes! For some unknown reasons, a gene within a cell can become faulty. That can change how the cell works and can cause abnormal cells to grow uncontrollably. Mutations of BRCA1 and BRCA2 genes are directly linked to breast and ovarian cancer. Unfortunately, a parent can pass on a copy of a faulty gene to his or her children. If you happen to inherit a faulty gene that can cause breast cancer, you have a higher risk of developing breast cancer. That's what the genetic or hereditary connection is." Dr. Vimal tried to explain the genetics-related reason of breast cancer to Shailender in as simple terms as she possibly could.

"But Dr. Vimal didi, I don't know if my mother or sisters had any of these genes. Perhaps they did or perhaps they didn't. How do I find out if I have them too?"

"Well, we can not find anything about your mother or sisters but we can find out about you, dear."

"Is there a specific process involved in getting Shailu tested to see if she carries these mutated genes, Vimal?" Usha didi asked.

"Yes, yes of course. The medical technology is really evolved to a phenomenal degree now. This testing is done via a simple blood test. The blood is analyzed in specialized labs to determine this. Before the blood testing, however, the process involves first a meeting with a genetic counselor or a geneticist, then an oncologist, that is, a cancer specialist, and also a psychologist."

"So many specialists? What's the purpose?" Shailender asked. She was getting more and more interested in Dr. Vimal's explanation, and at the same time quite nervous too, by now.

"The purpose is usually to review the family history, to explain mutation of breast cancer genes and most importantly, advise the patients what steps to take, in case the blood test comes out positive. The psychologist helps them deal with the stress."

"I am so glad I have you and Usha didi, I don't need anyone else." Shailender looked so honest, Usha didi and Dr. Vimal just smiled at her.

"Shailu, the decision to submit to cancer susceptibility testing is not an easy one. What if it's positive? Will you be able to take it?" Dr. Vimal asked. Shailender suddenly became quiet and looked very nervous with her question.

"Vimal, you may be right there but I think we should go ahead and do the blood test on Shailu." Usha didi took some courage and suggested to Dr. Vimal on Shailender's behalf.

"Shailu's family history is really a family mystery, and there's no one else that she can count on or ask for. This way, we'll rule out all the possibilities of getting breast cancer in young age. That's what she is really scared of." Usha didi told Dr. Vimal.

"Okay then, it's settled. I'll arrange for the blood test immediately." Dr. Vimal said.

Usha didi and Shailender left Dr. Vimal's clinic after thanking her.

Initially scheduled to go for only two or three days, Usha didi returned from her tour after almost a week. The night had set in already when she reached home. She was surprised to see the front door unlocked. She entered. It was dark everywhere.

"Shailu, Shailu, where are you?" She called for Shailender from the front room.

There was no answer. She locked the front door and went inside.

Usha didi went to her own room, put away her briefcase and all other stuff, and went into the kitchen. Shailender wasn't there either. She peeped into the little room that Shailender called her 'little palace'.

There she was, sitting on the floor with her eyes fixed on her toes, in the dark. Usha didi turned on the light. That startled Shailender a little. Giving a light jerk to her body, she got up and slowly lifted her head to look at Usha didi. There wasn't the usual joy in her actions she would normally express, especially when Usha didi returned from her trip. Her face looked like she had cried for hours.

"It's all over Usha didi. All over. I am following Ma and my sisters very shortly..." Then she ran towards Usha didi and holding her hand tightly, started crying convulsively.

"What are you talking about? Stop crying and tell me everything..." Usha didi walked Shailender to the front room and seated her on the sofa comfortably.

"My blood test result came out positive Usha didi. I'm going to get breast cancer and before I know, I'll be on the way to the heaven to meet my mother and sisters."

"Stop it, Shailu, stop it right now and tell me everything." But Shailender wouldn't stop crying at all.

Usha didi got up and dialed for Dr. Vimal's clinic. Fortunately, Dr. Vimal was still in her clinic.

"Vimal, this is Usha didi speaking.

What's with this girl, can you tell me?

She is just crying since I got home.

Oh, I see. Her blood test has been found to be positive, um hum...

And, she does have those mutated genes present in her blood sample, does she?

There is a possibility of onset of breast cancer any time? I see...

No, no, she is alright I think... just quite scared...

What do we do now, Vimal?

Removal of breast altogether?

Both breasts?

But isn't that a little over reactive remedy, you think?

Oh I see...that's a sure way of eradicating the possibility of breast cancer completely... Oh, okay...

Yes...okay...Vimal..."

Just as Usha didi was conversing with Dr. Vimal on the telephone, she heard some loud noise behind her. She hurriedly hung up the telephone and looked back. What she saw there, she couldn't believe her eyes.

Shailender had stripped off almost all of her clothes and was running around almost naked in the room, shouting madly, 'you think you'll kill me, you demon, I'll kill you first, you vicious evil ...' Then she laughed loudly and started shouting again. And all this while, she had her both hands pulling her two breasts as though she was ready to pull them out from their roots.

It was an awful sight, very sad too.

Usha didi was stunned and almost froze for a moment to see Shailender get so hysterical. She had seemed quite well-collected when she had entered the house just a few moments ago. But now, Shailender looked like she had lost her balance completely and gone totally wild.

Usha didi tried to hold her and calm her down but she seemed to have the energy of a boar. She could easily figure out what made her go wild like that. Shailender heard the telephone conversation with Dr. Vimal and figured out what would befall her now.

"Stop it, Shailu, stop it right now." Usha didi shouted at the top of her lungs. Shailender had never heard her shout in that tone and that loudly. She was startled for a moment, but only for a moment, then she started crying loudly, like a toddler. Usha didi picked up her sari that was lying on the floor.

"Come here." She ordered her in a loud voice again. Hearing that military like order, Shailender abruptly stopped her crying and hurriedly walked towards her.

"Sit down now." Shailender sat down on the floor, still almost completely naked. Usha didi took the sari and covered her body.

"Now tell me what happened to you?" Usha didi said in her usual gentle voice and Shailender started crying softly.

"I...I've the genes of that brutal demon in me..." Shailender managed to say a few words, "and these breasts are his kingdom. I'm going to kill him, kill *him*; he can not kill me..."

"Calm down, first calm down. No one is going to kill you. Vimal just told me everything about the test results. She told me what we can do next."

"I know what she is going to do now; she is going to cut off my both breasts, isn't it? Just like that patient she was talking about a while ago." Shailender was sobbing and talking at the same time.

"That's called preventative mastectomy. You *opt*, that means you make a choice of surgically removing your breasts *before* the onset of the disease. One can not remove genes from the body. But when there are no breasts, that's the part of the body these mutated genes invade, then these genes have to remain inactive. And that way, the woman is saved from getting breast cancer." Usha didi explained to her what the next step could be.

"Oh God..." Shailender just looked at her own chest.

"Of course, Vimal also said that if you..." Usha didi said.

"If you what...what?"

"If you wish to get married and have children, your daughter may also inherit these genes from you."

"Marry? Hah? Who will marry me, Usha didi, when I will look like this? No breasts, just a flat chest, that's so unattractive to any young man. And who will want to have children with me, especially knowing that I have inherited something like this? Who will be that stupid or broadminded?" Shailender said in a serious tone. She had stopped crying.

They both stayed quiet for a few minutes.

"Let us meet Vimal again. We will discuss everything with her in detail and see what we can do. Now, let us eat something. I'm tired from my tour and you have gone through tremendous stress since this afternoon, okay?" Usha didi got up and headed to her bathroom. She wanted to take a hot shower before her dinner.

Shailender also got up and started putting on her clothes. She wore the sari properly and headed to the kitchen.

She needed to warm up the food that she had cooked for her dear Usha didi.

Milestones on the Journey...

Dr. Vimal, Anita, Maya, Ritu and many other volunteers were sitting on the patio having their weekly meeting.

"The sessions on basic biology are proving to be very interesting ones. I myself am enjoying teaching them. Let us have them once every two weeks, instead of once a month, Anita." Dr. Vimal suggested and that was noted down by Anita.

"Quite honestly doctor, the information my daughters and their friends are getting from these sessions, Parth and I would love to have it too." Ritu said.

"How do you know what is discussed in those sessions?" Dr. Vimal was surprised to hear Ritu say that.

"We make it a point to stand just outside the room and listen to every word you say in that class." Ritu said and looked at Maya with a meaningful smile.

"You too, Maya?"

"Yes, doctor, me too. I thoroughly enjoy your lecture It is actually basic biological science about human body that we all should know." Maya said.

"I think it's very valuable information." Ritu said.

"Well, if you women find it so interesting and informative, then we'll hold such sessions even for the adults. How's that?" Dr. Vimal said.

Every one nodded.

Anita included that point on her agenda sheet. It was to be finalized that there would be a session on basic biology such as the ones they were having for the teenagers, every two weeks, one for the teenagers and one for the adults. Perhaps they would have them even in their Support Centre in future.

"Ladies, this is the pamphlet I have designed for our workshops." Anita started talking. She was chairing the meeting.

"It covers four major areas."

Then she laid a large piece of paper on the table and everyone started looking at it carefully. The title 'you are invited' was written in a sort of calligraphy.

It was followed by a statement, saying that they were starting a 'Peer Support Group for Cancer Patients and Survivors'.

"I like the title page." Ritu said.

"What are the four areas, Anita?" Dr. Vimal asked.

"Well, each area is covered by asking a question or two." Anita started explaining.

"The first area starts with two questions.

Question one is, 'are you a cancer survivor?' and the second question is, 'are you presently having cancer treatment?'"

"Isn't this too direct?" Maya asked everybody.

"I think so." Ritu said.

"Then what shall we say, ladies?" Anita asked them.

"How about, 'do you know someone who has cancer?' This way, cancer patients are invited without asking them a direct question; and if someone knows of a cancer patient, they can also attend our group." Maya suggested.

Everyone agreed. Anita made the necessary changes in her sheet of paper.

"The second area, covered again with a question is, 'would you like to talk to someone with similar experience?'..." Anita looked at everyone.

"I like this question. It covers the purpose of our support group." Maya said.

"I like it too. It encourages women to share their experiences, if they want to, that is." Ritu said.

"Yes. That's the real problem we face, isn't it?" Dr. Vimal said. She knew it too well how secretive many women were about their breast cancer because of many different reasons, including a social stigma.

"The third area deals primarily with 'counseling'. Breast cancer patients have some unique supportive needs. They need information about their disease as well as their treatment. There are too many misconceptions about various therapies that are used in their treatment."

"Excellent, Anita. I like this part very much. Getting accurate scientific information about the illness and learning about the benefits and side-effects of the treatment are very important." Dr. Vimal was happy to note that with accurate scientific knowledge about this disease and its treatment, awareness about this disease would also propagate through these sessions.

"Counseling will be given in psychological and social areas as well." Anita continued.

"Yes. Dealing with fear, depression or stress is very important, that would give the patients some psychological boost." Maya said.

"And what about social counseling, what's that counseling for?" Ritu asked Anita.

"Social counseling can help deal with some of the difficult social issues, such as talking with family members, children, changes in relationships, especially with your husbands..." Anita looked at Dr. Vimal and they both knew exactly what she meant.

"Excellent again, Anita." Dr. Vimal exclaimed.

She had seen too many family relationships destroyed because of women in those families developing breast cancer.

"The fourth area is a sad one; it's in the palliative care area..." Anita said and looked around. All the women were quiet.

"This is also a very important area we need to cover." Dr. Vimal started talking when she saw everyone becoming abruptly very quiet.

"Many people begin to grieve at the end of their illness. They develop a sense of mourning for their own death; they become very depressed and sad. At such times, we can provide them with some spiritual guidance and counseling. I'll talk to Meeraben if she can guide us in this respect."

"Oh I believe in spiritual guidance completely. I think some spiritual guidance and counseling is necessary even for those recovering from their illness. It would give them hope in their mental turmoil; and provide some meaning to their life..." Maya said.

This time it was Maya's turn to look at Dr. Vimal and exchange a meaningful look with her.

"Yes, I agree totally. Let us talk to Meeraben for these sessions as well." Dr. Vimal said.

"Excellent work, Anita." Ritu said and everyone in the meeting agreed.

The meeting came to an end. Major decisions were taken and finalized about various sessions to be conducted for the Cancer Support Group.

•••

When *Kumbhakarna*[17] Wakes up...

"Dr. Vimal, what is cancer?"

A session, conducted specially for teenaged girls, was going on in the living room of Maya's house.

After volunteering her house as a starting place for conducting all the sessions for the support group, Maya had taken special efforts to make all the necessary arrangements in her house. Three huge rooms of her house; drawing room, living room and family room, were assigned for these activities. She had rented a dozen chairs and four tables for each room, and had her servants arrange them neatly. Praful's old office room and all the bedrooms, except hers, were kept locked. People, especially Maya's co-workers, had full freedom to use the kitchen

17. One of the two prominent epics in India, named Ramayana, entails a story of a prince named Rama and a demon named Ravana, who was a king of Lanka. When Rama's wife, Sita, was kidnapped by Ravana, Rama declared a war against Ravana and defeated him. In that war, Ravana's younger brother, named Kumbhakarna, himself a vicious demon, helped Ravana fight against Rama.
The characteristic of Kumbhakarna was that he slept all the time, and therefore unlike all other demons, harmed no one. In the entire story of Ramayana, he woke up only once, to help Ravana fight the war against Rama.
Otherwise known to be a harmless demon, as soon as Kumbhakarna woke up from his deep sleep, his demonic actions started and he killed many people.
Ever since then, the name Kumbhakarna has been synonymous with sleeping! And the advice to all - Never wake up Kumbhakarna!

and dining room. The beautiful patio overlooking the backyard had become their favorite place for conducting weekly meetings with Dr. Vimal. They were all impressed and extremely pleased with Maya's beautiful house and her generosity, not to mention her efficiency in making all these arrangements in the house in such a short time.

Dr. Vimal herself was conducting this session. She had observed in her practice that often mothers found it difficult to talk to their children, especially young girls, about their breast cancer. Torn between their instinct to protect them from fears and the desire to be honest, most mothers avoided the subject altogether. A few, who had every desire to reveal their infliction by the disease with their children, were often confused as to how much information should be given to them, so that they would come to terms with their fears and emotions.

Before starting this session, Dr. Vimal hung two huge charts, both of human female bodies, each on either side of the wall. The middle portion of the same white wall was used as a screen for the slide projector that was kept on a stool a few feet away from it. There were ten girls attending this session. They were sitting on chairs in front of the wall facing the charts and the screen.

Ritu's girls, Sangita and Shruti, were among the attendees, and as one could imagine, they were instrumental in getting the word around among their friends to attend this session.

"Dr. Vimal, what is cancer?" One girl asked. She had her notebook open and a pen in her hand. So did most of the girls.

"Hum...what is cancer? In a normal process, cells in the body divide or reproduce, as the scientists say, only when new cells are needed. But sometimes some cells continue to divide for no reason and create a mass of tissue. Can anyone guess what this mass of cells is called?" Dr. Vimal asked around.

"A tumor, perhaps?" Someone answered.

"That's good. This mass of cells is called a tumor. These tumors can be benign, meaning not cancerous, or they can be malignant, meaning cancerous. In breast cancer, as well as in some other cancers, a cell of the tissue becomes abnormal and reproduces without any control or order, forming a malignant tumor." Dr. Vimal was explaining and the girls were writing it down in their notebooks.

"What happens when a tumor starts growing?" Someone asked.

"You know that all cells need food and nourishment to grow and divide, right? But when a few of the abnormal cells start growing and dividing without control, they also start consuming all the available food and nourishment leaving nothing for other normal cells. That affects the immune system, as well as the energy levels of the body, thus making it weak to fight the disease."

"But why do some cells grow without any control or order?" A girl, barely in her teens but with a serious face, asked.

"It is not an easy answer why some cells grow without control. Most of the normal and healthy cells have the capacity to reproduce, meaning, a mother cell divides into two daughter cells. This is also termed as cell growth."

Dr. Vimal walked to the projector and showed a couple of slides depicting cell growth and division to the girls. Then she displayed one more slide where two cells were touching each other. Pointing at this figure, she said,

"Cell growth stops completely when two or more cells come into contact with each other, just like you see here. This is a natural process of arresting cell growth. Scientists have termed this entire process, 'Contact Inhibition'."

"Contact Inhibition! Oh, that means 'Stop, when in contact with the other'! That's really neat..." some girls remarked.

Dr. Vimal found it amusing to see some girls getting entertained with this hard-core science.

"Unfortunately, some cells lose this property and therefore, they grow in such an uncontrolled manner that even when in contact with the neighboring cells, they can not stop growth. Scientists and cancer specialists use this characteristic property of cells to distinguish between normal cells and cancerous cells. And naturally, cancerous cells are the ones that create tumors." Dr. Vimal explained.

"But Dr. Vimal, you didn't tell us why some cells lose this property and therefore, continue to grow without any control or order?" The same girl asked again.

"Yah, obviously some cells don't obey the nature's law, why so?" This girl was sitting next to the previous girl. They both looked serious and also very much interested in Dr. Vimal's explanation.

"This is a good question. 'Why don't some cells obey nature's law?' Do you all know what genetic science is?" Dr. Vimal looked around and saw a few girls nodding and a few shaking their heads.

"Okay, in that case, let me explain in brief. Genetic science, as the name suggests, is the science of genes, and Genetics is the study of how living things receive common traits from previous generations. A gene is a hereditary unit that carries these traits. Genes are passed on from parent to child and are an important part of what determines the physical appearance of a person. A gene consists of a molecule called *DNA*[18], that occupies a spot on what we call *chromosome*[19]. It's the DNA that determines the characteristic of a person. We humans have forty six chromosomes in each of our cells, twenty three from the mother and the same number from the father. I'm sure you have learnt this in your biology course, right?" Again, Dr. Vimal looked around. This time she saw most of the girls shake their heads.

"Perhaps we should not get into too many details of this science. Just remember that we have most of our appearance and our behavior too, passed on from our older generations through the genes. Each cell in your body carries about a hundred thousand genes, and they are the ones who control how the cell functions, such as telling it when to divide and grow. All genes are given some duties to follow. Some genes are ordered to promote cell growth, some are checkpoint genes during a cell cycle and some are given the duty of carrying out the process of contact inhibition. All genes work like a clock work in healthy and normal humans. However, when some alteration or change takes place in some of these genes, that's what we call a mutation, the entire natural process can get affected. Most cancer cells are a result of mutated genes. And girls, even these mutated genes can be passed on by heredity from mother or father to the child." Dr. Vimal looked around. There was a pin-drop silence in the room. All the girls were writing her explanation down very promptly in their notebooks.

Dr. Vimal displayed a new set of slides for the girls and continued, "Cancer is now clearly understood to be a disease of abnormal gene function. We now understand that genes serve two major roles in

18. Deoxyribonucleic Acid
19. A chromosome consists of a single, very long DNA helix on which thousands of genes are encoded.

cancer; some cause development of cancer and others stop cancer from developing or growing. Genes that cause cancer are called *Onco* genes. Genes that stop or suppress cancer growth are called *Tumor suppressor* genes. Girls, do you know that we all have Onco genes in our bodies?"

"What?" The moment girls heard Dr. Vimal say this, they all looked shocked. Some of them dropped their pens in that shock.

"Yes, we all have Onco genes in our bodies. However, fortunately they are in like Kumbhakarna, in deep sleep."

"Kumbhakarna?" The girls looked amused for, they knew the story of this demon from the Ramayana.

"Hum...hum. They are like Kumbhakarna because they are all asleep! In a deep sleep! Their demonic action starts only and only if they wake up, and only then they become dangerous. Their 'deep sleep' state is called the 'dormant' state and their wake-up state is called the 'activated' state."

The girls were very pleased with Dr. Vimal's analogy of Onco genes to Kumbhakarna, and her entertaining explanation.

The session was going on for more than an hour, but there was no sign of anyone getting up or leaving. Anita walked in the room to remind Dr. Vimal about their meeting later on. That's when everybody, including Dr. Vimal realized that the 'class' was over.

"Well, we'll talk about Kumbhakarna in more detail next time..."

Dr. Vimal turned off the slide projector. All the girls gathered her

"Kumbhakarna? What were you teaching these girls Dr. Vimal?" Anita was totally confused with a mythological figure's name in a session that was supposed to be science based.

"See girls, even Anita, who herself is a breast cancer patient, doesn't know what *our* Kumbhakarna is..." Dr. Vimal teased Anita. A few of the girls giggled. Some girls inadvertently looked at Anita's chest, which did not escape Dr. Vimal's quick glance.

'This one part of a female body has gained an undue importance everywhere, in literature, arts, lyrics, and even the commercials...'

She thought to herself in that fleeting moment and felt a little amused.

"Well, aren't you going to tell me about *your* Kumbhakarna?" Anita said with a questioning face.

"I will, I'll tell you everything, one of these days for sure, how's that?" Dr. Vimal told Anita.

"When would the next session be, Dr. Vimal?" Sangita was asking her on behalf of all the girls.

"You inquire about that to your mother or Anita here. They are organizing all these sessions."

Dr. Vimal said and started walking out the door. The girls were dispersed shortly.

•••

Then Rama[20] Takes an Aim...

"As I said last time, we all have Onco genes in our bodies, but fortunately for us, they are in a dormant state, just like..."

"Kumbhakarna..." before Dr. Vimal could utter the name, some girls sitting in the front row said it simultaneously.

"That's right, just like Kumbhakarna. Now we need to know why Onco genes 'wake up'. Why do they get transformed from their dormant state to the activated state, for no apparent reason?"

Dr. Vimal looked around the room. It was packed to capacity with people from all ages, men, women and teenagers.

All the chairs from Maya's house were brought in the room and still some people were standing. Anita, Ritu and Maya were sitting in the front row.

"Detection of Onco genes has been one of the most important finds for the scientists. Just as finding of DNA and its helical structure turned into a magic wand for the scientists, so did the detection of these cancer causing genes. What makes the Onco genes get into their activated state is the question. The reasons given are manifold actually. Heredity plays a big role here. Gene function is disturbed with mutation and mutated genes can be passed on from parent to the child."

---

20. In the epic Ramayana, the story tells us that when Kumbhakarna woke up from his deep sleep, he started destroying and destructing everything, and killing people. No one could conquer him. Finally, Rama took an aim with his bow and arrow, and with just one arrow, killed the demon.

"But why does a gene undergo mutation, doctor?" somebody from the audience asked.

"Honestly speaking, we don't know the exact reason. Some doctors believe that the culprit could be pollution with its chemical carcinogens in the air that we breathe, some believe it's exposure to excessive sunlight which has high doses of UV rays, some say it's smoking, some say it's bad diet habits, all these are considered to be carcinogenic, that is cancer causing. Some even assign it to virus." "Virus?" People were surprised to hear Virus as the plausible cause for gene mutation or Onco gene activation.

"Yes, virus. Virus can cause simple cold and fever, and it can cause cancer too in human bodies." Dr. Vimal saw people had become suddenly very quiet and attentive.

"Virus may not be directly responsible, mind you, but with all the carcinogens I just quoted, they cumulatively affect the general health of the body, which in turn, reduces its resistance. At such times, if the body comes in contact with some virus, its immune system can not resist the attack; and that can prove to be the reason for the genes to mutate or Onco genes to get activated." Dr. Vimal looked at the audience; they were all listening intently to every word she was saying.

"It has been well established for some time now, that cancer, in essence, is a disease of the genes. It could be a multi-genic disease where more than one gene could become dysfunctional and cause cancer in the human body. Gene function of cell growth, regulation and maintenance is disturbed or lost due to mutation. Scientists have termed this as 'multiple hit theory' of cancer!"

Dr. Vimal looked around. There was a complete silence in the room.

She continued,

"There are many types of cancer, at least a hundred of them, but you can not pin point any one specific reason for any one type of cancer as the sole cause. Breast cancer is one among such cancers, where no single factor can be accounted for the disease. I wish it were so, for, then I could have advised to all my fellow women what to do or what not to do, to avoid breast cancer. But unfortunately my dear people, it is not so!"

"Why only fellow women, Dr. Vimal, we men have breasts too." One among the very few men that were attending the session, asked.

Dr. Vimal smiled at him. "You are right actually. Men have breasts too, but almost ninety eight percent of breast cancer patients are women. Seldom do you see a man being affected by breast cancer."

"Why so?"

"That is because breast cancer usually develops in the glandular tissue of the breast, specifically in the milk ducts and the milk lobules. These ducts and lobules are located in all parts of the breast tissue, including tissue just under the skin. As this part is rarely present in a man's body, so is the incidence of a man getting breast cancer." People looked satisfied with Dr. Vimal's explanation.

"Dr. Vimal, for women with breast cancer, if the breast is removed, then the woman should be free of it permanently, isn't it?" Some one asked.

"Well, yes, but that is an ideal situation. You see, the breast tissue extends from the collarbone to the lower rib margin, and from the middle of the chest, around the side and under the arm. In the breast removal surgery, which is called mastectomy, it is necessary to remove tissue from just beneath the skin down to the chest wall and around the borders of the chest. However, even with very thorough and delicate surgical techniques, it is impossible to remove every milk duct and lobule, given the extent of the breast tissue and the location of these glands just beneath the skin." Dr. Vimal said.

She paced around for a few moments in total silence, letting people absorb the information she had given in her explanation, and then continued further.

"Among many other risks we talked earlier, there is an additional risk for women in getting breast cancer. And that is having dysfunction in their hormone regulation."

Then Dr. Vimal walked to the projector and started showing a few slides to the people, with explanation, "Here are the pictures of a female body from age ten years to fifty years. Just look at them carefully. You can see that, as a female is growing in age, her body is undergoing tremendous hormonal changes. There is some hormonal change in her pre-teen or teenage that triggers her monthly periods; when she gets pregnant, her body starts synthesizing another set of hormones; when the baby comes, she nurses the baby with her milk that is a result of some more hormones; she undergoes even more hormonal changes during her menopause and her body stops getting periods or ability to reproduce. All this is going on in less than forty years in the female body, with so many hormones playing their specific roles at specific times in her life, for specific reasons. Now, just imagine, any one of these hormones not functioning at all or over-functioning or functioning at wrong time. Just think, what would happen?"

The listeners were silent again. One could hear only some faint sound of writing, as a few of them were jotting down some points.

"Dr. Vimal..." One woman from the audience broke the silence,

"As you explained, breast cancer can be a result of many things, such as genetic make-up, faulty hormones, and other exterior risk factors, right?"

Dr. Vimal nodded.

"And when all these factors come together, then the person, I mean the woman, may develop breast cancer, right?"

Dr. Vimal nodded again.

"You also stated that when a woman starts her periods at the right age, that is pre-teen or early teenage, then gets pregnant in relatively younger age, as in before or around thirty years of age, nurses her baby, because that's when the possibility of all the mutation is known to stop, right?"

"Um...Hum... go on..." Dr. Vimal said.

"Then she also stays away from all the external risk factors, such as pollution, excessive sunshine, smoking and all that; then tell me doctor, can a woman avoid breast cancer altogether?"

Dr. Vimal was impressed to see that this woman had listened to every word she had explained in the session. She was equally impressed with her question too.

She smiled at her and said, "Well, yes and no! It is good to follow all these things to keep fit and healthy. I would also say that this is a recommended way to avoid the possibility of getting this disease. Usually most of the women do follow this route, so I would say 'yes'. But..." "Oh no, the 'big butt'..." Some woman from the audience unknowingly exclaimed softly, but a few people around her heard her and chuckled.

"Yes, the 'big butt' indeed!" Dr. Vimal also heard her and chuckled a bit. Then she said, "Anyways, as I was saying, but, the genetic make-up of a person can not be changed drastically to reduce or rid away the risk of developing cancer. It is very difficult for a doctor to just assess a woman's lifestyle and her situation, and then *predict* if or when she may develop this disease, isn't it?"

There was a mixture of agreements and disagreements among the listeners. The questioner herself didn't look very satisfied with Dr. Vimal's answer.

"So, there is no specific rule as to when and in what situation a woman may develop this disease then, right?" Some other woman from the audience asked.

Dr. Vimal looked at her and noticed that she was sitting next to Virani.

"That's right. There isn't any rule or any specific situation assigned as such, for developing this disease." Dr. Vimal looked at Virani while answering the question.

"Any specific age in which a woman may develop this disease?" The same woman asked again.

"Cancer is believed to be a disease commonly occurring among the older adults now. Accordingly, the highest probability of a woman developing breast cancer is usually around or after menopause, that's around their fifty years of age or after..." Dr. Vimal was explaining, when she heard a loud voice shouting,

"That's a lie, a big fat lie...a total lie..."

Everybody, including Dr. Vimal, was stunned to hear such a loud shout in the middle of a quiet and serious session.

Dr. Vimal looked in the direction of the loud shout. It was none other than Virani. She was looking at the doctor and retorting at the top of her lungs. Dr. Vimal was shocked, for, she never expected such an outburst from Virani; especially when she herself was a group member, participating in the process of starting a Cancer Support group.

"I am not old, I'm young ..." Virani turned her face away from the doctor and towards the audience, and as though addressing the people gathered there, she continued in a loud voice.

"I had my period at age twelve, I had my baby at age twenty six, I nursed my son for six months; and you see this man..."

Virani pointed to Das who was sitting next to her.

"This man is my husband. I was a virgin until I married him. Just ask him, wasn't I a virgin, Das, until our wedding night? Did I fool around, Das, did I?"

Das felt a little embarrassed. He lowered his head down and wanted Virani to shut up and sit down, but in stead, she raised her voice even higher and as if attacking the doctor, shouted, "You doctors say that old people get this disease. Doctor, I am less than thirty years old. Tell me then doctor, why did *I* get this disease..., hum..., tell me why?"

Her face had turned red with anger, and as though it was the doctor's fault that she got cancer, she was yelling at her, "I don't smoke, I don't drink, I don't sunbathe, nothing like that. And still I got this disease, what can you do about it doctor, hum... and what can *I* do about it?" Her whole body was trembling.

"Rani...quiet...Rani...please..." Das was totally embarrassed to see his wife get up and yell hysterically like that, especially at Dr. Vimal, but Virani seemed to be totally out of control.

Virani ignored Das completely. She turned her attention to the people and continued her bellowing.

"And people, you know what? My cancer is at an advanced stage. It's *terminal.* Yes, it is t...e...r...m...i...n...a...l! Do you know what it means? Do you?"

And in a shrilly, almost hysterical sounding voice, she yelled,

"That means it's going to kill me soon. Yes, kill me. I'm never going to see my son go to school, not even KG..." She stood with her hands raised over her head and started crying profusely. Das held her hands tightly and started pulling her to take her out of the room.

'Rani... stop it dear...please...' As he was desperately trying to calm her down, she was crying even more, like a child, with loud voice, and continuously saying, "Please God...don't take me away so soon...please...let me see my son go to the school... just once...God please..."

Everybody in the room was frozen stiff to see this drama. Even Dr. Vimal was confused to see Virani, a soft spoken young woman like her, in this act. It was most unexpected. The whole scene was very, very sad and heart wrenching.

Das was trying to pull Virani out of the room, but it was as if she had gained the strength of a charging bull. Anita and Maya quickly came forward to help Das. The three of them finally managed to take Virani out of the room. There were more than a hundred people in the room, but the silence was almost deafening.

"Is it true, doctor, what that lady said?" Somebody broke the silence.

"Yes, unfortunately that's true. Virani is a young woman with one toddler son, and her breast cancer has been diagnosed at an advanced stage. Unlucky for her that it's a rare kind of cancer. I feel very sorry that I can not do anything for her..." Dr. Vimal sounded like she was getting a lump in her throat. She tried to control it and after clearing her throat, she continued,

"Unfortunately, we doctors can not predict when a woman will develop cancer in her breast. It is only *after* she develops it that we can diagnose it. We strongly recommend all kinds of methods for early detection because that could give a chance for control. However, cancer can only be *detected* and *not predicted*!"

Dr. Vimal took a few long breaths and continued.

"In a few cases, even after early detection, the disease progresses fast. In such cases, the most modern and advanced medical treatments also seem to fail. What can we doctors do? Absolutely nothing." From her voice, Dr. Vimal was sounding quite low in her spirits by now.

"But then, doctor, all those reasons you just stated..."

"Yes, and all those risk factor you discussed earlier..." a couple of women, almost simultaneously, asked Dr. Vimal.

"Those are after all, statistical data and measurements." Dr. Vimal tried to explain.

"Data is collected only after the fact, it is analyzed only after the fact, inferences are drawn only after the fact, and medical treatments are given based solely on the values obtained only after the fact. *Only after the fact*! That seems to be the big obstacle here, but what can we do? Right now, nothing much..."

"But doctor, each person is different, isn't it?" Someone asked.

"Yes, that's true. We doctors realize that each cancer patient is different from the rest, with a different body chemistry, different mental temperament, different everything, but the medical treatment that we give to all cancer patients remains more or less the very same, not terribly different from each other." As Dr. Vimal went on explaining more and more, her voice started going down further and further, to a point of sounding almost apologetic. Yet, she continued,

"We really haven't fully understood what cancer is, except that it is a disease of abnormal gene function. But then, we also postulate that most of the cancers are not inherited but arise from gene mutations that a person acquires during his or her life. Scientists and medical researchers are working day and night to comprehend this disease, but so far no success. We can not give any guarantees to any of our patients."

It was most unusual for Dr. Vimal, known to be a vibrant woman with a zest for life, and who would always encourage her patients for a positive attitude, to talk to people in such a depressing tone.

Even more unusual was for her to walk to her chair quietly and sit down in the middle of her session that she so loved to conduct. It was as if, she herself was helpless. She was looking quite frustrated and sad.

People were looking at each other wondering if she was going to continue, or if the session was over for the day.

"Does this mean we should stop all our efforts and research, doctor?" One young and bright looking woman was heard asking Dr. Vimal. There was a tone of slight anger in her voice. Dr. Vimal just looked in her direction with a mild surprise, but didn't say anything.

The bright looking young woman stood up and as if addressing the entire crowd, said,

"We humans worked hard and put an end to many diseases such as diphtheria, cholera, tetanus, chicken pox, by finding their vaccines. You know that all these diseases were killing thousands of people in the earlier times. But today, they are controlled through the vaccines. If some of you remember, not too long, children used to get vaccine for small pox as a part of their routine childhood immunization. My mother and father got them during their childhood. But, that is not true any more as this disease is almost eradicated from the face of the earth today. And the credit goes to the hard work of dedicated scientists and researchers. Infections used to kill hundreds of people earlier, but today? Today when we get any infection, we right away take antibiotics to control it. Rarely you hear or see someone dying of infection today. And the credit goes to the hard work of dedicated scientists and researchers. They have continuously strived hard in the pursuit of scientific knowledge to understand the 'whys and why-not's' of diseases and have come up with a solution for the benefit of health and wellness of humans and other living beings as well."

Then this bright looking young woman walked slowly towards where Dr. Vimal was sitting. Looking at the crowd in the front, she said,

"Look at the life expectancy today, people. Scientific discoveries have significantly increased the life expectancy of humans. Not too long ago, very few people survived after the age of fifty, but today? Today, people live for over seventy-five years of age. If someone dies at the age of fifty, we think that's too young to die, right?" She received a few nods from the audience.

Just then, Maya and Anita entered the hall after taking care of Virani and returned to their seats. The bright looking young woman smiled at them and walking closer to where they were sitting, continued, "We know of diabetes, hypertension, and many such chronic diseases and their reasons for developing. We have this knowledge only because of the hard work of dedicated scientists and medical researchers. They came up with medical treatments to keep all these diseases completely under control. Thanks to them, people lead a normal and healthy life even when they have diabetes or hypertension or any such chronic disease today. Credit for all the wonderful medicines for chronic diseases goes to the hard work of dedicated scientists and medical researchers. Why can't we think along the same lines for cancer as well?"

"You are right dear, we should..." Anita said softly with a smile on her face. She was sitting very close to the speaker. All the people in the room almost clapped for this bright looking young woman for her timely 'pep' talk.

All the while that bright looking young woman was speaking to the audience, Dr. Vimal was intently listening to her with a smile on her face. She looked as though she had taken a deep breath of fresh air and regained her energy. She stood up from her chair and walked towards that young woman.

"You know, I was hoping one of you would come up with some optimistic answers. Sometimes, I seem to get tired of carrying the torch of optimism all the time. Do you work in medical research?" She asked the young woman.

"Yes doctor. As a matter of fact, I'm a medical researcher, working in Oncology." The young woman answered.

"Then why don't you give some pointers about your field to our people today? You are an excellent speaker and hold a very positive outlook towards everything." Dr. Vimal was impressed with her earlier speech.

The bright, young woman readily agreed, and turning towards the people, she said,

"Dr. Vimal has just requested me to continue my talking to you all. It's my pleasure actually..." She smiled at the people and started talking,

"Cancer research is going on in every corner of the world today. Scientists are working day and night to overcome this disease. You learnt from Dr. Vimal earlier that there are Onco genes. These genes can cause cancer if activated. But ladies and gentlemen, I am very happy to tell you that scientists have also found genes that stop or suppress cancer growth. These are called tumor suppressor genes."

"I call them 'Rama genes'." Dr. Vimal interjected with a smile.

"Yes, exactly, Dr. Vimal. That's a new thing..."

"And I call Onco genes, the Kumbhakarna genes..." Dr. Vimal said with a smile.

"Oh that's a very apt description, Dr. Vimal." The bright, young woman looked genuinely impressed with these befitting names from mythology to medical terms.

She continued, "We all know the story of the Ramayana. When the demon Kumbhakarna wakes up, that is, when the Onco genes are activated, then our body sets out its Rama genes, that is, its tumor suppressor genes to take an aim at the Onco genes. Many scientists are working hard to develop technology based on these 'Rama genes' of human body. A good many cancer research laboratories are focusing their attention on gene therapy as a *cure* for cancer." The moment people heard the word 'cure' for cancer, there was a light applause.

"What's gene therapy?" someone asked.

"In one simple sentence, I would say, gene therapy is the insertion of functional genes into an individual's cells and tissues to treat a hereditary disease. You all know that we are born with a specific genetic make-up, but thanks to the hard work of scientists; in gene therapy, a defective gene is replaced with a functional one. Although the technology is still in its infancy, it has been used with some success." She was eloquent in explaining gene therapy.

Then she slowly walked towards the centre and as though staring at the people, asked,

"Do you know that scientists are working on finding a *vaccine* for cancer?"

Everybody in the room, including Dr. Vimal, was paying one hundred percent attention to this young woman. She continued.

"Many experts endorse the vaccine as a simple way to prevent deadly cancer. If vaccine is possible, and I think it will be, sooner than we think, then eradication of cancer could be achieved reasonably easily. Once its vaccine is discovered, it may become a part of the routine childhood immunization. Cancer will then be well under control, just like all those other diseases I mentioned earlier. The picture is very bright, my dear friends, very, very bright."

That young medical researcher then put her one hand on her chest where her heart was, as if to display her total respect, and said,

"Science has played a very important role in the entire history of mankind, and I assure you all, it will continue to do so in the future too..."

Then she slowly turned towards Dr. Vimal and said,

"Dr. Vimal, we now know that cancer is a gene-based disease. The situation is not that dismal or hopeless as you portrayed doctor. It is just a matter of time when we can control or cure that too. Really, just a matter of time..."

When people heard that, they started applauding this young woman whole heartedly.

"Right on..." A few said.

"That's the way it should be..." Others commented.

"Oh, that's wonderful." A few said.

"Even if it happens in our children's times, that would be okay..." there was a brief mutter among a few women.

With humility and a smile on her face, she accepted their admiration and sat down. The atmosphere in the room was filled with optimism and enthusiasm. People were looking at the young woman with genuine admiration and applauding her courage and knowledge.

The happiest person in the room was Dr. Vimal. This session had taken a course exactly how she wanted, in a very optimistic and positive direction.

'Rama does kill Kumbhakarna, after all, and not just in the story...' she thought to herself and declared the session adjourned for the day.

•••

Visualization Technique

Maya had organized a new kind of session for women, who had developed breast cancer, in her house. All the arrangements were made as per the requirements of Meeraben, her psychotherapist of almost two years now. There were no charts on the walls, no slide projector, no chairs, not even bright light; just a thick carpet on the floor for women to sit on and, since all the drapes of the windows were drawn, a dim light illuminating the room. In one corner was placed a CD player. Waves of beautiful soothing music were coming from the CD and filling up the room. The whole atmosphere of the room had a serene touch to it.

There were ten women, all breast cancer patients, sitting on the carpet in front of Meeraben. She was sitting in her usual lotus position. Her torso was straight and shoulders drawn back but relaxed.

"We have all gathered here today for getting to know a new technique. The scientists have termed this technique '*Visualization Technique.*'[21] It is utilized quite regularly in medical treatments, especially in the cancer treatment." Meeraben started talking to the ladies in her deep, soothing voice.

"My dear ladies, you all have heard many, many times the close relationship between our body, mind and spirit. Energy is created out

21. A partial credit of developing this technique is assigned to the contribution of a brilliant doctor named Elida Evans who did the psychological study of breast cancer patients early in the twentieth century.

of this relationship and that energy forms the basis of this new technique." Meeraben said.

"To tell you honestly, this technique may be new, but its concept is not. The concept, that there is a close relationship between our body, mind and spirit, is an age-old one. The technique is founded on this concept, which in turn, is based upon the principles of Hindu philosophy. This ancient philosophy vehemently states that the quality of thoughts has a direct influence on the body. Over the centuries, Hindu philosophers tried to gain access to their inner wisdom and strength, and learn more about the 'self'! Medical researchers have utilized this intrinsic yearning of mankind to explore the 'self' for developing many techniques to improve health and treatments to various diseases. One of these techniques that many scientists found very beneficial in medical treatments is Visualization. It is done through visual imagery that is, creating visual images. This technique today has an ever-expanding application in science and medicine, especially in cancer treatment."

Meeraben stopped briefly and looked at all the women. They were listening to her intently.

"I know, you all are breast cancer patients. Some of you are newly diagnosed, some are undergoing treatment and some have survived it for more than a year but afraid of its recurrence. This technique will prove to be extremely beneficial to all of you, I promise you that. As I said earlier, quality of thoughts create certain kinds of biological effects in our bodies. It is scientifically established now that negative thoughts create stress and anxiety. Stress and anxiety, in turn, release what the doctors call cortisones. Cortisones are degenerative stress hormones that are destructive to the body causing diseases. As against that, happy and positive thoughts release beneficial hormones such as endorphins and growth hormones which are regenerative and healing for the body. As you can see, all this is in your hands, ladies, in *your own* hands! By having positive thoughts and creating visual images of what you wish to see in your lives, you can heal yourself. This technique helps you keep your subconscious mind completely focused on what *you* want, and that is of course, getting well, isn't it?"

Meeraben looked around once and started talking again.

"Human body is the most efficient machinery Mother Nature created. If we couple its efficiency with this technique, utilizing visual imagery of positive things, then combating and defeating cancer is not too difficult.

We want to get better and we want to heal ourselves by the power of imagery, right? So let us now think of some positive things. Positive things are usually happy things, or things that make us feel happy. So, ladies, what happy things can we think of? What do you all like?"

Meeraben looked at all the women who were sitting silently and listening to her.

When she asked them questions, for a moment they all looked at each other. Then one woman said, 'ocean waves', another said, 'beach', one more woman said, 'coconut trees swinging gently with the wind'.

Meeraben smiled at the coincidence of all three answers focusing on only one topic, ocean beach with palm trees!

"Okay then, let us start a visual imagery of what you all like."

She closed her eyes and with her hands rested on her lap, started the mantra of 'Ohm...'

"Ohm..." Meeraben's deep and somber voice reverberated in the room.

All the women closed their eyes too. Each one tried to sit in the same position as Meeraben, but most of them couldn't.

They all repeated after her, "Ohm..."

Their voices resounded in the room.

This took place for a few minutes, Meeraben reciting 'Ohm...' and the women repeating after her, with their eyes closed.

As they were all chanting 'Ohm...' Meeraben started talking in gentle, deep voice.

"Imagine, you are standing on the beach in front of a vast ocean; its vastness seems boundless, extending past the horizon; its gentle waves are approaching you, touching your feet and ankles and receding back at precise intervals. Every time the waves recede, the sand underneath your feet tickles the soles of your feet and makes you giggle a bit. The sky above is as blue as the ocean. There is a light wind that is gently playing with the leaves of the palm trees that you see on the beach. The gentle swing of the leaves is making its silky sound, that is very soothing to you. Just imagine all this, my dear ladies..."

Meeraben opened her eyes and looked at the women. They were very quiet and had their eyes shut. All of them were obviously visualizing this beautiful scenery. Meeraben continued, "Imagine, a wave coming towards you, gently massaging your feet, receding back with some sand underneath your feet, thus tickling your soles and giving you pleasure…" She repeated this description over and over again at least twenty times, in a deep, soft voice with her usual soothing style. The women were lost in their imagery completely by now.

"You are having an immense pleasure with the ocean's playful waves. While standing and enjoying this ultimate delight, you are gazing at the horizon. Soon it turns orange red as the Sun starts to set slowly. The entire sky is gradually turning its color from beautiful blue to orange red; and so is the ocean. You are completely immersed in this heavenly scenery…"

Meeraben looked at all the women again. The expressions on their faces seemed like they were imagining a beautiful scene and soaking in the imagery.

Meeraben continued,

"You are gazing at the horizon, when suddenly an old, ugly warship props up at the horizon. You notice its prow and realize that it is moving towards you and approaching you very fast. You are confused momentarily. You can't make up your mind if you should get out of there or stay put. As the warship reaches the beach, you notice hideous looking pirates getting out of the warship and running towards you. You see the vicious expressions on their faces and want to run, but you can't. You just can not run. You are stuck in the sand. The same warm sand that was tickling your soles and giving you pleasure is now holding you back. You can not run and you have no ammunition to fight with those pirates, you are totally helpless…"

Meeraben looked at the women again. Although their eyes were completely shut, each of them had an expression of being disturbed on their faces. She noticed some tension as well on many faces. She continued.

"You are frustrated. You are scared too, as the hideous pirates have come very close to you and you are sure they could hurt you. But you can not defend yourself. Nor can you run for your life. You are getting mentally prepared to surrender to their vicious actions when suddenly you see another ship, a clean and beautiful one, approaching you fast. As it reaches the beach where you are standing, kind and gentle looking warriors jump out of the ship and come closer to you. You feel confident that they will rescue you and protect you from the frightful pirates. The kind warriors start fighting the pirates. You feel relieved that you have help just in time of your need. You start encouraging the warriors and seeing your courage and hope, they get stimulated even more to give a strong fight to the pirates..."

Meeraben again looked at the women. Most of them had an expression of complete release of their tension, some of them actually a happy expression, on their faces. She continued.

"After giving a fierce fight to the kind warriors, the pirates finally accept a defeat and try to run away to their warship. But the kind warriors chase the defeated pirates and destroy their warship. The pirates are drowned, finished and gone for good..."

Meeraben could clearly see the women imagining this scene from their facial expressions. She then advised the women to observe carefully faces of the kind warriors. "Look at the kind warriors, ladies. Whom do they look like? Do they look like your own self? Do they have your faces? Perhaps they do! They definitely do! They are a part of *you*, ladies, they are your own white blood cells! With your hope and will power you have given them strength! And the drowned pirates, that were about to attack you, were your cancer cells..."

The moment the women heard the word cancer, they opened their eyes almost as a reflex.

Meeraben smiled at them and said, "Yes, they were your cancer cells, but they are dead and gone now. You supported your immune system with your hope and positive thinking and that provided strength to the kind and gentle warriors of your body to fight and defeat the attackers, the cancer cells, completely."

She could clearly hear many sighs of relief from the women. Each one of them had an expression, as if filled with redemption, on their faces. They looked totally happy. Just one session of this technique, technique of Visualization to inculcate positive thinking, but it had done the trick.

She was sure, after a few sessions such as this one, the doctors would certainly find an improvement in their patients' health.

This thought made her feel quite happy and satisfied.

Meeraben closed her eyes and sitting in the same lotus position again, started uttering the mantra of 'Ohm...' in her deep, soothing voice.

All the women followed her, repeating the mantra after her. Their voices resounded in the room.

Their voices sounded a lot chirpier this time, she felt!

•••

Cancer–I am its Master!

The room was filled to capacity with people. There wasn't a room even for an ant to crawl inside. Most of the family members, friends and neighbors of all the women who were regularly partaking in these sessions based on a new concept of Visualization Technique were present there. So were many others who came to know about the sessions dealing with this new subject.

Initially started as a novelty and as an experiment, sessions on Visualization Technique were becoming very popular. Conducted initially only for breast cancer patients, they were gathering immense popularity among patients of other diseases and surgery as well. The enrolment was increasing day by day, and inquiries were steadily on the rise. More and more women, and sometimes men too, were expressing their desires to participate in these sessions. The sessions that were offered once every six or eight weeks initially, had their frequency increased to once every week. And yet, each one was full to its capacity every week.

The session that was about to take place right now was jointly organized by Anita and Maya, and jointly conducted by Dr. Vimal and Meeraben. Everyone in the room, except the participants, was curious about this new technique.

"When a patient sees the cancer cells being completely destroyed by her own immune system, she comes out of her imagery with her heart full of hope. She starts looking ahead for a brighter future.

Her whole outlook to life becomes positive and that positive thought does the magic..."

Meeraben started talking to the gathered crowd, in her deep, soothing voice, and everyone became attentive.

"But what does positive thinking have to do with cancer?" Someone from the crowd asked.

"What does it have? Almost everything." Meeraben said.

"Our immune system, let us call it the defense department of our body, gets a tremendous boost and a direct help from our positive thinking."

"Any scientific support for this thought or it's just a...?" a skeptic in the audience asked.

"Yes, there is enough medical support for this thought." Meeraben looked at Dr. Vimal and said,

"Dr. Vimal, perhaps your explanation may convince our audience here better." Meeraben requested Dr. Vimal with a smile.

Dr. Vimal agreed and started talking to the audience.

"When I give treatment for my cancer patients with radiation and chemotherapy after their surgery, I insist that they all take some treatment also for their minds during and after their medical treatments. I recommend them to go see Meeraben for such treatment."

People knew that Dr. Vimal was a bright doctor and a renowned cancer specialist. They started listening to her attentively.

"I presume that you are all familiar with the mind-body connection. I am a doctor of the *body*, I give treatment for the *body* of a patient. In my judgment, Meeraben is the doctor of the *mind*. I firmly believe in the Visualization Technique for, it is a *technique* based on this beautiful mind-body connection." Dr. Vimal looked around, people were listening to her with their full attention.

"Someone among you asked earlier if there is any scientific support for this type of technique. The answer to that is a definite *yes*! Meeraben explained to us earlier that when the patient comes out of her imagery, she is full of hope. Her thought process has taken a positive direction. The medical fact is that this positive thought that arises in her mind helps our immune system tremendously. You know that our immune system is a complex network of specialized cells and organs that has evolved to defend the body against attacks by "foreign" invaders. When functioning properly, it fights off infections by agents such as bacteria, viruses, fungi, and parasites. However, when it malfunctions, it can unleash a torrent of diseases. These diseases could include from simple allergy to cancer."

Dr. Vimal looked around. Not a single person in that room was even moving slightly.

She continued.

"We know that biological links between the immune system and the central nervous system exist at several levels. A new field of research, known as psycho-neuro-immunology, is evolving in the recent years."

"What's that?" A few people unknowingly uttered this question.

"Psycho-neuro-immunology." Dr. Vimal realized that this is a complex word.

She tried to explain in simpler terms.

"It explores how our immune system and our brain interact with each other to influence our health. You can imagine that emotions play an important role in modulating our bodily systems which in turn influence our health. For example, we have heard it too many times that stress is suspected to increase our susceptibility to various infectious diseases and even cancer. The power of the mind to influence bodily function has long been of interest to scientists. Now, evidence is mounting that *the immune system and the nervous system may be intricately interconnected.*"

Dr. Vimal looked at the people again, and when she noticed that they did not look confused or anything, she continued,

"Recent research has shown that an area of the brain just behind the forehead, called the left prefrontal cortex, is associated with positive emotion. With this finding, studying the connections between the nervous and immune systems has gained attention of the scientific world. Many scientists have turned to the brain to understand the mechanisms by which our mind influences our body."

Dr. Vimal was afraid if this was too much of a heavy dose of scientific matter to the people, but they all looked like they were 'with her'. So she continued.

"My dear people, the mind-body connection is real! New medical research shows that a healthy, active brain boosts your immune system function and keeping a *positive attitude* helps keep you healthy. This is a medical fact, not fiction!"

Dr. Vimal then looked at Meeraben and said with a smile,

"And as you can see, Meeraben's sessions of Visualization Technique, a technique that generates *positive attitude* among cancer patients, do have enough scientific support." Dr. Vimal finished her talk and sat down.

The listeners were so thrilled to hear Dr. Vimal's beautiful and articulate explanation about the current scientific research that a few among them tried to give her an applause, but she held it back by gesturing them not to clap, for, it was more like a tutorial session than a speech.

"You just heard Dr. Vimal explain the mind-body connection in scientific terms. You also heard from her that keeping a positive attitude does help your immune system to fight infections and even a deadly disease like cancer."

Meeraben started talking to the people.

"Now, my friends, we are going to present something totally different here. It may seem purely of entertainment to you, but it is as educational as Dr. Vimal's explanation about the medical science was... It may provoke your thought, it may make you think, judge it for yourself."

Meeraben looked for Maya in the audience and called her to the front of the audience. She requested Maya to say a few words before they started their 'entertainment' session.

"Friends, I have been taking Meeraben's psychotherapy treatments for the last couple of years." Maya said.

Wrapped up in a beautiful silk sari and wearing a light make-up and a select few ornaments, Maya looked very pleasant and dignified.

With total confidence, she started talking to the people.

"My daughter took me to Meeraben for the first time. Initially I gave my daughter some resistance, but once I started meeting Meeraben regularly, it was almost addictive, I would say. Now, you must be wondering why I went to her for any treatment at all, in the first place. Well, my friends, I am a breast cancer survivor."

The moment Maya said the last sentence everyone looked a little surprised, for, Maya looked too gorgeous to have survived any disease, especially breast cancer.

"Before, during and even after my cancer treatment, I needed Meeraben's visits. Before, because it was Meeraben who inspired me to take an action against the disease, so I did. During the treatment, I needed her to help me give a fight to the disease *mentally*, so I did. And afterwards, which is now onwards, I shall never let that bloody disease recur in my life." Maya looked at everyone and then asked,

"Do you know how I will keep cancer out of my life for ever?"

"How..." A few people said with utmost curiosity.

"I will not allow the cancer to recur in my life because I *am its Master*..." Maya said emphatically and looked around.

The crowd got a little confused with her statement. Some took it jokingly and laughed; others looked doubtful about Maya, whispering among themselves, 'is she for real?'; a couple of them started getting ready to leave as they didn't want to waste their time in Maya's antics.

"Please come here Meeraben, tell these people what I am saying is the truth." Noticing minor ripples of disagreement in the audience, Maya called Meeraben to support what she told the people.

"What Maya is saying is one hundred percent true, ladies and gentlemen, I can vouch for it." Meeraben said.

"When she first came to me with her daughter, she seemed quite skeptical. She was not even sure if she should meet me again after that first meeting. Fortunately in that first meeting I found out that Maya had a cancerous lump in her breast, but she was reluctant to do anything about it. She wanted to die. She wanted to end her life since her life had no meaning, in her judgment. As you can imagine, I was surprised to hear that at first, but slowly and steadily, she started realizing her folly and her mistaken judgment. That's how it all started."

"This lady, who looks so good and collected, wanted to die?" A couple of women sitting in the front row asked with surprise.

"Yes. And how her mental disposition is now totally transformed into the opposite direction is something you all must hear. Maya and I have prepared a brief skit, and through this skit, we can demonstrate that. Would you like to watch our skit?" Meeraben asked.

Each and every person in the audience nodded, including the ones who were getting ready to leave. They sat down to watch the skit.

"This is Maya talking..." Meeraben told Maya to stand on the right side, facing the audience. "And I am assuming the role of Maya's cancer, so this is Maya's cancer talking..." Meeraben herself stood on the left side, facing the audience. The moment she said 'Cancer talking...' people got a little jolt. They got quite curious.

Cancer :Do you realize I am your friend?

Maya :Friend? How so?

Cancer :Do you remember, after you lost your husband unexpectedly, you wanted to die too. You wanted to commit suicide actually, but you didn't have enough guts to do that, remember?

Maya :Yes, yes I remember, so?

Cancer :So, I thought, since you want to die but you can't because you are timid, let me visit you. Let me, the Cancer, kill you and save your trouble of committing suicide.

Maya :Oh, I see. Hum, how thoughtful of you...

Cancer :Yes, very thoughtful. You felt no one needs you any more, you thought your life was totally empty, you were exceptionally lonely, so I thought let me be her friend, let me be her close companion, so I developed in you...

Maya :But I have my three lovely children...

Cancer :Who cares? They were busy in their own lives. They didn't need you either, that's what you used to tell yourself all the time, remember? You convinced yourself that when your husband died, everything else in your life died too, remember? You used to just sit in one room day after day, night after night, without talking to anyone, even to your children, without doing anything. You really looked like a zombie, so I thought I must help you end this miserable life of yours. But alas! You screwed up my plan altogether.

Maya :Your plan, plan of what?

Cancer :My plan of ending your life, of course.

Maya :And how did I screw that up?

Cancer :By going to that, that cunning, double-crossing woman...

Maya :Cunning woman, you mean that psychotherapist? What did she do to you?

Cancer :You went to that woman and she convinced you that your life is not empty at all. She convinced you that your children, all three of them, needed you. She told you that you were needed by the society as well, since you have so much to offer. When you were convinced that you were in need after all, a feeling that you yourself needed badly for your own existence, the first thing you did was get rid of my roots. Ouch, how it hurt me then, you have no idea...

Maya :You are sick, a bloody sick devil...

Cancer :Oh, how I loved it when you were in total despair, how you saw nothing but darkness everywhere. I had beautifully rooted in you. I loved it when you were completely distressed, full of sorrow. That made my roots stronger. You, sitting alone in the corner, feeling hopeless, provided me with ample of food for my growth. That was my nourishment.

Maya :You are despicable, don't talk to me.

Cancer :But, with that woman's psychotherapeutic treatment, you started taking interest in life, you became hopeful for life. How terrible!

Maya :My God, you are a monster.

Cancer :You call me a monster, but I played a very important role when that woman was teaching you, do you realize that? I am the one who carried a major weight in your lesson for learning to lead a good life.

Maya :You? You taught me something?

Cancer :Yes I did, my dear lady, believe it or not, I did. That woman taught you that if you remain hopeful, happy and if you always think positive...ouch, even saying these words gives me an ache in my groin; anyways, she said that that will make you healthier and help you fight me better. The role I played in this valuable lesson was that, it was *me* who demonstrated to you clearly that by you remaining positive all the time and never ever entertaining any pessimistic thought, you can develop a very strong immunity that can destroy me. It was me, the Cancer, the disease people are so scared of, who taught you this! Now you see my role? I had to run away to make you feel as a conqueror.

Maya :My, my! Aren't you egotistical?

Cancer :You may call me egotistical, or you may call me conceited; but the truth of the matter is that, my dear lady, when someone defeats *me, the Cancer*, in the war, that someone is known to be a *survivor* by all, isn't it? Have you anytime heard anyone being called a 'typhoid-survivor'? Or a 'malaria-survivor'? Hum, have you?

Maya :Well, I must admit it, albeit grudgingly, what you are saying is true. I am called a 'survivor' by all because of defeating you, the cancer. Hey, but you were not that easy to defeat, okay?

Cancer :I know that. And I must admit I had a lot of fun in giving you a fight.

Maya :Fun, did you say fun? How so?

Cancer :It was something like a gorilla-warfare between us, don't you think? There were a few times when you used to feel really depressed. Those times gave me enough nourishment to grow. I was almost sure at times that you were going to wave a white flag in our war! But then...

Maya :Sorry to interrupt you, Mr. Cancer, but, let me tell you something you may not know. Thinking positively all the time is very difficult, you know. It is hard to remain optimistic all the time, especially when one is going through the tough ordeal of cancer treatment.

Cancer :Oh! I can imagine that. It must be putting a big responsibility on the patient, the fighter, too, right?

Maya :Right. You got it.

Cancer :But then, as I was saying, in your case, that woman with her 'psycho-tools' would come on the scene and inculcate some 'positive poison' in you. And then, there you were, full of ammunition to give me a fierce fight. Oh! how I hated those tools and that poison of positive thinking! I couldn't take it anymore. Finally, I had to accept my defeat and run away.

Maya :Ah ha! See...

Cancer :But hey, you know what? Even during my fleeing, I felt very proud of myself.

Maya :You felt proud? About what?

Cancer :That I was so successful in teaching you such a valuable lesson of life. A lesson you could learn only because of my presence in you for a short time. Something you would have never learnt otherwise. It was only with *me* on your mind that you made such a concerted effort the whole time to develop a positive attitude and try to remain happy, isn't it? Tell me honestly now, don't I deserve a little credit in your learning?

Maya : Well, yes, I suppose. You do get some credit. Ever since I have had a fight with you, Mr. Cancer, I don't take anything for granted any more. I have developed such a tremendous fighting spirit now that I can face any situation without fear. The most valuable lesson I have learnt from this war with you is about the direct correlation between beautiful, positive thoughts and physical health. Now you can never accompany me, and even if you do, you can never defeat me! Mr. Cancer, you may be scary but you are in *my* control, because I am your Master!

People were stunned to watch this skit and see the importance of positive thinking so beautifully demonstrated. Many got goose pimples on their bodies while watching it. It was very emotional too. A few women in the audience had tears running down their cheeks.

Meeraben, with her deep and soothing voice, was superb in acting. For Maya, it wasn't acting at all. It was her own, real-life experience, and therefore, she had poured all her emotions in the demonstration.

Anita and Dr. Vimal got up from their chairs and started applauding for Maya and Meeraben; they just couldn't control their own enthusiasm. The whole audience joined them spontaneously in their applause.

The session for that day was declared adjourned by the organizers. There was a long line up of people for registering in the forthcoming sessions on Visualization Technique.

•••

Cancer–It is my Teacher!

A session for discussing 'advantages of positive thinking to health' was going on in a hall. The number of people attending such types of tutorial sessions had gone up to such a phenomenal level that the room dedicated in Maya's bungalow for such lectures was no longer sufficient. Therefore, with Anita's help, a hall was rented specially for these sessions. Anita and Maya were the main organizers of these lectures. The main speaker for today's session was Meeraben, the psychotherapist. It was in the presence of Dr. Vimal.

Meeraben entered the hall and saw around. It was a big hall, packed to capacity with people, mostly women, women of all ages, shapes and sizes. They were all sitting on the floor. In one quick glance at their clothing and the gold jewelry or lack thereof, she could assess that they were from all economic strata of the society. The hall was actually the dining area of the same community college where Dr. Deven Dixit had been teaching before his retirement. The floors were cleared off all the chairs and tables and covered with some simple, rolling-type jute mats, for sitting on the floor. This was a very popular and one of most efficient ways of accommodating a much larger audience in a smaller area.

A few men were standing around, bordering the seated crowd of women on the floor. Meeraben walked across the hall led by Anita and Maya to the far side of the hall. There was a small piece of carpet laid out on the floor, with a single microphone on a stand in the middle of it. She was requested to sit in front of the microphone, on the floor.

That was no problem for Meeraben as she would always sit in a lotus position on the floor. She sat comfortably in front of the microphone. Maya introduced Meeraben to the audience and then walked towards Anita and Dr. Vimal and sat with them who were also sitting on the floor on the rolled mats

Meeraben cleared her throat, and dismounting the microphone from its stand and taking it in her hand, greeted the audience in her usual deep, soothing voice. She thanked them for coming all the way from various areas of the city for this lecture, and started to address the topic of the speech. "Today's lecture, as you all know, is arranged specifically to talk to you all about the advantages of positive thinking related to your health. And it is primarily focused on breast cancer. As you all know, I am not a doctor or a cancer specialist like Dr. Vimal, nor am I a breast cancer survivor like Maya or Anita. I am a psychotherapist. As Dr. Vimal calls me sometimes, I am a doctor of the mind!"

In spite of a big crowd, there was a pin drop silence in the hall. Dr. Vimal, Maya and Anita looked around and could actually feel the eagerness on people's faces. As organizers of this event, they felt satisfied.

Meeraben started stressing the various points of positive thinking, and how helpful it can be, narrating a few anecdotes. She was a motivational speaker and with her voice, her speech had a spell binding effect on the audience. She was about to ride on a high tide of emotion in her speech, intending to take everyone in the audience with her, when right in the middle of her speech, one man darted in the direction towards someone sitting on the floor and with his hands thrown out in air, started speaking in a very loud voice in that direction. "This is exactly what I have been telling you over and over again. Don't you get it? "

As though not at all cognizant of the crowd around him, he kept on shouting out in one specific direction,

"It is *you* who has to decide to get well, it is *you* who has to take the reigns of your life in your hands..."

He was emphasizing the '*you*' part of his sentences with both his voice and his right fore finger pointing out straight at someone in the audience.

Meeraben looked startled. So did everybody. They all started looking, first in the direction of that man and then in the direction of his pointed finger. He was looking at a young, frail looking woman who was sitting on the floor. She looked startled too for a moment and then started to cry silently. There was a toddler sleeping soundly on her lap. The toddler also woke up and started crying with a loud sound. The whole audience was taken aback with this commotion.

Dr. Vimal looked at the man and the frail woman he was talking to. They were none other than Das and Virani. Dr. Vimal knew instantly what was going on. She hurriedly approached Das and tried to take him out of the hall. Maya and Anita darted towards Virani and helped her get up with her toddler and walk outside the hall. Amma, who was sitting next to Virani, quietly got up and followed them too. However, just as Virani managed to reach the door, Das ran towards her, hugged her tightly with her crying child squished in between them, and started saying,

"Rani, this is exactly what you need to do, don't you understand? Believe in yourself, like that nice lady said, have faith in your doctor and the treatments, don't let the disease defeat you. Do it for me, Rani, do it for our baby, and do it soon, Rani, time is running out on us now...."

Dr. Vimal tried her best to quiet him down, but she was not successful. He had become too emotional, and obviously swept away with Meeraben's speech on positive thinking.

In utter dismay, people watched this drama for a minute or so. They were all staring at the two people, Das and Virani, alternately. But those two seemed totally oblivious to the surroundings and the people around them. Dr. Vimal and Anita finally managed to get this young family out of the hall and out of everyone's sight. Maya took the microphone in her hands and in a commanding voice requested everyone to quiet down, apologized to Meeraben and when everything was settled down, requested her to continue the speech.

Meeraben spoke for almost an hour after the incident. However, that scene never left her or any body's mind. What everyone had seen there was almost a dumbfounding, real life drama. It was very intense too. The whole thing had an intriguing effect on people, especially Meeraben. The lecture was over and people slowly dispersed. Dr. Vimal, Maya and Anita were also getting ready to leave the place when Meeraben approached them and requested them to brief her up with some details about this young family, and if possible, arrange to meet them in person.

"Didn't that young woman, Virani, attend our very first meeting in the community centre when we talked about organizing and starting a Cancer Support group, doctor?" Anita asked.

Dr. Vimal nodded.

"She sounded so calm and balanced at that time, didn't she?" Maya asked.

Dr. Vimal nodded again.

"Yes, she certainly did, but lately, things have gone a little haywire with her..." Dr. Vimal said.

"You saw that young man, he is her husband. His name is Das Prakash Rao."

Dr. Vimal started telling Anita, Maya and Meeraben about Virani.

She obviously wasn't too concerned with the doctor-patient confidentiality, as those three women were her team members in the fight against breast cancer for all breast cancer patients.

"He is a middle management executive in a local bank. He calls her Rani. That toddler on her lap is their only son and the older woman is his mother, they call her Amma. Rani worked in the same bank as a teller. Six months after the birth of their son, she starting working again. During her maternity leave, she was nursing the baby. In spite of weaning the baby completely, she found out later that she still has some lumps in her breasts. Thinking that the lumps must be of milk, she ignored them for quite some. When she noticed that those lumps wouldn't go away, she disclosed this to her mother-in-law and then her husband. That's when Das brought her to me for a full check up. She has been my patient since then."

After narrating Virani's complete story to the three women, Dr. Vimal abruptly became very quiet and just took a few long breaths.

"Why, what happened doctor?" Anita asked her.

"To tell you honestly, ladies, after her check-up, I was absolutely flabbergasted to find out what she has developed..." Dr. Vimal said.

"What does she have, doctor?" Maya asked.

"This young woman has developed a relatively rare kind of breast cancer, it's called Inflammatory Breast cancer. And her cancer is fairly advanced. Not much can be done for her, really."

Dr. Vimal looked visibly upset after mentioning the disease to Meeraben, Anita and Maya, which disturbed those three women too.

Dr. Vimal took a few long and deep breaths again, and said,

"It is always at Das's insistence that Virani reluctantly comes to me for some consultation. It is also at his insistence, that she joined our group, but her heart is not in it, I can see that very clearly. And amazing as it may sound but she has refused to take any of my treatment for her cancer. According to him, her interest is somewhere else since the diagnosis of the disease..."

"Where?" All three of them inquired.

"Well, it's a life-changing medical diagnosis for them, right? So I advised her to quit her job and focus completely on the treatment of cancer. She doesn't want to do either of them, though. According to Das, she is completely changed since the diagnosis of the disease. Cancer has damaged her sense of self. She has denied herself a normal life as a wife or a mother. She feels hopeless, and feels her life is finished already...."

When Dr. Vimal was telling them all this, Maya remembered her own days after Praful's demise in a flash of that second. And so did Meeraben, remembering Maya's state of mind at that time. They both exchanged glances at each other for a second and quickly turned towards what the doctor was saying.

"It has already killed all her dreams, I can see that. Do you all recall her tantrums a few days ago in one of our sessions?" Dr. Vimal asked them. They all nodded.

"Yes, yes, I remember them very well. Virani kept on yelling about her young age and called you a liar. She even questioned your medical expertise when you said breast cancer is primarily an older age disease." Anita said.

"Yes, and another myth she firmly believes in is that breast cancer happens to women who are not virgins on their wedding nights..."

Dr. Vimal said.

"What?" All three of them exclaimed.

"Yes. That's why she was stressing that point on that day as well, do you remember?"

"Yes, I remember." Meeraben said.

"How ignorant! Who told her all this nonsense...?" Anita asked, not directing it at any one specifically.

"That must be the figment of her own imagination, obviously. No where is it written in literature or said by any doctor or a scientist." Dr. Vimal said.

"I think, that sometime, somewhere, if somebody writes something about breast cancer and happens to write something about multiple sex partners in the same context, especially in the West, then that can be totally misunderstood by some people..." Meeraben said.

"Especially in the East." Anita joined Meeraben in completing what she was saying.

"That's so true." Maya said.

"Being a virgin on the wedding night has absolutely nothing to do with getting this disease, I tell her all the time, but she doesn't believe me." Dr. Vimal continued.

"Not just that, every time I say something to her about the treatment for cancer, she ignores me completely and pulls this tantrum of crying and yelling loudly. Fortunately, Das is very sensible; he is not giving up so easily."

"Oh Good for him." Anita said.

"As of late, Virani has taken up a totally different activity for herself, I was told by Das." Dr. Vimal said with a very serious face.

"What kind of activity?" All three of them asked almost simultaneously.

"She wants Das, her husband, to meet some girl of *her* choice from their native town in Karnataka, and marry her."

"What?" All of them almost screamed as though struck with lightening.

"Yes. Virani feels that she herself arranging a girl, who would be a good wife to Das, a good mother to her son, and a good daughter-in-law to her mother-in-law, would let her die in peace." Dr. Vimal said.

"No..., really?" The three women almost didn't believe Dr. Vimal.

"That's true. I couldn't believe it either. When I heard it for the first time, I was thunderstruck myself, just like you three are.

'Is she for real?' I wondered. But I know her mental condition now. She's making a big fuss about her medical condition now. She says all the time that that's going to kill her shortly. I understand her frustration. I just can't imagine what her husband must be going through. He complains all the time to me about this hideous activity of his wife finding a girl for him, but he is afraid that she would become hysterical. As it is, she complains to him that he is not giving her a few good and happy last months of her life. I can see he loves her very much but he can't do anything anymore."

Anita, Maya and Meeraben were quiet for a few seconds, looking very serious and sad.

"What about her mother-in-law? Virani seemed quite attached to her when I took her out of the hall..." Anita asked.

"Well, she sympathizes with her completely, but apparently, advises Das to do what his wife wishes to do." Dr. Vimal informed.

"What do you mean?" They all asked the doctor.

"I mean, that old woman, although she loves Virani, is quite willing and actually helping Virani find a girl from Karnataka for Das."

"Oh my God!" Maya said.

"Unbelievable, really. We need to do something for this young woman, and soon. We need to put some sense in her." Anita said.

"I think I can work on her. Dr. Vimal. Please give me that assignment. I will try to work on her..."

Meeraben looked like she was ready to take upon the challenge; a big challenge of putting some sense into Virani's head.

"Meeraben, you will be facing an uphill battle, you realize that, right? Virani is convinced that her cancer is going to kill her very soon. She is ignoring everyone's requests, everyone's advice, refusing to take medical treatment as well. She insists that she will die in peace only if she accomplishes this mission of finding a girl for her husband and therefore she is focusing all her energies on it. She is actually in a rush to do this." Dr. Vimal warned Meeraben.

"Dr. Vimal, I want to start my psychotherapy work on this woman right away. I don't think we should let her waste her precious time in all this nonsense." Meeraben seemed confident.

"My best wishes to you, Meeraben, remember this patient is a case of total absence of hope, coupled with grotesque ignorance. She does not seem to realize the seriousness of her disease or the emergency of medical help for her well-being. She seems completely oblivious to the crisis in her life."

Dr. Vimal warned Meeraben, but deep down, she felt happy for Virani and confident in Meeraben's skills. All of them left with heavy hearts for Virani.

"Ohm..."

The mantra in Meeraben's deep and soothing voice resounded in the room. She was sitting in her usual lotus position with her eyes closed. In front of her, sitting on the floor were Maya, Anita, Das and Virani. It was with great difficulty that Das was able to convince Virani to visit Meeraben. After listening to her lecture in the previous week, she some what reluctantly agreed to meet Meeraben. That was a good start.

Meeraben was determined to work on Virani's psychology. Maya and Anita had volunteered to help her in that difficult project. All three of them had been overtaken by awe and grief after hearing the tragic story of Virani's family from Dr. Vimal. A day was decided to meet at Meeraben's clinic, and accordingly, Dr. Vimal had suggested Das to take Virani to the clinic.

"Kindly repeat after me, everybody..." Meeraben said. Maya and Anita started repeating after her, and in a few minutes, Das joined them too. But Virani kept quiet. She looked a little apprehensive, a little timid too. There were only four of them in the room at the time. That's how it was purposely arranged.

"This is how we start the Visualization Technique, in a completely serene atmosphere, with this mantra, as it has a tremendous meditative quality." Meeraben explained to Das and Virani, and started reciting the mantra again. Maya, Anita and Das repeated after her again. Virani listened to them, but still looked reluctant to participate in the process.

"Would you like to try reciting Ohm, Virani?" Meeraben asked her directly, but she shook her head.

"It might make you feel better, just try it for a minute..."

Meeraben insisted but Virani shook her head vigorously this time, indicating she was not at all interested in participating in any of that.

Ignoring her reluctance to join them, Meeraben still continued reciting the mantra and the other three people kept on repeating after her, all of them with their eyes closed. During the recitation, Meeraben just once opened her eyes and glanced at Virani. She was looking at her wristwatch, checking the time. That gave a clear indication to Meeraben that Virani was totally disinterested in trying out the new technique or even being there. She closed her eyes again and while reciting the mantra, decided to try a different route to get Virani involved in the process.

"Maya, would you kindly assume Virani's role now?" Meeraben stopped reciting and gently asked Maya.

Maya was ready, she nodded willingly. But hearing her own name, Virani looked a little startled. Das looked a little confused too. Maya got up and stood on the right side of the room, facing Anita, Das and Virani.

"And I will assume the role of Virani's Cancer. The Cancer will be talking to Virani now..." Meeraben got up and stood on the left side of the room, facing Anita, Das and Virani.

The moment she said 'Virani's Cancer...' Virani got even a bigger jolt. She looked quite curious and started watching the two women, standing in front of her, with keen eyes.

Maya in Virani's role, started talking to Meeraben, who had assumed the role of Virani's Cancer.

Virani :I am soon going to die.

Cancer :That's what you have been saying since the day of your diagnosis. Ever since then, you are behaving as though you have been my prey, and it's only a matter of short time. You just can't think of anything else, anything except your death, can you?

Virani :No, that's not true. I'm going to die very soon, that's for sure, but my death is not the only thing on my mind. There is another thought that's been on my mind too, a very important one.

Cancer :What's that?

Virani :I am looking for a good woman, who would be a good wife for my Das and a loving mother to my Kittu.

Maya and Meeraben momentarily looked at Das and Virani, they both looked disturbed, but they did not get up and leave. 'The drama could continue', they thought and quickly assumed the roles again.

Cancer :What? What are you saying?

Virani :That's right. Ever since you imposed your presence in my life and invaded my body, I can't think of anything else. I have made it my mission, you know, and I'm trying very hard to attain it.

Cancer :I see. So, since I invaded your life, as you put it, you accepted immediately that you are going to die. Is that it? You don't want to fight me, don't want to defeat me, you don't want to even try to win over me, is that it? This reminds me of someone who had the same defeatist attitude just like you. She was also waiting for her death, same like you. She didn't love her husband or her child either.

Virani :You arrogant scoundrel, what nonsense are you talking?

Cancer :Hey, there's no need to swear at me, okay? I am saying what I am noticing. You really don't love your husband and your son, otherwise you wouldn't wait for your death like this. You would try every way to make sure that you live as long as possible for them.

Virani :Oh ho, ho...! What a gem of wisdom? How pretentious of you? First you invade my life, get ready to kill me, then you become judgmental and question my love for my dear husband and son; and as if that is not bad enough, you pretend to teach me words of wisdom in that condescending tone of yours...

Cancer :Okay, in that case let me ask you directly, do you love your husband?

Virani :Of course, I do! What kind of stupid question is this? You have no idea how much I love my Das.

Cancer :And how about your son?

Virani :Another foolish question! Of course I love my son. Kittu is our love child. We call him the blossoming of our love, mine and Das's.

Cancer :In that case, you silly woman, when you have two such loving people in your life, how is it that you are waiting for your death? I know I am growing in you, but why aren't you giving me a fight? Why not? You call me foolish, but look who really is behaving foolishly? You know fully well who my real enemies are. My victim's self confidence, faith in her healthy and loving family support and friends and their loving support, these are all my bitter enemies. They build up her positive attitude. And that is my most fierce enemy! I always wish to live and grow, but with a healthy attitude, you can certainly overpower my wish. Attitude is very vital, my dear woman. Wake up now, come out of that jungle of hopeless, dismal thoughts...

Virani :Stop it, stop right this minute. I am appalled at your series of accusations. You accuse me of feeling hopeless, you accuse me of not having a positive attitude, but have you looked at yourself anytime? Have you assessed yourself? If not, let me tell you, Mr. Know-it all! You are one of the deadliest of all types of breast cancers. Once you get in some one, you don't give that person any chance. It is *you* who made me feel this way. In addition to that, you didn't give me even a simple indication of your development in me.'

Cancer :Well, yes, as you put it, I may be a deadly one; and no, I didn't give you even a simple indication of my development. Both are true, but the only answer I have for both is, *'it is your fate'*!

Virani :Oh, so now it's my fate...

Cancer :Yes, it is your fate. Let me tell you something that I have observed with you humans. Most of you humans believe that every human life is controlled by two major factors. The first and the foremost is fate and the second is her or his genetic make-up. No one can alter or run away from these two controlling factors, according to your belief, isn't it?

Virani :So, what you are saying is; it's mainly my own fate that was responsible for you developing in me, is that it?

Cancer :Well, yes, but let me also tell you something very important; I'm sure you will be happy to hear it.

Virani :What's that?

Cancer :Although your fate and genetic structure are not in your hands, since these are God-given certainties of your life, as you humans put it; you still have one very, very powerful tool in your own hands. And that is your *Free Will*. My dear woman, free will is also a fact of human life. You can utilize this tool to overpower or at least modify many turns of your life dictated by fate or anything else. In your case, fate and genes dictated my presence, cancer, in you, agreed; but with your own free will, you can take the best medical treatment, employ the best possible therapy, utilize your family support to the best level and with all such positive steps, defeat me completely. Honestly, when and in whom I should develop is really not in my hands, you know? But when I develop in humans, I very earnestly try to teach them this valuable lesson. And I have noticed that most of them do learn this lesson from me very quickly.

Virani :But not all of them?

Cancer :No, not all. Occasionally, I do come across an odd one, like...

Virani :Like me?

Cancer :Well, yes, like you. But fortunately such odd ball students also eventually come around on the right track, for they have their family members to help them learn this lesson.

Maya and Meeraben both looked at Virani momentarily. Noticing that she was totally engrossed in their presentation, they continued with it.

Virani :My, my, aren't you sounding totally pedantic, and quite conceited too?

Cancer :Probably, yes.

Virani :Then tell me this, Mr. Schoolmaster, supposing I do learn this valuable lesson from you and give you a fight, as you put it, still death is inevitable for me, isn't it?

Cancer :Oh, ho, ho...now look who is pretending to be a great philosopher? My dear woman, this is the most profound, age-old statement. There is nothing new in it. Death is inevitable to all mortals! Then how can you avoid it? You obviously didn't get my point. The point I'm trying to make here is that, those in whom I develop, they realize the mortality of their life instantly. With my advent, it suddenly dawns upon them that there's an end to their life. Their life is not endless or eternal. It is almost as if they wake up with a jolt from a deep sleep, deep sleep of total ignorance, shall we say...

Virani :Hum...

Cancer :Hey, can I share a secret with you?

Virani :What's that?

Cancer :These humans, who wake up instantly from their deep sleep, and that's because of me of course...

Virani :Of course...

Cancer :They start living their life so fully and beautifully, it almost amuses me to see that change in them. They try to *live every moment* of their life. And as I said earlier, that's solely because of this realization of mortality that I teach them. On one hand, they give me a fight with all possible ammunition, and on the other, they try to fulfill all their desires. Those, who love nature, go for nature hikes; those, who love painting, do painting; those, who love to travel, go on site-seeing journeys; and so on. They refuse to postpone anything anymore. It's so amusing to me, I tell you.

Virani :Amusing? Why do you find it *amusing*?

Cancer :Well, whenever I see them busy in all such activities, I just laugh to myself with amusement. I really find it funny and equally perplexing as to; why does this, *supposedly the most intelligent species of the universe, need someone like me, a deadly disease, to realize that they are all mortals?* Why? Don't they know the simple Truth of the universe that anything that is born is sure to die sometime? Don't they?

Virani :Hum...that...well, yes, they do, actually.

Cancer :Then why do they realize it only after they come face to face with *me*, the Cancer? As soon as I enter their body, why do they behave as though suddenly some alarm clock just went on and woke them up? Umm, why? *Am I some kind of an alarm that they need*?

Virani :Well, I don't know about that, but what you say is certainly something to ponder upon.

Cancer :Honestly, you humans crack me up! You need *me* to teach you this basic thing of life. Ha, ha, ha!

Virani :Well, don't get so amused at our folly. Now, tell me one more thing, Mr. Alarm clock, what if your alarm doesn't sound in time?

Cancer :There you go again, talking negatively. Do I end anyone's life instantly? Do I? Don't I give some time to every person for a fight? Don't I? I am not that cruel, you know. In many, many instances I give plenty of time to all my hosts to give me a fair fight. Many do, but a few don't. To those who don't, I want to tell them over and over again, 'come-on people, don't despair, don't give up, fight with me'; stressing upon the fact that, that is something totally, totally in their hands, and their hands alone, not mine.

The dialogue between Meeraben and Maya was barely over when Das turned to Virani and holding her tightly in his arms, said, "Rani, did you hear that? Did you hear that Rani? It's all in your hands and your hands alone darling..."

His eyes were full of tears, ready to overflow anytime. And so were Virani's.

They both stood there in a close hug, with tears running down their cheeks continuously for a few minutes, while Anita, Maya and Meeraben watched them silently, hoping this presentation achieved some success.

•••

A Forum for Women

"How was your breast cancer diagnosed?" One woman was asking another. They both looked like they were in their sixties.

"It was diagnosed with a mammogram." She answered.

"What's that?" The first woman asked.

"It's a kind of an x-ray photograph they take of your breasts..." The second woman tried to answer.

"But isn't x-ray used only for bones and skeletons?" The first woman asked again.

"I honestly don't know how it works." The second woman was not all that knowledgeable about mammograms, either.

"I can tell you briefly about it, if you wish..." A younger woman overheard their conversation and volunteered to join in the conversation. "A mammogram is an x-ray test of the breasts, as you said. It is used to screen for breast problems, such as a lump, and to see whether a lump is fluid-filled or a solid mass."

"What does it do exactly?" The two older women asked the younger one.

"You see, many small tumors can be seen on a mammogram before they can be felt by hand to a woman or her doctor. So, to screen for breast cancer in women without symptoms or to detect breast cancer in women with symptoms at early stage, a mammogram is always preferred. Cancer can be treated and controlled when it is discovered in an early stage, isn't it?" The younger woman answered.

"Is there any risk in getting a mammogram?" The first older woman asked again.

"That I really don't know." The younger woman answered.

"Oh, I know that." A fourth woman joined the group. "Mammography technique uses, after all, some kind of mild radiation. So, there is always a slight risk of damage to the breast cells or breast tissue due to low levels of radiation used for this test, isn't it? But, the risk of damage from the x-ray is very low compared with the potential benefits of the test."

"Yes, yes, that's for sure." Rest of the women agreed.

This conversation was taking place in a session that Anita and Maya had organized in the usual place, in Maya's house. This session was meant only for women, for sharing their experiences with each other. There was no definite structure or an agenda for today's session; instead, anyone who wished to share their experience was encouraged to do so in a general, friendly conversation with others.

The room was packed with women of all ages, and not necessarily all were breast cancer patients or survivors. There were quite a few women who themselves did not have breast cancer, but knew of someone who did, in their family and friend circles. A few women were wearing black scarves on their heads. Obviously, they were undergoing chemotherapy and covering the absence of hair on their heads.

"Maya, you are so lucky," someone said when she saw Maya approaching the group.

"Lucky? How so?" Maya was unaware what was being talked about in the group.

"We were talking about the mammogram..." One woman from the group informed her.

"And, we were thinking about you, you are so lucky, you didn't have to lose your entire breast..." Another woman said to Maya.

"Oh that? Yes, that's for sure. It's my daughter who takes the credit for it. She insisted I see Dr. Vimal and that's when I had it done. The mammogram detected a tiny lump in my breast. When tested it was found to be malignant. Fortunately it was at a very early stage, so I got away with just lumpectomy." Maya said.

"Were you there when this psychotherapist, what's her name..." One woman said to another in a different group, sitting in a different location within the room.

"Her name is Meeraben." The other woman answered.

Both these women were very well dressed and looked like they were also over sixty years of age.

"Yes, Meeraben. When she conducted a special session on a new technique called Visualization Technique, were you there?"

"Yes, I was. And it was simply fantastic. I am going to register for her sessions. I think that'll help me. Perhaps you should join it too. You know, sometimes I feel that it's *me* who invited my breast cancer."

"Why do you say that?"

"Ever since I was a little girl, I had this habit of trying to do everything perfectly, no short cuts. Everyone called me a 'little Miss Perfectionist.' As I grew up, that habit grew too, and before I knew it, I became an obsessive, compulsive worker."

"Yes, I believe that. I have seen your house, it's spotless, your children were always very well dressed up, and you took them to a million places to learn different things. And the meals? You always took extra efforts to prepare full, well balanced meals. Never any shortcuts, like we do. And you worked outside home on a regular job too. I often used to wonder, 'where does this woman get this much time and energy'?"

"Well, all that hit me finally. I got totally exhausted. Completely burnt out, may be. With not enough sleep and rest, my immunity started dwindling down. Dr. Vimal said that exhaustion didn't cause the cancer, but coupled with my stress, it didn't help me either. Now she has given me strict orders to take a minimum of seven hours of sleep at nights and a few minutes rest during the daytime, as a part of the medication."

"So, do you?"

"Yes, since this devil of a disease entered me..."

"That's good."

"You know, before Meeraben starts her session, she always asks women what makes them happy?"

"Really?"

"I think I am going to say, 'a comfortable bed and a soft pillow...'"

Both the women laughed at this, and then decided to register themselves for the sessions on Visualization Technique conducted by Meeraben.

"This mastectomy is so very inconvenient to me, you have no idea..."

"What do you mean, inconvenient?" A few women had formed a small group and were chatting in yet another location in the room. Most of the women in this group looked quite athletic and seemed like they were barely over forty years of age.

"You know I played badminton every evening for at least two hours before my breast cancer, right? But since this breast surgery, I can barely play two games now."

"How come?"

"I'm right handed, and guess what? I lost my breast precisely on the right side. My hand hurts like crazy when I play longer..."

"The same with me too. It's such an obstruction for me too." Another woman joined the group.

"What do you play?"

"I am an instructor for javelin throwing."

"Oh, really? That's wonderful."

"Were you the champion in college days?"

"Yes."

"I think I have heard about you. Oh, you were good..."

"Thank you, but not any more. With my right breast gone to cancer, it has imposed a limit on my right hand activity. Honestly, I am not sure if I can continue my instruction in javelin throwing, any more."

"At least, you all have vigorous games that you worry about. In my case, I am a calligraphy artist, and still I can't pursue it anymore..." Yet another woman started talking with this group.

"Your right breast too?" They asked her.

"No, it's my left one." She answered.

"Then?"

"But I'm left handed." She said.

"Oh, no..." All of them said together and laughed mildly.

"Are you women doing your arm exercises regularly?" Anita overheard their conversation and walked towards the group, asking everyone who complained about their left and right hands hurting.

"What's that?" The whole group turned to Anita.

"Soon after the mastectomy, Dr. Vimal advises all her patients to do a special exercise that she calls 'wall climbing'. It helps muscles around the breast area to strengthen. This is how it's done."

Then Anita walked to the nearest wall and standing with her face to the wall and feet about six inches away from the wall, she said,

"To begin this exercise, stand like this, facing the wall. Then place your hands on the wall, shoulder width apart and on the same level with each other. Slowly 'walk or crawl' your hands up the wall until you feel slight tension. Stop and hold this position for about thirty seconds." A couple of women from the group joined her and started copying her.

"Remember to breathe, ladies. Now, slowly push your hands up the wall a little bit further."

"That's good." Anita said.

Slowly, all the women in that group joined them in the exercise.

"If you can go high enough, put one hand over the other and hold. Slowly release the stretch and walk the hands down to the original position. Repeat with the other hand on the top."

"How many times do we do this exercise?" Someone asked her.

"Oh, I would say at least fifteen to twenty repeats every time and preferably two or three times per day. I did it, I still do it and that seems to help me a lot."

"Which side did you lose madam?"

"Left side." Anita answered and smiled at the group. Just then she spotted Ritu talking to another group of women. She walked towards them and joined them in their conversation.

"Why me? I kept asking this question."

Ritu was talking to a group of women who were around the same age as hers.

"I was angry when I was diagnosed with my breast cancer. I was on the top of my career in music and I have two young daughters; they both have aspirations of becoming musicians too. Do I have enough time to teach them music with this condition?" Ritu said within a sad tone.

"Yes, you are right. I had exactly the same feelings. Why me? What did I do to get this horrible disease? And that too, so early in life? I have three young children you know. Do I have enough time to raise them?"

The woman became a little emotional.

"Yah, same here. I have two boys, both under ten years of age. And here I am, diagnosed with this horrible disease..."

This woman also became a little emotional.

"You know, I never thought *I* would get cancer. I knew my next door neighbor got breast cancer. Shortly after that, I came to know that one of my cousins got it too. But I never imagined that *I could be the next victim...*" Another woman said with tears in her eyes.

There was a brief silence in the group.

"How do you handle this feeling, Anita?" Ritu asked her as she saw her approaching the group.

Anita was known by all to be a very compassionate social worker, and considered to be the wise one by many.

"I overheard your conversation. What you ladies are discussing is one hundred percent right, actually. The first thought that comes to our mind is 'why me?' right?" Anita asked the women in the group. "Yes. I felt that 'someone up there' was punishing me." One woman said, with a tone of distress.

"I always questioned, 'what did I do to deserve this calamity in life?" Another woman said, sounding a bit angry.

"Oh, I know the feeling. You are all right in feeling this way. You feel angry and helpless at the same time." Anita started talking.

"Believe me, I felt exactly the same way when mine was diagnosed. But then I realized, cancer doesn't have its favorites. It picks up any one, unfortunately even the innocent bystanders, if you will! There is no one invincible. When it develops in you, you have no choice but to accept it."

"Hum..." A couple of women let out an exclamation with a disconsolate tone.

"Well, you just accept it, I suppose." Ritu said.

"Grudgingly, of course!" One woman said.

"Well, ladies, to tell you all honestly, I have adopted a bit of a philosophical attitude for that. You see, cancer creates fear among us, and that fear is fear of death; more like, fear of an early or untimely death, right? You try to learn to cope with that fear." Anita said. "That's hard." Someone said.

"Yes, no doubt about that." Anita continued,

"But employ your own way for coping with it. Each person's way of coping with fear could be different. For example, Ritu, you could start the music training for your daughters immediately, without wasting any time. That will keep you fully occupied mentally. As the goal of training them comes closer and closer, the degree of fear will automatically become lesser and lesser. The biggest advantage in all such activities would be that you will not have time to dwell on cancer or its fear. Do you agree, dear?"

Ritu nodded with her eyes full of tears and hugged Anita.

Anita continued,

"The very same thing applies to you two young mothers as well. I would say, start getting involved with your children as much as possible, in their school projects, in games they play, in everything. Read them different books. Children have an excellent memory, you know. They don't forget what they learn during their childhood. Try not to leave any 'could have's or 'should have's while raising your children, especially after diagnosis of cancer. Children are your legacy, and they will remember you all their lives if you get involved with them."

The two women were quietly listening to Anita's wisdom.

Anita felt good that her advice was proving to be quite useful to these women. She continued.

"And do get some spiritual help for yourself too. Personally for me, I believe in the concept of the Supreme Being, or God, as some call it. That faith alone can overpower the fear of death."

All the women in that group felt that they received some solace from Anita.

"And during all this time, do not forget to get proper treatment for your disease, okay?" She smiled at all of them and walked towards another group of women.

There were only three women in this group and they were all standing quietly, not talking to any one or with each other, just watching everybody in other groups.

"How is it going, ladies?" Anita inquired in an effort to get them involved in talking with each other. But instead of saying anything to her, they just shrugged their shoulders and kept quiet.

"Madam, could I ask you a personal question?" One of the three women finally opened her mouth.

"Oh sure." Anita said.

"When your cancer was detected and you had surgery, did your husband move out of your bedroom, permanently?" Anita noticed that the woman who asked this question had her eyes full of tears. She could see a lot of pain in that woman. And perhaps in the other two women too, for that was the reason they were so quiet, not talking to anyone about anything.

What was Anita to answer to the question? Should she have told her how Deven was behaving, or how he had changed completely from his original self or that they had not had any intimate relationship, since her surgery? But she said nothing of the sort. She just couldn't.

In stead, she just smiled at them and as if she never heard the question, moved on to another group of women, who were discussing the breast removal surgery and its pro-s and con-s! She joined the group with a question,

"Do most of you have had a surgery...?"

Most of the women nodded to her question.

"With one breast removed, does that make any of you feel a little lop-sided, with one breast gone, that is?" One woman asked the group.

"Yes, I do." Someone from the group said.

"I do too, but only after I take off my bra." Another woman said.

"What do you mean?" the first woman asked her.

"I wear a special bra. It has one cup fully padded. That way, it looks normal, and more importantly, that helps me feel good."

"You know, I am seriously thinking of reconstructive plastic surgery now. My husband keeps saying, 'it doesn't make any difference to me, one breast, two breasts', but..." some other woman started talking.

"Hey, if your husband doesn't mind it, why are you doing it?" Someone interrupted her.

"I want it for my sake. I can't look at myself in the mirror like this. Even during bath, I still get an eerie feeling putting soap on the empty side." That woman said and then shuddered.

"I know exactly what you mean. It's an awful feeling. All these years, you have two breasts, a nice pair, and now suddenly, there is only one..."This woman also shuddered.

"An only and a lonely one..." Some other woman tried to joke.

"Plastic surgery is improved so much, there's so much advancement happening in it, I say, why not?"

"Yah, why not?" Many women agreed to the idea of having reconstructive plastic surgery for them.

"I think I'll have to have this surgery, really." One woman sounded quite serious when she talked. "My husband doesn't understand my feelings. It makes me feel incomplete, a less of a woman, when he comes to me at night time, if you know what I mean..."

Many among them agreed with her.

All this while, Anita was quietly listening to them, trying to grasp their feelings and emotions and assessing their marital situations and love relations; at the same time, comparing them with her own relationship with Deven. She had seen pain in the eyes of a woman earlier, who she felt definitely belonged to her own category. She was sure there were many more like her in today's forum.

-'A session for men, especially for the husbands of breast cancer victims, is an absolute must,' she thought to herself and decided to organize one with the help from others, and continued listening to the women's talk in the same group.

The women were still busy talking about the plastic surgery.

"Hey, do you know that lady over there. She somehow looks familiar..." someone pointed to Shaina, who was helping Maya and Anita that day.

"Yes, I know her. Of course, I don't mean personally. She is one of the top models of our country, do you know that? She is pretty much in every magazine and on TV for some advertisement or another... " One woman answered.

"What is she doing here, with a perfect figure like that?"

"Well, someone told me that her breasts are not real..." One woman said while lowering her voice, as if she was sharing a big secret.

"What?"

"Um, Hum..."

"You mean she is also a breast cancer survivor?"

"Yes, she is, however, indirectly ..." Anita informed them. All the women, who had seen and admired Shaina in her various commercials, were stunned to get this new and unexpected piece of information about her. "Why don't I call her here and request her to talk to you all. Would you like that?"

"Yes."

"Yah."

"Oh sure, if it's possible..."

"Would love it, really..."

The response from the women was overwhelming.

Anita decided to call Shaina and have her talk to the entire room full of women. It was Shaina's turn to address the women's forum that day.

Shaina stood in front of everybody. She was beautifully dressed up in a light blue pant suit with fine red stripes, with a bright red belt at the waist. She was wearing bright red colored, high heeled sandals and the same colored small bow in her hair. In that custom-made, designer suit with its right accessories, she was looking absolutely stunning. All the women were staring at her.

Shaina started talking directly to all the women.

"I know you are all looking at me right now, assessing everything I am wearing, right from my hair clips to my sandals. And as you are looking at me with a keen eye, I am noticing a surprise on most of your faces. Many of you, perhaps all of you, must be wondering what am *I, a model with a perfect figure*, doing here. Am I right?" She looked at all the women in the room and saw them nod.

She even heard a few of them, especially those in the front row, utter a few words to that effect.

She smiled and continued.

"The other day when I was trying on some new style of bras, I glimpsed at myself in the changing room mirror, and believe me, I did a double take. Was that gorgeous young woman with the spectacular cleavage really me? I wondered. It's almost ten years now, since I have had my own natural breasts removed, and replaced by these beautiful fake ones..."

The moment she said it, the whole audience felt some kind of a jolt. No one knew about it. She looked at the audience with a confident smile again and said,

"But ladies, I'm convinced that I'm the luckiest woman on Earth. I did lose my natural breasts, yes, but far from fearing that my femininity has disappeared, I feel very fortunate. Thanks to reconstructive surgery, I've attained a beautiful, permanent figure with two brand new breasts that my surgeon designed specially for my height and slim waist. Do you know why I had my natural breasts removed?" There was a pin-drop silence in the room.

"I had my natural breasts removed because they were like a ticking time-bomb for me. There was a very high probability that I'd inherited a defective gene which was confirmed with the genetic testing. That meant that I stood a very high, almost ninety per cent chance of developing breast cancer, compared with the average of less than ten per cent." Shaina looked at the audience again and with a serious face, continued telling her life story.

"I must be three or four years old when my mother died of unknown cause. She was less than forty years of age when she died. When I was ten years of age, my older sister died, again of unknown cause. Two years later, my middle sister died, again of unknown cause. They both were in their late twenties. We were living in a small village in North India, in the foothills of the Himalayas. No one had heard about breast cancer there. People didn't know what cancer meant. Knowing about things like genetics or genetic history was far from imagination of these people."

Women were getting engrossed in Shaina's personal story by now. Shaina continued telling her story.

"By some wonderful turns in my life that was purely a stroke of good luck, I met dear Usha didi. Her place in my life, I honestly can't describe, it's deep down in my heart. I moved with her to Mumbai. Again, with sheer luck, I met Dr. Vimal at Usha didi's place. As you might know, Dr. Vimal is Usha didi's student. When Dr. Vimal came to know about my family history, she, with my request and Usha didi's consent, did the special blood test on me. Dr. Vimal gave me the bad news when the report was back. I did carry the faulty BRCA1 gene. You all know what it is, right?" Shaina looked at the audience.

All the women were listening intently to her life story. A few among them nodded their heads.

"To those of you who don't, I would suggest, do talk to Dr. Vimal. She has a mastery over explaining it beautifully in layperson's terms. Anyways, when I heard this from her, my stomach lurched and I lost my control and went berserk. I knew what lay ahead of me, perhaps the same as Ma and my two older sisters. I was extremely stressed; I wanted some kind of assurance of not getting breast cancer. That's when I took the option of having my healthy breasts removed. I knew instantly that, a preventative mastectomy, as Dr. Vimal calls such type of surgery, would guarantee me my peace of mind. So ladies, I have had a preventative bilateral mastectomy, where you opt to surgically remove your both breasts *before* the onset of the disease. A preventative double mastectomy may sound horrific, but I felt it was the only way to be free of the curse of breast cancer. Much more importantly, I've probably saved my life."

"But then, these beautiful breasts of yours, they look so natural too..." A few women expressed their doubts.

"They *look* natural but they are not. That's the artistic accomplishment of a wonderful surgeon. He was a good friend of Dr. Vimal. The love and trust of my Usha didi and these two wonderful doctors have been incredible."

With this last sentence, Shaina got a little emotional and had to wait for a few seconds to collect herself. She took a few long, deep breaths and continued.

"I took the decision of removing my natural breasts as a prevention of the disease, but the thought disturbed me too much. I started getting nightmares where I would look at my chest and it was empty. No breasts. I started becoming depressed again. Usha didi talked to Dr. Vimal again about my nightmares. That's when Dr. Vimal suggested reconstructive surgery for me, and introduced me to her surgeon friend. I was so relieved when Dr. Vimal and her surgeon friend explained to me that he would build me new breasts at the same time of removing my own breasts. Living without breasts may suit some women, but not me. I was only twenty years of age then. Just imagine, a twenty year-old young woman, how would she feel losing her both breasts?"

Shaina's eyes were full with tears, so were most of the women's in the audience.

She had moved the whole audience with her personal story.

Shaina took a couple of long, lung-full of breaths again and continued her story.

"The surgeon explained the entire procedure, how it's done and all that, to me. From that moment on, I started preparing myself. I was promised by Dr. Vimal that her surgeon friend was one of the finest in his field and the implants he would insert in my breasts' place would never look fake. Lo and behold! That's exactly how it was! Not even a small scar anywhere! To this day, no one, I mean, not a single person knows my secret. You all know that I model bras too, but the most experts in that industry too, have not doubted it." Shaina looked around and said,

"I've never relied on my breasts for sex appeal or anything like that, mind you, but I realize that these fake breasts gave me my confidence and my self-esteem of being a woman. I would suggest every woman who has to undergo mastectomy, for one or both breasts, must have this reconstructive surgery. It does improve the quality of your life."

Then giving a little lighter tone to her story, Shaina said.

"As my new fear-free life started, I changed my name from Shailender to Shaina, and dropped my last name altogether. As you all know, my fake breasts have given me a tremendous opportunity to become one of the most sought after models of our country, and have made me quite rich." With this sentence, she smiled at the audience. All the women spontaneously clapped for her speech. They instantly developed a great liking for her.

"Tell us about your operation please, Shaina." A few of them requested her. Shaina looked at Anita and when she saw Anita gesturing positively, she continued her story-telling.

"Well, this is how it all happened. Usha didi took me to the hospital as per the schedule. Dr. Vimal had booked a room for me which was next to the cancer ward. It was full of women, some were in their thirties, and some were as old as in their seventies. They were all fighting for their lives. It was a chilling experience. Actually that's when it dawned upon me that I also carried genes for breast cancer like them, but I'd been given a choice over my destiny which they'd been denied. Immediately I stopped feeling sorry for myself or for having to lose my breasts. I admit I was frightened but Usha didi stayed with me all night and I managed to sleep." Shaina was creating an elaborate picture of her operation day in front of her audience.

"The next thing I remember was Usha didi calling out my name and Dr. Vimal's voice saying, 'Yes, she's definitely got some shape.'

She was obviously talking to the surgeon. I was lying on the bed, covered with the hospital sheet. I got curious. I wanted to look at what Dr. Vimal was talking about. I knew it was about my breasts. My hands were trembling as I lifted the sheets to look underneath. I didn't know what to expect, a flat chest, a huge scar, a new set of breasts, what? Finally, I managed to look under the sheets. There it was, the miraculous cleavage created by two brand new breasts. They were wrapped in some kind of transparent plastic or something, so I could see them. I was happy. Very, very happy. They looked perfect to me. As it was, I had no pain at that stage because I was full of painkillers. Looking at those perfect breasts, I got a little excited too. I smiled, and seeing me smile, poor dear Usha didi burst into tears." Shaina had to fight her own tears at that moment.

'This girl really loves her Usha didi…' Anita said to Maya softly. And Maya nodded.

"As the excitement of beating the cancer and having new, perfect breasts started wearing out, I started remembering my own natural breasts.

'What happened to my natural breasts?' I inquired with one of the nurses.

'They are in the garbage,' she told me bluntly, pointing at the dustbin.

I felt a momentary stinging pain in my stomach, for I didn't even get to say a final 'goodbye to them'! I shed some tears for my natural breasts. For the next few days, I was horribly uncomfortable because of the surgery. I couldn't move and had to lie on my back. But within a week or so after the operation, my wounds had healed well and I could lift my arms to comb my hair. Usha didi would visit me every single day in the hospital. Two weeks later, my stitches were removed and I came home. My new breasts were so heavy I had to wear a support bra for the first almost three months. It's because large quantities of saline had been pumped in to help stretch my skin. Although, I felt sad to lose my natural breasts, these new ones soon made me feel that they were a part of me.

'These are my breasts from now onwards', I told myself." Shaina waited for a few seconds, took a few breaths and then continued.

"Although I never had cancer, the fear of having it would have haunted me all my life, especially after knowing the fact that I had a family history for it. Now, I can safely say that it's gone for ever. I feel incredibly blessed to have been able to change my destiny, with Usha didi and Dr. Vimal's help. That has given me a new zest for life. I feel lucky. How many other people are that lucky?" Shaina looked at the sky for a moment, as if offering her sincere thanks to the Lord above, and continued,

"I have joined this support group and have promised Dr. Vimal, as well as Anita and Maya and everyone involved, to help in whatever they need my help for. I want to make the most of my life. That's a promise to me and to you all."

In a thunder of claps, Shaina bowed politely with her slender, shapely body, to one and all. The session for that day was over with a great success.

•••

A Forum for Men

"One very important thing we must do is, avoid the numbers game. That's one big mistake I did..." Dr. Deven Dixit was standing and talking to a group of men.

A session organized specially, and only, for men, more like for husbands of the breast cancer patients, was going on in one of the rooms in Maya's house. No woman was in sight in this session. Anita, with the help of her husband, Deven, and Virani's husband, Das, had arranged it specifically for men.

'When you had your breast cancer detected, did your husband move out of your bedroom?' A woman had asked Anita during the women's forum. Since then, that question was resonating in her ears constantly. The pain she had clearly heard in that woman's voice and seen on her face never left her thought.

'Having a forum for only men is a must', she had concluded and with that decisive conclusion, tried to calm her own disturbing thoughts.

"What do you mean, numbers game, Dr. Dixit?" Someone asked.

"I'll explain. When the doctor told us that my wife had developed breast cancer, I was absolutely flabbergasted, but instead of collecting myself and supporting my wife, I, like a bloody fool, blurted out in loud voice, 'oh, that means my wife's days are numbered now.' I can't even imagine what my wife must have felt at the moment." Deven became a little upset and stood still for a moment.

"But fortunately for me, my wife, that's Anita as you all know, is a very strong and courageous woman. She pulled her own tremendous courage and during the entire cancer treatment, gave *me* the courage to pull through it. The doctor had told me in no uncertain terms, 'take care of her', which I did; but I failed miserably in another very important area..." Deven stopped to wipe his brow for a few moments.

"What's that?" Someone from the audience asked again.

"Dr. Vimal had told me very emphatically, 'be very supportive', but I wasn't! I made her feel like less of a woman, if you all know what I mean..."

"I know exactly what you mean, Dr. Dixit..." Another man stood up and started talking to the group.

"When my wife's breast cancer was detected, the first thing I did was, pull my bed out of our bedroom and move it to the next room. I have been sleeping there ever since then. She underwent mastectomy, a complete treatment of radiation and chemotherapy as well. It is almost two years now, but still I am in the room next to hers." The man tried to cover his face with one hand and was on the verge of crying.

"Do you know...", With quivering lips, he continued talking, "I haven't seen her chest yet, I simply can't...I have no guts to look at her...", and then he broke down completely.

The whole atmosphere in the room became quite tense for a few minutes. No one talked.

"Is it the fear that we can not face? Fear of death of our spouse?" Some one from the audience pulled his courage and asked.

"Yes, yes, fear of losing wife..." Some other man supported the first man's question.

"Or is it the fear of not being able to function normally?" Another man inquired.

"What do you mean?"

"Ever since my wife has had her surgery and lost her breast, I have not been able to 'function' as a husband, you know...", and then with a slight hesitation, he said, "I mean I just can't 'make love' to her, I just can't, because, because...", not being able to express properly, he just stood quietly.

"Because when you see or feel with your touch the flatness of her chest, you almost immediately get something like erectile dysfunction, is that it? You just don't seem to..." Another man said.

He had, as if, hit the nail right on its head. He didn't even have to complete what he wanted to say when Deven got up and interrupted him,

"Yes, that's it. That's exactly it." Then he looked around and said, "I'm glad I'm not alone in this."

"You too, Dr. Dixit?" A few men, who knew Deven quite well, sounded surprised that a very-well educated person like Deven would also have this problem.

"Yes, my friends, me too. It has been more than two years now. I know very well that sexual excitation begins as a state of mind, and not body. Accordingly, I do get excited and feel like having some intimacy with my dear wife every so often. However, every time I approach her with that purpose in mind, the moment I see that part of her chest which is totally flat and bare, that's it. It is as if I instantly lose my vigour. I grow weak in my limbs, I start feeling terribly exhausted, I panic and then I have to, almost immediately, withdraw myself from the thought or action of intimacy completely."

"I always thought that it's the love between two people that matters the most. But now I am really confused. How is it that we tend to forget this important principle?" One man said after listening to Deven.

"Yes, now, I wonder about that too. I love my wife very much, so, her having or *not* having breasts would not carry that much importance in our 'love making'. Well, at least that's what I thought. But she lost her one breast to cancer and since then, I have lost my desire for her." Another man iterated his experience. "Honestly, it's damn confusing to me..."

'So, is it fear or confusion?" Some one asked.

"I think it is both, fear and confusion..." Some one said.

"Fear, I can understand. It's connected directly to death by cancer, but why confusion?"

"Confusion, because we don't know whether she would feel good about our advances or she would feel awkward about it?"

"That's exactly how my story goes too. And we both are musicians..."

Parth was present in the group too, and a few people recognized him.

"I fell in love with my wife way back when she was just an up coming artist. We got married, had two beautiful girls, and now, out of no where, this lightening struck us. It's like our whole life was totally devastated. Ritu, that's my wife, lost her both breasts."

Parth closed his eyes and took a deep breath to control himself from crying.

"I pretended to be very brave, only in front of her of course; for her sake and for the sake of my two girls. But whenever I was alone, I would cry my guts out. I was scared out of my wits, but I didn't want anyone to know that. Some one asked earlier about fear and confusion. Friends, I think I am filled with both, fear and confusion. And to add to that, my Ritu didn't just lose her breasts, she lost her singing too with cancer." Parth couldn't control his emotions any more. He started crying profusely.

Some people in that room had heard of Ritu Bose, the famous singer, and also that she had lost her singing to cancer. Now, they were witnessing her husband crying and grieving. The entire atmosphere in the room was filled with grief. No one spoke for a few minutes.

"I think, there is no single answer or solution to this problem. Each couple has a unique situation and that can be solved by that couple alone, no one else..." Das stood up and started talking to the people. He was one of the helpers of this session.

"Making love is a very personal matter." He said.

"My name is Das Prakash Rao. When my wife's cancer was detected, she was only twenty eight years of age. We have one son; he was not even out of diapers when her breast cancer was detected. And that was just a few months ago."

"Oh, no...", "Really?", "Oh, shit man..."

Comments coming from all the men in the room were full of sympathy for Das, although they themselves were husbands of breast cancer patients.

"And as if this was not catastrophic enough, my wife's breast cancer is one of those rare kinds, which doesn't give much time to the patient for surviving..."

The moment Das said this, everyone in the room got very serious. No one could utter a single word. Not even of sympathy. It was as though he had given them a huge electrical shock.

However, Das stayed relatively calm and continued talking,

"But my friends, I do want to tell you that we have forbidden her breast cancer to enter our bedroom. We make love to each other as passionately as before. Her breast cancer, I call it the *bastard coward*, has no room in it." Every one was stunned to hear his brave statement and his strong conviction behind it. Das did look fairly calm, at least outwardly.

"I consider this passionate activity, an intercourse, with my wife done with a deep sense of love and affection, as *meditation*. You all must have experienced it. Making love has a tremendous meditative quality in it. I do not wish to give it up, or have it polluted with confusion or fear. That is how I genuinely feel and that's exactly how I convinced my wife too. Thank God, she also believes in this now."

Everyone was dead silent. They looked shocked but at the same time, looked full of admiration for Das. He kept quiet for a few moments and then continued,

"Not enough research is done in my wife's cancer case. They don't know at what stage her cancer could be, or how far treatable it is. And therefore, they have given her only a year, or two at the most, to live..." At this point, Das's voice started cracking up, but he still continued speaking,

"Friends, I urge you, do not waste your precious time with your wife in fear or confusion. I personally don't! And I honestly urge you again; make the most of every single day. That's what I do!"

Das cracked up completely and started crying silently. Many men in the room were also crying silently. There was a total absence of sound in the room for a few moments. It is a *myth* that men don't cry!

"What Mr. Rao just said makes a hell of a sense, guys. Let us not waste this precious time in futile way, like fear or confusion. My wife displayed tremendous courage when she went for her surgery. She has expressed her courage so many times afterwards too, when she would go for her chemotherapy or radiation. It was always *her* who would hold *my* hands and give *me* courage. I feel so ashamed of myself now." Some one new got some courage to stand up and speak to the group.

"Talking about feeling ashamed, do you know how I feel?" Another man stood up and asked a question to the audience. "Along with fear and confusion, I feel extremely embarrassed and awkward too." This got immediate attention from the people.

"What do you mean, embarrassed and awkward?"

"My dear people, in my case, it's *me* who has developed breast cancer, not my wife." He said with his head turned as downwards as he could. "When I went to the hospital with my wife for the initial surgery, most of the people including some of the hospital staff first suspected my *wife* to have breast cancer. When they came to know it was *me*, I almost saw an expression on a few of their faces as though they had seen a clown or something. And that was not the only time this happened. I get this type of experience almost all the time, when I go for my treatments. My wife has a problem telling anyone in our friend circle, or sometimes even in our extended family members, that *I, the husband*, has had breast cancer. My disease is as serious as women's, but we don't seem to get much sympathy from anyone..."

This man was almost on the verge of crying, but he continued,

"In my cricket club, where I was considered to be a valuable player, a couple of my own teammates made fun of me. One asked me jokingly, 'so, what size are you choosing for your reconstructive surgery? Lemons or oranges?'

Immediately another answered, 'watermelons...' and they all laughed loudly. What do I say to that? Since cancer was going to hit me anyways, I wish it was some other form of cancer..."

He cupped his mouth slightly and started crying softly.

Some men were stunned to hear all this. They didn't know that men too can get breast cancer.

"What this gentleman said is true. Whether it is the husband or the wife, breast cancer is a family disease. And to do away with fear or confusion, or embarrassment, we must face this disease with courage and full family support."

"But how will we achieve this?"

"How do you handle it?"

There was a slight chaos in the room, with people asking various questions and talking among themselves.

"With communication and openness." Deven stood up and said loudly. "Communication and openness is the answer to all our questions, fear and confusion. And to our embarrassment too."

"Communication with whom? Openness about what?" Some men asked.

"Communication with our partners. Openness about our own feelings and fears. Combining both, we communicate our fears and feelings, even embarrassment, to our loved ones, especially our partners, and we express frankly and openly about how and what we feel about this disease." Deven said.

There were a few questioning faces among the men.

"To explain it better..." Deven said after looking at their faces. He started talking as though he was now ready to give one of his famous lectures in his English literature class.

"Let me quote my own experience. For more than two years now, I have been carrying this intense fear within me. I don't think I'm scared of my wife's disease, *per se*, I think it has to do with that empty area on her chest when she lost her one breast to cancer. That empty spot reminds me continuously, every single day, of her death as a result of cancer. But I have been hiding my fear all this time. And to hide it successfully, I pretended to read philosophy books. I thought this philosophical reading would camouflage my fears while giving me some courage to face it eventually. But alas! It did neither. My wife is a smart woman. She recognizod my cowardice. She made me realize that I was only deceiving myself, and not her. So finally one day, with her insistence, I opened up to her completely. It felt so good, I tell you, my friends. There is nothing like open communication..."

Deven pulled out a handkerchief from his pocket, wiped his brow and forehead that was shining with a few sweat beads, and continued again. "Today for the first time, I heard that I am not the only one feeling this way. There are many among us who are going through exactly what I have been facing these last two years. I feel somewhat encouraged, even better, to see that I wasn't the only husband who was a coward."

Then Deven directed his gaze at Das and said,

"When I heard Mr. Rao say, 'making love is a kind of meditation,' it struck my inner chord. Just like him, I also firmly believe that there is a beautiful, meditative quality in 'love making'.

When he said, 'don't waste your precious time', it hit me hard as a blatant reality of my own life that I'm a husband of a cancer survivor. Therefore, my time with my wife is very precious."

Then Deven walked closer to the window and as if talking to himself, he said,

"I have already wasted enough time of our lives in futile ways, let me not waste it any more. This is a promise to me that when

I go home today, I am going to hold my Annie in my arms and tell her face to face,

"Let me not to the marriage of true minds,
Admit impediments.
Love is no love
Which alters when it alteration finds.
Or bends with the remover to remove.
Oh no! It is an ever fixed mark.
That looks on tempests and is never shaken..."

Deven completed the recitation that came to him so very naturally. He looked around. Everyone was staring at him as if they were totally spell bound by his beautiful recitation of Shakespeare's poetry, in that passionate, resonating voice of his. He himself realized in that instance, that that was his original voice. It had come back to him.

He felt extremely elated. And totally liberated! As though, he was set free from the captivity of some grotesque oppressor!

With deep satisfaction, Deven was about to sit down when he looked outside. Through the window, he saw Anita, standing in the corridor, looking at him, with tears running down her cheeks.

'She heard me...', he felt sure and instantly knew, things were going to be back to normal in their lives, like they were before, before her breast cancer was diagnosed.

•••

And the Journey Ends Successfully!

Anita

"Annie, I will be back at the usual time..." Deven entered the veranda twirling his car keys in his hand. He was all ready to go to the club for playing his favorite sport of badminton. Anita and her daughter, Devnita were sitting in the veranda chatting with each other. They looked at him. He was dressed up meticulously in white shorts, white tee-shirt, white socks and white wrist band on his right hand.

"Okay dear. Don't forget Devnita's friend is joining us for dinner today, so don't be late." Anita said.

"No, I won't be. Annie, do you want me to pick up something on my way home?" Deven asked while putting on his white canvas shoes.

"No, we are okay." Anita said.

"Alright then, see you later, my two sweet ladies..." Deven picked up his racket and left.

"Did you see how wonderful he is now? He is back to his normal self..." Anita said to Devnita.

"Yah, Mom..." Devnita said. After finishing her studies at the university, she had joined a firm as an employee in a neighboring city. She was visiting her parents during her vacation time.

"Mom, Daddy sounds exactly how he was when I was at home. He looks also a lot better, compared to how he looked then, that is."

Devnita said. She knew very well what had taken place for those two years between her parents after her mother was diagnosed with breast cancer.

"Yes. And do you know, he has been requested to join the college as a Professor Emeritus in the department of English?"

"Oh really? And..."

"And he is seriously considering it. I'm also encouraging him to accept it. I myself am getting more and more involved with all these social activities with the Support Centre for breast cancer patients, so I want him to be busy too."

"More importantly, Mom, Daddy likes his work very much. I don't think he can live without studying or teaching English lit. You know what I mean?"

"Oh absolutely, dear. That's his passion, not just profession. I honestly can't figure out what had gone wrong in these past two years..." Anita sighed.

"With all those dry philosophy books and reading some weird sounding hymns, and all that..."

"They are called *shloka*, dear..."

"Well that's what I meant."

"Your Daddy reading all those shloka in that weird dry voice was really..." Anita was about to complete what she intended to say when Devnita interrupted her, saying, "...something that I could never fathom Daddy could ever be like that, right?"

Anita nodded full heartedly.

"Uhhh..."

"Uhhh..." They both shivered and sighed together.

"Mom, let's leave it now. Let's not think of it. He is out of it already. That's good. You weren't exactly normal either when he was reading those shloka day and night. Remember?"

"What do you mean?"

"Remember, you used to sit on the kitchen stool for hours together, thinking of the past. Any time I telephoned you, your answer would be, 'I am sitting in the kitchen, looking out the window.'

And when I would talk to Daddy, his answer would always be, 'I am sitting in the veranda, reading a philosophy book...' It used to really puzzle me sometimes, you know? 'What's wrong with my parents these days?' I used to think and feel worried.

It's so good to see both your lives being back to normal now, Mom." Devnita got a little emotional. She cared for her parents.

"By the way, how is the Support Centre work going on, Mom?" Devnita changed the topic to Anita's favorite one.

"Fantastic. Most of the sessions are almost full now."

"What kind of sessions are they?"

"Oh, there are quite a few of them, and of a wide variety. There is one for only women, one for the teenaged girls; one session is a general one, meant for all the family members and friends of breast cancer patients. Dr. Vimal conducts all the sessions that are educational and mainly science based. That's for giving accurate information about the disease. Then there is a psychotherapist named Meeraben who conducts a few sessions for developing psychological power of the patients, through a new technique called *visualization technique*." "That sounds wonderful, Mom."

"Yes, it is coming along just as we had hoped for when we planned. Many women come and tell us that they are getting the benefit from all these sessions. Hey, do you know that there is also one session meant only for men?" Anita asked Devnita.

"Oh really?"

"Yes. Actually, I think that's what brought on the change in Dev

That's what made all the difference in Dev's attitude."

"So, you can say from your own experience that the concept of this Support Centre is very good, and very useful too."

"Yes, most definitely, indeed!"

They both laughed, and then became suddenly very serious.

"Mom, when I got the news of your diagnosis, you have no idea how much I cried. For almost two days and nights, I just couldn't stop crying. My roommates were trying to console me, give me courage but nothing worked. Then, when I found out that you were very, very courageous, faced surgery and the following treatments very bravely, I felt a bit better." Devnita looked into Anita's eyes and continued,

"Mom, I knew fully well that Daddy wasn't with you in your fight with cancer. He did take care of you initially, yes, but he was one scared cat, I know that. And then, Oh my God, he became so much aloof emotionally. Mom, how did you face it alone?"

"That was hard, dear. Emotional support of the husband is the most needed one, especially at such times, but..."

"That's when I realized your true strength. Mom, I really want to be like you..." Devnita's eyes were full of pride for her mother, when she complimented her.

"...and not like your Daddy, a scared cat, right?" Devnita and Anita both got startled and looked towards the gate. Deven had already walked inside the gate, and was climbing up the steps to enter the veranda.

"Oh my dear Daddy, I didn't mean that way..." Devnita got up and hugged him when he entered the veranda.

"That's okay dear. Your mother is a strong woman and a very smart one too. She was the victim but then, *she* was the one who was like a rock..." Deven had a big smile on his face and he looked like he meant every word he said.

"...rock of Gibraltar..." Devnita completed Deven's sentence, with a smile on her face too.

"Stop it, you two..." Anita said, with genuine admiration for her dear family.

"You came back early today..." Anita commented on Deven's return from the club.

"Annie, I was gone for almost two hours..." Deven said while still holding Devnita in his hug.

"Oh Daddy, we didn't even realize how the time passed in our little talk." Devnita was enjoying her Daddy's bear hug.

"What's that in your hand Dev?" Anita saw a small package in his hand.

"It's a package."

"Well, I can see that. What's in the package?" Anita asked him.

"Jasmine flowers."

"Oh, honey..." Anita took the package from his hands and had a big smile on her face.

"Annie, come here, join the hug..." Deven said and she instantly joined them in the hug too.

It was after a very long time, two long years that those three were having a group hug. It felt the same as before; before Anita was diagnosed of her breast cancer!

'Thank God, the journey through this ordeal ended successfully...' each one of those three was thinking.

•

Ritu

"...kaun karat tori binati piyarava..."

A young singer of classical music, barely twenty years of age, was sitting in the singer's specific pose on the stage and singing. Clad in a bright pink sari and a matching blouse, which made her youthful looks even more charming, she was stringing a Tambora gently with her fingers. With her eyes closed, she looked totally engrossed in her singing.

The hall was packed to capacity with music connoisseurs and every one in the audience was swaying with her music, the whole audience looking like a meadow swayed by gentle wind.

'So young and yet such a mastery on classical Raga?' Many people in the audience clearly had this expression on their faces.

The Raga that she was improvising at the moment was one of her favorite ones, Raga Bageshri, a Raga in which she had started her advanced training of classical music She was trained by one of the top singers of India, none other than her own mother, Ritu Bose. Yes, this was Sangita, Ritu's first born child. With this concert, she was fulfilling her own ambition of being known as a promising young singer, and more importantly, her mother's dream of seeing her daughter sing in front of a knowledgeable audience someday. That day had arrived today; and both their dreams were being materialized.

Sangita opened her eyes momentarily and looked at the audience and smiled. Then her gaze moved to the very first row of people and fixed on one person. That person was none other than her mother, Ritu Bose, sitting on a soft cushioned chair, wrapped up in a woolen shawl. Sangita smiled again and closed her eyes, ready to resume her singing again. In that brief moment, she had read the expressions on her mother's face, which had instantly told her that her own ambition was fulfilled and her mother's dream had come true.

Sitting next to Sangita was her father, Parth Bose, accompanying her on the Tabla, creating magic with his fingers. And behind her was sitting her younger sister, Shruti, stringing the strings of a second Tambora. Together they were making the music of such a fine quality that everyone in the audience was mesmerized by it.

This was all the result of a strong determination coupled with tremendous hard work of Sangita, Shruti, Parth and most importantly

Ritu, the breast cancer survivor. With Dr. Vimal's help in medical treatment, Meeraben's help in developing psychological powers, and with the help and encouragement of her own family and friends like Anita, Maya and others in the Support Centre, she had been able to achieve what she had otherwise imagined to be impossible. And that was surviving the disease for many years without fear or depression, and pursuing the dream of training her daughters. Her rigorous training to her daughters was clearly getting recognition with Sangita's performance today.

Ritu was sure Sangita would be the nightingale of the country of tomorrow, as she herself was, yesterday!

Ritu was listening to her daughter and while listening, continuously shedding tears. They were tears of contentment, of pride, of fruition, and above all, tears of extreme happiness that she had a hard but successful journey through her breast cancer.

Just as she looked at Parth, she noticed two large tears dribble from his eyes onto his Tabla. She knew exactly what they meant too!

•

Maya

"Ma, did you get the list completed?" Kirti was sitting on the patio and asking her mother with a shout as Maya was sitting in her bedroom.

"I'm almost done dear..." Maya answered from her bedroom, but Kirti couldn't hear her.

"Go to your grand mother's room and see if she has finished her list. Run..." Kirti told her three year old son, Deepak.

Deepak ran towards Maya's bedroom and instead of going straight inside, he stood in the doorway and said, "knock, knock."

"Who is there" Maya looked up from her writing pad and asked him with a smile.

"Boo." He answered.

"Boo who?" She asked.

"Don't cry little girl..." Deepak said in his usual cute way and started giggling. This was his favorite game that he loved to play with his grand mother.

Maya got up from her table and walked towards the door where he was standing. She picked him up and started kissing his cheeks and hugging him. Just then, his little cousin came running towards them. Maya tried to pick her up too. The grand mother tried to hug the two together in her arms.

Kirti had a baby boy just about three years ago, and almost immediately following that event, her younger sister Arti, also had a baby, a little girl, she named Piyaa. Ever since Kirti and Arti had their babies, Maya's life had changed completely. Her days reverted back to being full, all seven days of the week, offering Maya no time to think of her once falsely imagined notion that 'no one needed her'!

Deepak and Piyaa needed their grand mother even more than their mothers did, for every minute of the day, and their grand mother loved every minute of it. Kirti and Arti had moved back to Maya's town with their young families and depended on Maya's help for everything; right from looking for an apartment to stay to buying furniture, etc.; and most importantly, for looking after their young ones.

Right now, Maya was preparing a list of people to invite for a grand function she had arranged for her son. Anand was about to visit his mother after a few years of stay in Canada, and she was all too excited to receive him. She was hoping he would meet a suitable girl as his bride, in this gala function. Therefore this list was very important.

With the two grandchildren in her two arms, Maya came outside onto the patio.

"Hey guys, don't trouble Grandma..." Kirti told the little ones. "Ma, I don't think you should carry them like that..." Kirti was being careful for her mother.

"That's alright. They are not that heavy." Maya slowly lowered them onto the floor. They ran towards their mothers.

"Ma, how's the list coming along? Did you put the name I gave your earlier?" Arti asked her mother.

"Yes, I did, but are you sure..."

"Yes, Ma. I am one hundred percent sure." Arti interrupted her.

"Sure about what?" Kirti asked Arti.

"Do you remember my classmate, Dhiroo Patel?" Arti asked Kirti.

"Yah... what about him?"

"His uncle lives in Canada. That's a huge family, with many uncles and all that. They are into Motel business. And as I understand, there are a couple of beautiful and educated girls in that family. If Ma can invite just one member from that family, that's enough to get the word around..."

Kirti and Arti laughed together. They knew fully well how this 'facilitated' marriage business worked in India, especially in families like theirs.

Just then, they heard the telephone ring and their maid answer it. She came outside in a few moments and giving the chord-less receiver to Maya, said, "Madam, its Anita Madam from the Support Centre for you." Maya took the telephone and started talking and discussing something. After a few minutes, she hung up.

"Is every thing okay Ma?" Kirti asked.

"Yes, yes. I have given my house for the activities of the Centre, right? So Anita wanted to know how long should they keep the sessions closed so that can we have the house all to ourselves."

"And?" Both the girls asked her simultaneously.

"And I said we need it just for two weeks, the two weeks that Anand is here. I told her that during that time, we would be having all kinds of family activities here. Other than this time, they can have our house for conducting all the sessions, same as before. I have no problem giving our house for the Centre's activities." Maya said.

"Really Ma?" Arti asked.

"Yes, really..." Maya said with full conviction.

"That's commendable, Ma" Arti looked very much impressed with Maya's generosity.

"How's the work of the Centre going on?" Kirti asked her.

"Absolutely wonderful. You know girls; it's the Centre that saved me, really. That's where I have been meeting many women who are breast cancer survivors, but having a very positive attitude towards life. Meeting them and seeing their will power teaches me a lot about living. Of course, Meeraben takes the credit of my first step towards it, but these women also have helped me in the past, and still help me a lot, indirectly. The mother you see today, was not so a while ago, and now..." Maya got a little emotional.

"And now, she is even more feisty and stronger than before." Kirti and Arti completed her sentence.

"Honestly, Ma, we don't know what we could have done without you..." Kirti held Maya's hand and said with a genuine feeling of appreciation. Arti became emotional too.

"My dear daughters, I need you too very badly, even more than you know." Extreme emotions overtook Maya, and she couldn't speak any more. They all started laughing at each other, and at the same time, had their eyes full of tears.

All three of them knew very well that Maya's journey through that dreadful period was one uphill battle, but a very successful one, after all!

•

Shaina

"Okay, so you have lost your hair due to chemotherapy. But that does not mean you should hide from the world until your hair grows back..." Shaina was talking to a small group of women in one of the sessions that were still conducted in Maya's bungalow.

Since the day Shaina talked to them openly about herself, her experiences and her life story in the 'Forum for Women', she had instantly become very popular among all the members of the Support Group. That included men as well.

"But Shaina, it is almost impossible for me to go out like this..." One woman took off the black scarf from her head and complained while patting her hairless head with her hand.

"Yah... I wear a nice sari, a matching blouse, I wear nice bangles and then tie this ugly black scarf on my head. I can't do that..." A second woman said.

"The black scarf looks kind of repulsive, you know..." Another woman said and the rest of the women agreed with her.

"Listen, going out without a scarf is impossible, yes, and then wearing a black scarf may be repulsive too; but is that the only way you can cover your heads? With a black scarf?" Shaina asked them.

"Then what do you do?" Shaina had become an expert for all the questions and tips relating to beauty for those women.

"You may want to change the color of the scarf sometimes, matching your dresses, saris, or whatever you are wearing. There are beautiful scarves available in all kinds of material like silk, tissue, fine cotton, etc. in the market. Go to the shopping places, look for the ones you like and buy them."

The women listened to her intently.

"There is another alternative too. You could use wigs." Shaina said.

"Oh, but the wigs are very expensive."

"Yah, they are kind of pricy..." Many women complained.

"As it is, a lot of money has been spent in my medical treatment; if I start spending for wigs and all such things, it would be almost impossible for me to make the ends meet, Shaina." One woman said.

"Who is going to look at us any way?" Another woman asked a genuine question.

"I'll be happy if my *husband* looks at me..." A third woman said with a slight complaining tone in her voice.

"Yah, we are not models..." Some of the women laughed. However, there was an undercurrent of a bit of sarcasm coupled with a bit of sorrow in their laughter. At least, Shaina felt it that way.

"Ladies, ladies, you don't have to be a model to want to look good. It is not necessary that you should be in the fashion industry or some such field and then only you are permitted to take care of yourself and look good. Perhaps no one looks at you, not even your husbands, but *you do.* Don't you? Aren't *you* important to yourself? I narrated my personal story to you all just a few days back, remember? It wasn't so much cancer, but losing both my natural breasts at my age of barely twenty years, was like everything coming to a sudden stop. It was like my life coming to an end, remember?"

Then she walked towards the window and as if looking outside and talking to the trees, said,

"It was a big shock to learn that that was the only viable option for me to live free of fear of cancer. It took nerves of steel to come to that point." At this point she turned her face towards the women and looking at them face to face, said,

"But I told myself, 'what didn't kill me made me stronger!' After I got the reconstructive surgery and saw that my new breasts have added a big plus to my figure, I didn't just stop there. I started working hard to get every inch of my body beautiful. Ladies, I owe it to me, the new me, just as you owe it to *you*! The brave survivors of breast cancer!"

Then she asked some of them, "I told you my background, right?"

Some of them nodded whereas, a few others shook their heads.

Looking at those who didn't know about her, Shaina said,

"I come from a very small village in North India. To see anything even closely connected to models or fashion for me was almost next to impossible there. The very first time I saw anything like that was in Usha didi's house. She had a few modern magazines on her coffee table. I distinctly remember, one of them had a glossy advertisement with a picture of a young woman with beautiful figure and shiny hair and teeth. 'Can this really exist?' I had wondered, because I had never seen anyone having such beautiful body, hair or teeth, in my village. 'Are these women real?' I even asked Usha didi once. Her answer was, 'yes, they are real, they are called models.' Then she told me, I still remember very well,

'these women take extra care of their bodies and hair and teeth, and eat less and work hard to maintain their beauty.'

Since then the only thought that would crop up in my mind about a thousand times a day was 'I wish I could be a model.'

I was that much fascinated by the models. By a strange turn in life, or whatever, I did achieve to be one of the top models of the country! It took tremendous hard work on my part. My dear friends, at the base of all this was my strong desire and determination. I *wanted* to look good." She was so convincing, everyone was attentive to her talk.

"But Shaina..." Someone was about to ask her something. "I know, I know. You are going to say, 'we are not models.' And I know you are not, but does that mean you can neglect your bodies? Neglect your hair and skin and all that? Neglect how you look? Neglect your *desire* to look good? Aren't you *living* still?"

Then she walked closer towards them, held a couple of women's hands in her own hands and said,

"You are women; you *want* to look good, because, when you look good, you *feel* good too. And..." Shaina gave herself a few seconds to look at all the women and then said,

"...that's one more sure way of showing your family, friends, and the whole world that you have beaten your cancer!"

She had a beautiful smile on her face when she completed what she wanted to say to the women.

"Shaina is getting really good at this..." Anita commented to Maya as they were also standing at the back of the women's crowd and listening to her.

"I think we should get her even more involved in talking to women, and advocating them." Maya said.

"Maya, how about requesting Shaina to be our 'Patient Advocate?' She is good, she is young and most importantly, she is dedicated to this work; and ..."

"...and she will add some pizzazz to this work of building a Support Centre." Maya completed Anita's sentence. They both had the very same thought.

Shaina has been working, ever since, as the 'Patient Advocate' of the Support Centre. Women just adore her. They like to consult with her for all their needs in their physical appearance. They feel proud to tell their friends that they are associated with a top class model of the country after surviving breast cancer. Because so has *she*!

She has also helped them feel that there need not be any taboo or inhibition in talking or discussing about breast cancer.

Shaina's journey through the fear of this dreadful disease has ended very, very successfully!

•

Virani

"Kittu, what do you want for a snack in your recess time, son?" Das was asking Kittu as he was getting ready for his senior kindergarten school in the morning. Amma was helping him with his clothes, but he seemed to be more interested in looking at the pictures of bears in the book.

"Krishnadev, get ready fast, dear..." Amma kept on saying and he was co-operating reluctantly.

Finally when he was ready, Amma and he came out of his room.

"Come on, let's go..." Das Prakash said and he put some snack in Kittu's little backpack.

The backpack was a blue colored bag and had a huge picture of a teddy bear on it. Das said 'good bye' to Amma, and he and Kittu set out to walk to Kittu's school. Kittu's school was at a walking distance from their house. Their daily schedule was, Das would drop Kittu at his school and then go to his bank; then in his lunch time, he would pick up Kittu and bring him home to Amma, and then go back to the bank again and work until the late hours of the evening. This schedule was followed every single day of the week, except Sunday, since Kittu started going to the senior KG about five months back. That's also when Virani's cancer entered the terminal stage.

As they were walking, Kittu suddenly stopped, turned back and started looking at the balcony of his house. Then he waved a 'good bye' to the balcony and turning back, started walking again with his father. There was *nobody* in the balcony.

"Kittu, what are you doing?" Das asked his son.

"Waving 'bye bye' to mommy..." Kittu answered matter-of-factly.

"What?" Das was stunned, and for a moment lost his self control.

"I said I was waving to mommy..." Kittu said again quite seriously while walking.

"But mommy is ..." Das was about to say 'not there', but he couldn't.

"Daddy, I see her sitting there waving to me." Kittu said.

Das couldn't say anything.

In the last few weeks of life, Virani used to sit in the balcony every morning waving 'bye bye' to Kittu when he left for school. She did get to see her son go to the school, for those few weeks. After giving a fierce battle to her breast cancer, and surviving it for almost five years, she had requested the doctor to let her be home and die in peace in the midst of her dear family.

"Daddy, do you remember the book?" Kittu asked Das.

"Which one?" Das managed to quickly come out of his thought about Virani's last few days with them.

"The name is, 'Three Big Bears'" Kittu said.

"Yes, of course I remember." Das said. He knew what Kittu was going to say afterwards.

"Mommy used to read that book to me every night before I went to sleep. Remember?"

"Um…Hum…"

"You know what else, Daddy?"

"What?"

"Mommy is in Heaven now."

"Is she?" Das started getting a little apprehensive about what Kittu was going to say.

"Um… Hum…! She told me that that's where she is going."
"I see." Das said quietly.

"And she also told me that we will be meeting again in Heaven. But she told me that I can't go there right now."

"Oh?"

"That's right. She said it will be many, many years, like hundred years, before I can go to heaven and see her. Is it true Daddy?"

"Yes."

"Mommy knew so many things, and she told me so many things. I will never forget her, Never, never, never…And you know what Daddy?"

"What?"

"That's why I am going to say 'bye bye' to her every day when I leave for school."

Das couldn't say anything. His eyes were already deceiving him by getting filled with tears, he didn't want to lose his control in front of his son, especially when he was about to drop him at the school.

"Daddy, do you know the story of a huge bear that mommy told me?"

Das, on the verge of getting extremely emotional, just shook his head.

"I will tell you that story tonight. It's so funny..."

Kittu started talking about the story and chuckling to himself intermittently. He was telling his father how his mother, while pretending to be the big bear, had even acted up some of that part of the story.

As they approached the school, Das said 'bye' to his son and started walking towards his bank. His mind was walking even faster than him.

"Did you see that Rani, did you?" He looked at the sky and asked his wife, as though she was looking at him from the sky, peeping through the clouds.

"Kittu is going to tell me the story you had told him. And he is going to wave 'bye bye' to you every day when he goes to school. Rani, did you see that?" Das looked at the sky again.

"Rani, this is exactly what I was telling you. Fortunately, you cooperated. You developed positive attitude and took medical treatment to defeat your breast cancer, and instead of just one year, you got full five years to live with me and your son. Did you hear what our son said to me just now, Rani? Did you? He said that he will never forget you, Rani."

Das's monologue with his wife was going on, on a full speed. He was so much engrossed in it that he almost felt a nod from Virani to his question. As though to reciprocate to her nod, he said,

"Rani, we won the battle! We really did. You are now carved in our son's mind, permanently. With him remembering you so well, we'll be talking about you all the time. And that way, you will be with me all the time too."

Intense emotions and memories of his dead wife overpowered Das. Suddenly he stopped walking. Kneeling down right there on the footpath, and looking at the sky, he said loudly, "Rani, your journey has ended very successfully, my darling. You know why?"

And as if he had a sudden revelation, Das wiped his eyes dry and said, "Because with Kittu around for a hundred years, even death is not the end, my dear, even death is not the end!"

•••

Scientific Information given in this Book

More than ever before, women are taking an active part in their breast health in India and many other Far Eastern countries of the world. There is a growing concern and understanding of breast cancer, the second most common form of cancer among women in the world.

Cancer is now clearly understood to be a disease of abnormal gene function. Genes are segments of DNA that contain instructions on how to make the proteins the body needs to function. They govern hereditary traits, such as hair color, eye color, height, etc. as well as susceptibility (likelihood of being affected) to certain diseases, such as cancer. In humans, genes are located on 23 pairs of chromosomes, one of each chromosome pair coming from the mother and the other from the father. Each chromosome contains thousands of genes that are passed from the parents to the child. The genes are present in every cell of the body.

Each cell in the body carries about 100,000 genes. Genes control how the cell functions, such as telling it when to divide and when to grow.

We now understand that genes serve two major roles in cancer; some contribute to the development of cancer and others stop cancer from developing or growing. Genes that can cause cancer are called Onco genes. Genes that stop or suppress cancer growth are called Tumor suppressor genes.

Even some of the healthy genes sometimes change or alter. This change is termed as mutation. The cause for mutation could be manifold; such as exposure to large doses of radiation, exposure to excessive sunlight, smoking, bad diet habits, stressful lifestyle, etc. Mutated genes can cause cancer to start. This explains why most cancers are not inherited but arise due to gene mutations.

It is observed that cancer risk increases with age. The reason could be that the older a person gets, greater is the risk of gene mutations in that person.

It is not the cancer that is inherited, but the abnormal gene that can cause the cancer is what is inherited.

What is cancer?

Cells in the body normally divide or reproduce only when new cells are needed. However, sometimes cells divide for no reason, creating a mass of tissue called a tumor. These tumors can be benign, meaning not cancerous or malignant, meaning cancerous.

In breast cancer, as well as in some other cancers, a tissue cell becomes abnormal and reproduces without control or order, forming a malignant tumor. Cancer cells can break off from the tumor, travel to other parts of the body, and form new tumors. This process is called metastasis. Metastasis is a late stage of cancer.

Breast cancer and Heredity[22]

The greatest risk factor for breast cancer is observed to be heredity.

A woman is at even greater risk if she has a close relative, a mother, aunt, or sister, who has breast cancer, developed before age of forty years.

What is the breast cancer gene?

Genetic breast cancer incidence makes up about 5-10% of all breast cancers.

More than one faulty gene has been found in women with breast cancer.

There are two known breast cancer genes. They are BRCA1 and BRCA2.

Women, who have BRCA1 gene mutation, have about 60% lifetime risk of developing breast cancer. It is believed that women with these mutations also have significantly higher risk of developing ovarian cancer.

22. I have discussed this topic by creating a character, named Shaina, in this book.

Unlike women who are carriers of well-recognized genetic mutations, like that of BRCA1 or BRCA2 genes, most women do not have any evidence of genetic alterations that would increase the risk of breast cancer. The increased breast cancer risk in this group of women may be related to a group alteration of genes rather than a single gene mutation. Such genetic alterations as a group may have increased predisposition to development of breast cancer.

It is also difficult to separate impact of environmental factors in these cases. The role of environmental factors is difficult to quantify and the extent of the impact caused by common environmental factors is difficult to judge.

Risk for developing breast cancer?

Breast cancer is an extremely complex disease and it's difficult to pin-point any one single risk factor directly responsible for developing of the disease.

The first and the foremost risk factor could be being a *woman*! If you are a woman, there is a risk of developing breast cancer. (Men very seldom develop breast cancer.)

In many cases, it's not known why a woman, any woman, develops breast cancer. In fact, 70 percent of all women with breast cancer have no known risk factor.

What are the risk factors of breast cancer?

Heredity - The greatest risk factor for breast cancer is heredity. That is, having a mother, aunt or sister, who has breast cancer. A woman is at even greater risk if her relative developed breast cancer before 40 years of age.

Age - A woman's risk for breast cancer also increases as she grows older. Just to quote the observation: A woman who is 35 years old has a one-in-622 chance of developing breast cancer, while a woman who is 60 years old has a one-in-24 chance.

Other risk factors include:

- Late menopause (after age 55)
- Getting period early in life (before age 12)
- Having first child after age 30
- Never giving birth
- Being obese after menopause

- Taking hormone replacement medicine
- Race (breast cancer occurs more frequently in Caucasian women than in Hispanic, Asian, or African-American women)

Do most women with breast cancer have a family history of the disease?

No.

Women with a family history of breast cancer account for only 20-30% of all women with the disease. (This also means that about 70% to 80% of women with a family history of breast cancer do not develop the disease).

If a woman has a close relative who has breast cancer, then there is an increased risk. A woman should keep a careful watch of her breast health.

Does having a benign breast condition mean having a higher risk?

Benign breast conditions mean breast conditions that are not cancerous, meaning, breast that have cysts or lumps which are benign. They rarely increase the risk of breast cancer. Some women have a condition called hyperplasia which means excessive cell growth. This condition, otherwise benign, is known to increase the risk only slightly.

Ways to protect from breast cancer

- Examine your breasts each month
- Get a mammogram, especially after age 40
- Have your breast examined by a doctor or a nurse once a year

Where do breast cancers form?

Breast cancers may develop in the glandular tissue of the breast, specifically in the milk ducts and the milk lobules. These ducts and lobules are located in all parts of the breast tissue, including tissue just under the skin. The breast tissue extends from the collarbone to the lower rib margin, and from the middle of the chest, around the side and under the arm.

In a mastectomy, it is necessary to remove tissue from just beneath the skin down to the chest wall and around the borders of the chest. However, even with very thorough and delicate surgical techniques, it is impossible to remove every milk duct and lobule, given the extent of the breast tissue and the location of these glands just beneath the skin.

Stress related to breast cancer[23]

Scientists have found that stress doubles a woman's risk of developing breast cancer. The rationale for this link is that, excessive, sustained stress may cause suppression of the immune system, which in turn, may affect the hormonal balance in the breast.

Women diagnosed with metastasized breast cancer who have also endured previous traumatic or stressful events see their cancer recur nearly twice as fast as other women.

However, further research is needed before any direct correlation between stress and increased breast cancer risk is established.

What is BCT?

Breast Conserving Therapy (BCT) consists of removal of the lump, termed as lumpectomy.

Lumpectomy, followed by radiation and hormone therapy, is considered to be a safe, effective treatment for non-hereditary or sporadic forms of early breast cancer. However, for hereditary breast cancers, the use of BCT is controversial due to conflicting data about increased risk of recurrence in the treated breast and development of new tumors in the untreated breast.

About Inflammatory Breast Cancer[24]

Inflammatory Breast Cancer ("IBC") is known to be an especially aggressive type of breast cancer that can occur in women of any age (and, although extremely rarely, in men). It is unique because often, there is no lump in the breast and therefore is not detected by mammography or ultrasound.

Inflammatory breast cancer causes breast changes in the nipple and surrounding areas. Other symptoms include rapid increase in breast size, redness, persistent itching, skin hot to the touch. IBC often initially resembles metastasis, and is sometimes misdiagnosed as an insect bite.

As mentioned earlier, inflammatory breast cancer is a rare but very aggressive type of breast cancer in which the cancer cells block the lymph vessels in the skin of the breast. This type of breast cancer is called "inflammatory" because the breast often looks swollen and red,

---

23. I have discussed this topic by creating a character, named Maya, in this book.
24. I have discussed this topic through a character named Virani, with the help of creating a doctor's character, named Dr. Vimal, in this book.

or "inflamed." IBC accounts for less than 5 percent of all breast cancer cases in the world.

It is more likely to be diagnosed in younger women compared to non-IBC breast cancer. Like the other types of breast cancer, IBC can occur in men also, but usually at a much older age than in women.

Symptoms of IBC

Symptoms of IBC may include redness, swelling, and warmth in the breast, often without a distinct lump in the breast. The redness and warmth are caused by cancer cells blocking the lymph vessels in the skin. The skin of the breast may also appear pink, reddish purple, or bruised. The skin may also have ridges or appear pitted, like the skin of an orange, which is caused by a buildup of fluid and swelling in the breast. Other symptoms include heaviness, burning, aching, increase in breast size, tenderness, or a nipple that is inverted (facing inward).

These symptoms usually develop quickly, over a period of weeks or months. Swollen lymph nodes may also be present under the arm, above the collarbone, or in both places. However, it is important to note that these symptoms may also be signs of other conditions such as infection, injury, or other types of cancer.

How is IBC diagnosed?

Diagnosis of IBC is based primarily on the results of a doctor's clinical examination. Biopsy, mammogram and breast ultrasound are used to confirm the diagnosis.

IBC is classified as either stage III IBC or stage IV IBC breast cancer.

Stage III IBC is locally advanced cancer. Stage IV IBC is cancer that has spread to other parts of the body.

IBC tends to grow rapidly, and the physical appearance of the breast of patients with IBC is different from that of patients with other stage III breast cancers. IBC Stage III is an especially aggressive, locally advanced breast cancer.

Chemotherapy

Chemotherapy is one of the prime therapeutic measures of breast cancer treatment, (including IBC).

The purpose of chemotherapy is to control or kill cancer cells, including those that may have spread to other parts of the body.

Most of the breast cancer patients undergo surgery that is done for removing the tumor from the body; (it could be lumpectomy or mastectomy), and radiation therapy to the chest wall that is done for destroying the remaining cancer cells. While both radiation and surgery are local treatments that affect only cells in the tumor and its immediately surrounding area, Chemotherapy is a systemic treatment that affects cells throughout the body.

Treatment consisting of chemotherapy, targeted therapy, surgery, radiation therapy and hormonal therapy is used to treat most of the breast cancers, including IBC.

Breast Cancer Preventative Mastectomy[25]

In hopes of avoiding future disease, some women at very high risk of developing breast cancer elect to have both breasts surgically removed, a procedure called *bilateral prophylactic mastectomy.* The surgery aims to remove all breast tissue that potentially could develop breast cancer. Preventive breast cancer surgery also may be considered if a woman has already had breast cancer and is therefore at increased risk for developing the disease again in either breast.

A recent study suggests that prophylactic mastectomy may reduce the risk of breast cancer by as much as 95%.

Who should have bilateral prophylactic mastectomy?

The decision to proceed with prophylactic mastectomy is an individual decision. Various factors such as an estimate of individual breast cancer risk, the ability to monitor the patient for early breast cancer and, most importantly, the patient's concerns and feelings, need to be considered in making this decision.

According to the scientists and doctors, only those women who are at very high risk of breast cancer should consider surgery. This includes women with one or more of the following risk factors:

- Presence of mutated BRCA genes.
- Previous cancer in one breast
- Strong family history of breast cancer.

Appropriate genetic and psychological counseling is strongly recommended before the prophylactic mastectomy, to discuss the psycho-social impacts of the procedure.

---

25. I have discussed this topic by creating a character, named Shaina, in this book.

General Information about Puberty and Normal Breast Development among females[26]

Puberty refers to the process of physical changes by which a child's body becomes an adult's body, capable of reproduction. Puberty is initiated by hormone signals from the brain to the gonads (ovaries in females and testes in males). In response, the gonads produce a variety of hormones that stimulate the growth, function, or transformation of brain, bones, muscle, skin, hair, breasts and reproductive organs.

Growth accelerates in the first half of puberty and stops at the completion of puberty. Before puberty, body differences between boys and girls are almost entirely restricted to the genital organs.

During puberty, major differences of size, shape, composition, and function develop in many body structures and systems. The most obvious of these are referred to as secondary sex characteristics. In a strict sense, the term *puberty* refers to the bodily changes of sexual maturation rather than the psycho-social and cultural aspects of adolescent development.

Adolescence is the period of psychological and social transition between childhood and adulthood. Adolescence largely overlaps the period of puberty, but its boundaries are less precisely defined and it refers as much to the psycho-social and cultural characteristics of development during the teen years as to the physical changes of puberty.

What is Normal Breast Development?

Breast development is a vital part of puberty in the human females. Unlike other mammals, however, human females are the only ones who develop full breasts long before they are needed to nurse their offspring.

Breast development occurs in distinct stages, first before birth, and again at puberty and during the childbearing years. Changes also occur to the breasts during menstruation and when a woman reaches menopause.

The breasts are usually fully mature by 18 years of age. When fully mature, the secondary mound underneath the areola blends in with the surrounding rounded breast shape. The nipples project outward.

26. I have discussed this topic through a character named Ritu, with the help of a doctor's character, named Dr. Vimal, in this book.

Milk glands and ducts fully develop. (They don't start producing milk until the baby is born to the female.)

Open, relaxed and comfortable communication is the most important thing one can do for the child during puberty. A child who is not comfortable talking to adults will act according to whatever is suggested by her biological impulses, her peers or the media and culture around her. Young girls want their mothers to be their main source of information about puberty. They appreciate a mother's stories of her own experiences.

You can help your child by opening discussions from an early age and making them fun and pleasant. Do not tell your child she is a woman because she is menstruating. A 10 year old who's wearing a bra and a maxi pad needs to know she is still a child, or else she might be unfairly shoved into adult specific pressures that she is not psychologically prepared for, and might be forced to miss out on crucial developmental stages.

When does breast development begin?

Breasts begin to form during fetal development, with a thickening in the chest area called the mammary ridge or milk line. By the time a female infant is born, a nipple and the beginnings of the milk-duct system have formed.

Breast changes continue to occur over the lifespan, with lobes, or small subdivisions of breast tissue, developing first. Mammary glands develop next, and consist of 15-24 lobes. Mammary glands are influenced by hormones activated in puberty. Shrinkage of the milk ducts, called Involution, is the final major change that occurs within the breast tissue. Involution typically begins around the age of 35 years.

The duct system also begins to grow. Usually, the onset of these breast changes is also accompanied by the appearance of pubic hair and hair under the arms. The maturing of the breasts begins with the formation of secretory glands at the end of the milk ducts. The breasts and duct system continue to grow and mature with the development of many glands and lobules. The rate at which breasts grow varies greatly and is different for each young woman. Generally, there are five stages of breast development in girls.

Hormonal Evolution

Cells of multi cellular organisms need to communicate with each other to regulate their development and organize growth and cell division. Hormones contribute to these processes by acting as messengers between cells, telling them what's happening elsewhere and how they should respond.

A hormone is a chemical messenger that carries a signal from one cell (or group of cells) to another. All multi-cellular organisms produce hormones, and they are often transported in the blood.

Contact Inhibition Theory[27]

Contact inhibition is the natural process of arresting cell growth when two or more cells come into contact with each other. Oncologists use this property to distinguish between normal and cancerous cells.

When used in the context of reproduction of living cells, the phrase 'cell growth' is a 'shorthand' for the idea of growth in cell **population** by means of cell reproduction. During cell reproduction, one cell, also called the 'mother' cell, divides to produce two daughter cells.

Cancerous cells typically lose this property and thus grow in an uncontrolled manner even when in contact with the neighboring cells.

In brief, it is the momentary stopping of a cell's growth and reproduction when it runs into another cell.

General Information about the science of Genetics

Genetics is the study of how living things receive common traits from previous generations. These traits are described by the genetic information carried by a molecule called DNA. The instructions for constructing and operating an organism are contained in the organism's DNA. Every living thing on earth has DNA in its cells.

A gene is a hereditary unit consisting of DNA that occupies a specific spot on a chromosome and determines the characteristic in an organism.

Genes are passed on from parent to child and are an important part of what determines the physical appearance and also behavior, including the fact that a gene determines what traits a whole family (such as the grandfather, great grandfather, etc.). Genes are passed on through the chromosomes, each chromosome consisting of a single, long DNA helix on which thousands of genes are encoded.

What is gene therapy?

Gene therapy is the insertion of genes into an individual's cells to treat a disease. It may also be helpful for treating hereditary diseases

27. I have discussed this topic with the help of creating a doctor's character, named Dr. Vimal, in this book.

in future. Although the technology is still in its infancy, it has been used with some success.

Visualization Technique[28]

Over the centuries, human beings have developed many techniques to gain access to their inner wisdom and improve learning. Especially practiced in the older cultures of world, this theory holds true even in today's technological times of the modern world.

Visualization is a technique that entails creating images, diagrams, or some kind of animation to communicate a message. Visualization through visual imagery has been an effective way to communicate both abstract and concrete ideas since the dawn of times.

Visualization today has ever-expanding applications in science, education, engineering (e.g. product visualization), medicine, etc.

Guided health imagery, a technique to help patients relax their muscles and open their minds to images of health and healthy living, has long been used to help surgery and cancer patients, as well as for reducing pain and reversing negative thoughts resulting from traumatic events

It is well known that the quality of thoughts create certain kinds of biological affects. For example it is well known, and scientifically established, that negative thoughts create stress and in turn, release stress hormones in the body, called *cortisones.*

A cortisone is a degenerative hormone and is destructive to the body causing illness and disease in it. By contrast, positive, happy thoughts do the opposite. They release beneficial hormones such as beta endorphins and human growth hormone within the body, which are regenerative and healing to the body.

Creating visual images that one can refer to, or see in passing during the day is a good way of keeping the subconscious mind more focussed on intentions (in this case, to get well).

Using the visualization technique does not mean one does not attend to proper eating, rest, and using medicines that are appropriate, but by using these techniques, a person will drastically improve the bodies ability to realize itself to full health sooner.

---

28. I have discussed this topic with the help of creating a psychotherapist's character, named Meeraben, in this book.

Body-Mind connection

A new field of research, known as psycho-neuro-immunology, is exploring how the immune system and the brain may interact to influence health. For years, stress has been suspected of increasing susceptibility to various infectious diseases or cancer. Now evidence is mounting that the immune system and the nervous system may be inextricably interconnected.

Biological links between the immune system and the central nervous system exist at several levels.

The immune system is a complex network of specialized cells and organs that has evolved to defend the body against attacks by 'foreign' invaders. When functioning properly it fights off infections by agents such as bacteria, viruses, fungi, and parasites. When it malfunctions, however, it allows a torrent of diseases, from allergy to arthritis to cancer to AIDS to develop.

It is believed that through the language of hormones, the immune cells and the brain cells communicate with each other. The immune cells detect the arrival of foreign invaders, and through the chemical signals (hormones), alert the brain cells. The brain cells, then, send signals (through hormones) that guide the traffic of 'fighting' cells through the lymphoid organs.

Thus the body-mind connection is real. New research shows that disorders in the immune system can cause disease; and a healthy and active brain boosts the immune system function well. It helps keep a person healthy.

In brief, keeping a positive attitude (function of the mind) is vital to the well being of a human being (the body itself).

•••